70 Quotes of Amma

Celebrating the Wisdom and Compassion of
Sri Mata Amritanandamayi on her 70th birthday

Swami Amritachitswarupananda Puri

Mata Amritanandamayi Center
San Ramon, California, USA

70 Quotes of Amma
Celebrating the Wisdom and Compassion of
Sri Mata Amritanandamayi on her 70th birthday

By Swami Amritachitswarupananda Puri

Published by:
Mata Amritanandamayi Center
P.O. Box 613
San Ramon, CA 94583-0613, USA
Website: www.amma.org

Contents

Foreword

In this ever changing and wonderful universe, all of us are searching for happiness. Our life experience however, is interspersed with both happy moments and disappointments. A majority of our lives is spent in earning a living, the pursuit of pleasures and achievements and in supporting a family. Youth quickly passes away, leading to old age. Then there is death, always lurking around the corner. Are we not meant to be happy in life? Are we simply resigned to a life of ups and downs? The Truth, the scriptures say, is that we are created in God's image and are meant to experience supreme peace and infinite happiness. The question then is, how to gain that supreme peace?

The ancient Rishis and the great Seers, all have deeply investigated this paradox of life and have handed down to us the solution through the teachings of the Upanishads in the east and and other ancient masters in the west. They tell us from their own experience, that supreme happiness is completely attainable by one and all, in this very life itself.

The essence of the ancient teachings is the same. As the great sage Ashtavakra puts it "One only is, was and will be". Call that One as Brahman, or Atman or by any other name. That One alone exists or rather, that One is Existence-Consciousness itself. All these colorful names and forms in the universe are simply transitory appearances on that One Reality. Each one of us is one hundred percent exactly that One reality. Even though this is the core of all spirituality, most of us are not ready to grasp this Truth in its pure form. Spiritual masters like Amma, help us to realize this Truth, by holding our hand and gently guiding us one step at a time.

It is my great pleasure to introduce this book of 70 Quotes of Amma, which is being released on the occasion of Amma's 70th birthday. For many decades, Amma has been a spiritual guide and a source of inspiration for countless individuals all over the world. Since Amma is always established in that state of Oneness, her words offer profound insights into the nature of reality, the power of love, the importance of compassion, and the urgency of spiritual fulfillment. They are a testament to Amma's constant abidance in the Truth, her deep understanding of the human experience and her steadfast love for humanity.

Swami reflects on Amma's words, elaborating and often citing from the Bhagavad Gita and the Upanishads, to help us further meditate on Amma's words. Any one who sincerely reflects on these divine teachings of Amma, with a sincere desire to progress on the path of freedom, will benefit from them.

As we celebrate Amma's 70th birthday, it is most fitting that we reflect on her spiritual teachings and take full advantage of them to realize the Truth. May our beloved Amma continue to inspire and uplift us all for many years to come.

Raghu Mannam, Atlanta, Georgia, USA
September 2023

Introduction

Amma, also known as Mata Amritanandamayi, is a spiritual leader, humanitarian, and a beacon of divine love and compassion. For the past several decades, she has dedicated her life to serving humanity and spreading the message of love and selflessness. As she celebrates her 70th birthday, we take this opportunity to reflect on her teachings and the tremendous impact she has had on the world.

This book, with "70 Quotes of Amma", is a compilation of some of her most inspiring and thought-provoking quotes. Each quote offers a glimpse into Amma's wisdom and her deep understanding of the human experience. Her words resonate with Truth and compassion, and offer guidance on how to navigate life's challenges with equanimity and humility.

As we read through these quotes, we are awestruck by the depth of Amma's insights and her unwavering commitment to the well-being of all beings. Her teachings remind us that we are all interconnected, and that true happiness can only be found through acts of selfless service and the cultivation of love and compassion.

This book is a tribute to Amma's life and work, and a celebration of her 70th birthday. It is our hope that these quotes will inspire readers to live their lives with greater purpose, compassion, and love, and to work towards the betterment of humanity.

We extend our heartfelt gratitude to Amma for her tireless service to humanity, and for the gift of her wisdom and love. May she continue to inspire and uplift us all for many years to come.

Swami Amritachitswarupananda Puri

Amma

1. *"Amma sees everything as part of the whole, as an extension of Her own Self. On Amma's shoulders, there are tears of devotees, some with joy they cried, some with despair they wept. My children's happiness is Mother's food. "* – Amma

In the profound teachings of Amma, the embodiment of love and compassion, we find a deep understanding of the non-dual nature of Existence. Her words convey the essence of Oneness, where everything is seen as One and as an extension of the divine Self.

When Amma speaks of seeing everything as part of the whole, she reminds us that the boundaries we perceive between ourselves and the world are illusory. In the realm of non-duality, there is no separation between self and others. We are all One, woven together in the fabric of existence. Just as the body is made up of countless cells, each with its own unique function, so too is the universe composed of diverse beings, each contributing to the harmonious functioning of the whole.

Amma's compassionate heart extends to all beings, embracing their joys and sorrows as her own. She is fully present with the tears the devotees shed, whether they are from moments of blissful ecstasy or deep despair. She understands that these emotions are part of the human experience, and she holds them with immense love and compassion. In her presence, devotees find solace, knowing that their experiences are seen and acknowledged by a divine mother who encompasses all.

The quote highlights Amma's profound understanding that her children's happiness is her nourishment. She recognizes that true fulfillment lies not in seeking external validation or personal gain, but in selflessly serving and uplifting others. By embracing her children, she nurtures them with boundless love, providing them the strength and support they need to navigate life's challenges.

In the Advaita (non-dual) vedanta philosophy, this quote reminds us that the true essence of our being is Love. Love is not limited to individual identity or personal attachments. It is an expansive force that transcends boundaries and embraces all of creation. When we recognize this Truth, we begin to experience the unity of existence and see ourselves in every being we encounter.

Amma's teachings call us to embody this non-dual understanding in our own lives. By extending love and compassion to all beings, we cultivate a deep sense of oneness and dissolve the illusory barriers that separate us. In doing so, we awaken to the Truth that we are not separate individuals, but unity expressions of the divine.

Amma invites us to expand our awareness beyond the limited perception of the individual self and recognize the inherent divinity that resides within us and all of creation. As we embrace this understanding, our actions become rooted in love, compassion, and selflessness. We realize that by nourishing the happiness and well-being of others, we are nourishing our own spiritual growth and deepening our connection with the universal consciousness. Amma's teachings inspire us to see the world through the lens of non-duality, where every interaction becomes an opportunity for selfless service and unconditional love. By embracing the oneness of existence, we can transform our lives and contribute to the collective awakening of humanity.

Let us heed Amma's words and embrace the profound Truth of non-duality, recognizing that we are all One. By treating the joys and sorrows of others as if our own, we embody the divinity within us and contribute to the creation of a more harmonious and compassionate world.

In the Bhagavad Gita, we find a verse that beautifully resonates with Amma's profound teachings on the non-dual nature of existence:

He who sees the Supreme Lord dwelling alike in all beings, the Imperishable amidst the perishable, truly sees.

This verse encapsulates the essence of non-duality, emphasizing the importance of perceiving the divine presence in every living being. Just as Amma reminds us to see everything as the whole and an extension of the divine Self, the Bhagavad Gita teaches us that the true vision of wisdom lies in recognizing the Supreme Lord dwelling within all beings.

When we cultivate this vision, we go beyond the limitations of individual identities and external appearances. We see the underlying unity that connects us all, transcending the boundaries of caste, religion, race, or nationality. In this realization, the divisions and conflicts that arise from a narrow perspective dissolve, and we embrace a broader understanding of non-duality and oneness.

When we embrace this perspective, our actions and interactions are infused with love, compassion, and respect for all beings. We no longer discriminate or differentiate based on external factors but approach every person with a sense of reverence, recognizing the divine spark within them.

This aligns with Amma's teachings on love, compassion, and service. Just as she urges us to see the world through the lens of unity and extend kindness and support to all.

As we cultivate this non-dual vision, we begin to experience the Truth that we are not separate individuals but unity expressions of the divine. We realize that the path to Self-realization is paved with love, compassion, and the recognition of the divine presence within ourselves and every being we encounter.

Story
In a peaceful monastery nestled amidst lush mountains, there lived a humble and wise monk. This monk, named Deva, was known for his deep spiritual insights and his unwavering commitment to the path of non-duality.

One day, a young traveler named Ram arrived at the monastery seeking solace and guidance. Ram was burdened by the struggles and conflicts of the external world, longing for inner peace and clarity. Hearing about this monk's wisdom, he sought his counsel.

Ram approached Deva with reverence and shared his journey, expressing his desire to find a deeper understanding of life and the oneness of all things. Deva listened attentively, his compassionate eyes reflecting the wisdom he had acquired through years of introspection and spiritual practice.

With a gentle smile, Deva began to share a story that would illuminate the essence of non-duality and the unity of all beings.

"In a distant kingdom," Deva began, "there lived a wise and benevolent king named Raja. He was loved and respected by his people for his fairness, compassion, and deep sense of unity. The king understood that every individual, regardless of their background or status, was integrally the whole."

"One day, the king fell gravely ill, and news of his condition spread throughout the kingdom. People from all walks of life gathered at the palace, offering prayers and hoping for his recovery. Among the concerned crowd was the young prince."

"This young prince, like many others, had experienced the king's love and guidance. He believed in the king's vision of unity and wanted to carry forward his legacy. With a heavy heart, he approached the royal physician, seeking an update on his father's health."

"The physician, a wise and experienced man, spoke to the young prince with utmost compassion. He said, 'Prince, your father's condition is critical, and his time in this physical realm may soon come to an end. However, he has left a powerful message for you and all his subjects."

Intrigued, the young prince listened intently as the physician continued, "Your father wishes for you to remember the profound Truth of non-duality. He said, 'Son, love is the thread that binds us all. We are one, and our actions ripple through the fabric of existence. Embrace this understanding and lead with compassion, for that is the true mark of a wise ruler."

Young prince, deeply moved by his father's words, embarked on a transformative journey of self-discovery and spiritual growth. He sought the guidance of sages and wise beings, delving into the teachings of non-duality and the unity of all beings.

Years passed, and the young prince eventually ascended to the throne, becoming a king in his own right. Guided by the wisdom he had acquired, he ruled with love, compassion, and a deep sense of unity. He became a beacon of light, inspiring his subjects to embrace the truth of non-duality and extend kindness and support to all.

Through his actions and leadership, this King transformed the kingdom into a harmonious and prosperous realm. People from all walks of life found solace and acceptance within the kingdom's boundaries, as the King's reign was marked by the recognition that every being was integrally the whole.

ॐ

Goal of Human Life

2. *"This human birth is intended for the purpose of realizing our true nature: Bliss. Do not miss out on the precious opportunity to find your eternally blissful Self by running behind temporary joys."* - Amma

Amma reminds us here that the goal of human life is to realize our true nature, which is infinite happiness. This infinite happiness or Bliss (Ānanda) is realized to be our fundamental essence, along with Beingness and Awareness (Sat-Chit-Ānanda). Amma's profound words remind us of the precious opportunity we have in this human birth to awaken to our eternal blissful Self. She urges us not to be swayed by temporary joys and distractions that can cloud our understanding of our true purpose.

In the journey of life, we often find ourselves chasing after fleeting pleasures, seeking happiness in external objects and experiences. However, Amma reminds us that true and lasting happiness lies within us, in the recognition of our divine essence. Our ultimate goal is to realize our inherent nature as pure consciousness, transcending the limitations of the body, mind, and ego.

Amma's words here invites us to reflect on the purpose of our lives and the choices we make. It is a call to shift our focus from the transitory and ephemeral to the eternal and unchanging. While the world around us is ever-changing and impermanent, our true nature remains constant, untouched by the fluctuations of life.

To attain this realization, we must turn our attention inward and cultivate self-awareness. Through practices such as devotion, meditation and serving others selflessly, we gradually cut through the layers of conditioning and false identifications that veil our true nature.

Advaita Vedanta teaches us that our true essence is beyond the limitations of the body, mind, and ego. It is the infinite, unchanging consciousness that witnesses everything but stands untouched. It is the substratum. It is complete in itself, all experiences of pleasure and pain are temporary waves in the ocean of this consciousness. This realization brings forth a deep sense of inner peace, contentment, and joy that is independent of all external circumstances.

Amma's words serve as a reminder to prioritize the pursuit of Self-realization above all other pursuits. Amma, both through her words and her presence, inspires us to seek the eternal happiness that is our birthright, rather than being consumed by temporary pleasures that often lead to suffering and dissatisfaction. It is an invitation to go beyond the superficial and delve into the depths of our Being.

In the journey towards Self-realization, we may encounter challenges, distractions, and moments of doubt. However, Amma's guidance encourages us to persevere and not lose sight of our ultimate goal. It is a call to detach ourselves from the transitory and embrace the eternal, to realize our true nature as Sat-Chit-Ananda. It is an invitation to turn inward, and discover. May we heed Amma's wisdom and embrace the path of Self-realization, finding eternal happiness within ourselves.

Story

In a peaceful village nestled amidst lush greenery, there lived a wise sage. The sage was known for his profound wisdom and his ability to guide others towards Self-realization. People from far and wide would seek his counsel and guidance, hoping to gain a deeper understanding of life's true purpose.

One day, three young individuals approached the sage with a desire to get advice on how to achieve their goals in life. They believed with the sage's advice and blessings, they would achieve their goals and thus find ultimate happiness. They had heard of the sage's wisdom and were eager to learn from him.

The sage welcomed the three seekers with a warm smile and invited them to sit beside him under the shade of a mighty banyan tree. He began by explaining the fundamental teachings of Advaita Vedanta, emphasizing the importance of realizing our true nature as infinite happiness.

As the sage shared his wisdom, the three seekers listened attentively, their hearts filled with curiosity and a deep longing for self-discovery. They asked questions, seeking clarification and guidance on the journey of life.

They learned to detach themselves from the transient pleasures of the world and to focus their attention on the eternal essence within. Through the sage's guidance, they gradually developed a profound understanding of their true nature. They realized that they were not separate individuals but interconnected with all of existence. They discovered the divinity within themselves and recognized the same divinity in every being they encountered. No longer did the fulfillment of external goals matter. They understood that all actions performed as an expression of the fullness within, are fulfilling, no matter what stage of life one finds oneself in.

ॐ

Spirituality

3. The foundation of spirituality is not blind faith. It is enquiry, it is an intense exploration within one's own Self. Look within, observe the thoughts, and trace them back to their source. Always be convinced, 'I am the nature of Sat-chit-ananda (pure being-awareness-bliss).'" - Amma

Unlike religion, spirituality is not built upon blind faith but rather on the pursuit of knowledge and self-inquiry. It is an inward journey, a profound exploration within one's own being to unravel the true nature of Existence. Amma here is guiding us to rise beyond just belief in something higher, and to delve deep within ourselves and discover the essence of our being.

Self-enquiry, or Ātma Vichāra, is a profound process of introspection and investigation into one's own Self. It involves turning inward, observing thoughts, and tracing them back to their source. This essay explores the transformative practice of enquiry, highlighting its significance in gaining self-awareness and realizing the ultimate truth.

Understanding Self-Inquiry

a) Enquiry is an intense exploration within one's own being, seeking to uncover the deeper layers of consciousness.

b) Through the process of such enquiry, one is able to perceive that the body, mind, emotions, feelings and all events in the world arise and pass away in time, but the seer of these remains.

c) Enquiry involves questioning the thoughts, beliefs, and identities that shape our perception of our personalities.

The first step in observing the mind is to develop a keen sense of self-observation. One must also cultivate a certain degree of detachment from the constant stream of mental activity. This practice allows us to gain insight into the patterns, biases, and conditioning that influence our thoughts and behaviors.

Through such investigation, as we practice delving deeper into the origin of thoughts, seeking to uncover their source, and attempt to remain as this pure Seer. This process leads us beyond the realm of conceptual thinking and into direct experience. We come to realize the eternal, unchanging nature of the Self.

Benefits of Self-enquiry

a) Enquiry liberates us from the grip of identification with thoughts, emotions, and external circumstances.

b) It leads to a deep sense of inner peace, contentment, and freedom from suffering.

c) Enquiry opens the doorway to Self-realization, where we directly experience the unity and interconnectedness of all existence.

Through enquiry, we transcend the limitations of the mind and experience the eternal essence that resides within us. So, embracing the practice of such enquiry empowers us to live authentically, with clarity, and in harmony with the deeper truths of our existence.

The essence of spirituality lies in self-inquiry, in observing our thoughts, and tracing them back to their source. Through this introspection, we begin to unravel the layers of conditioning and beliefs that veil our true nature. We question the very fabric of our personalities and seek to understand the fundamental Truths of life.

Amma reminds us that at the core of our being, we are Sat-chit-ananda – pure Being, Awareness, and Bliss. This realization is not merely an intellectual understanding but a direct experiential knowing. It is the recognition that our true nature transcends the limitations of the physical body and the fluctuations of the mind.

The Bhagavad Gita, resonates with Amma's teachings. In Chapter 2, verse 45, Lord Krishna says, "Nistraigunyo bhavarjuna," which translates to "Be beyond the three modes of material nature, O Arjuna." This verse emphasizes the need to transcend the limitations of the mind and the transient nature of the external world.

The path of Advaita Vedanta teaches us that we are not separate from the divine or the ultimate reality. We are one, integral parts of the vast cosmic tapestry. The exploration within ourselves leads us to the realization that the divine essence permeates everything and everyone. We recognize the inherent oneness of all beings and transcend the boundaries that divide us.

As we embark on this inward journey, it is essential to approach it with an open mind and a willingness to question our deeply ingrained beliefs. Blind adherence to dogma and external rituals is not the essence of spirituality. True spirituality is a personal quest for truth and Self-realization.

Through self-inquiry and the exploration of our true nature, we come to understand the impermanence of external phenomena and the eternal nature of our Being. We begin to recognize that the external world is subject to change and flux, while our true essence remains constant and unchanging.

Amma's guidance encourages us to embark on this transformative journey of self-discovery. It is through intense self-exploration, contemplation, and introspection that we come to know ourselves as the Sat-chit-ananda, the pure being, awareness, and bliss that we inherently are.

Story

In a distant kingdom, there ruled a wise and just king. This king had a deep longing to understand the nature of life and the purpose of his existence. Despite his wealth and power, he felt a profound emptiness within, as if something essential was missing.

One day, the king heard of a renowned sage who resided in a secluded hermitage on the outskirts of the kingdom. Known for his profound wisdom and spiritual insight, the sage was said to have the ability to guide seekers on the path of Self-realization. Intrigued by the sage's reputation, the king decided to seek his counsel.

The king, accompanied by his trusted ministers, embarked on a journey to the hermitage of the sage. As they arrived, they were greeted by a serene atmosphere, surrounded by lush greenery and the calming sounds of nature. The sage, known for his ability to perceive the innermost thoughts and desires of individuals, welcomed the king with a warm smile.

Sensing the king's quest for spiritual understanding, the sage began to impart his wisdom. He spoke about the illusion of material wealth and the fleeting nature of worldly pleasures. He emphasized that true fulfillment could only be found by transcending the ego and realizing one's true nature.

Intrigued by the sage's teachings, the king humbly asked, "How can I transcend the limitations of my ego and find true fulfillment?"

The sage smiled and replied, "Your journey towards Self-realization begins with understanding the impermanence of both inner and external circumstances and identifying with the eternal essence within you. It is through self-inquiry, contemplation, and the practice of detachment that you can transcend the limitations of the ego."

The king, determined to embark on this inner journey, asked the sage to guide him. Over the following days, the sage imparted timeless teachings to the king, sharing stories of enlightened beings and scriptures that illuminated the path of Self-realization.

As the king delved deeper into his spiritual practice, he realized that his true essence was not bound by his royal identity or material possessions. He began to experience a sense of inner peace and contentment that surpassed any fleeting pleasure derived from external achievements.

With newfound wisdom and a compassionate heart, the king returned to his kingdom, inspired to lead his people with greater understanding and empathy. He started initiatives to alleviate the suffering of the less fortunate, providing food, clothing, and shelter to those in need. His actions were not driven by ego or personal gain but by a genuine desire to serve and uplift others.

ॐ

4. *"Spirituality is receptivity, the ability to accept all experiences of life without reacting to them."* - Amma

Spirituality is often misunderstood as a practice of detachment or renunciation, but from the perspective of Advaita Vedanta, it is described as a state of choiceless receptivity to life. Amma's profound quote reminds us that true spirituality lies in our ability to accept all experiences of life without reacting to them with the extreme reactions of love and hate.

In the Bhagavad Gita, Lord Krishna imparts the same wisdom to Arjuna on how to cultivate this receptive state of being. In Chapter 2, verse 14 says,:

mātrā-sparśhās tu kaunteya śhītoṣhṇa-sukha-duḥkha-dāḥ
āgamāpāyino 'nityās tans-titikṣhasva bhārata

O Bhārata, the non-permanent appearance experiences
of happiness and distress, heat and cold, appear and
disappear in due course. They arise from sense perception,
and one must learn to tolerate them without being
disturbed.

This verse encapsulates the essence of spiritual receptivity. It teaches us that the ups and downs of life, the joys and sorrows, are transient and subject to change. True spirituality lies not in trying to control or manipulate external circumstances, but in developing an inner resilience that allows us to remain centered and at peace amidst the ebb and flow of life.

To understand this further, let us explore the concept of non-duality in Vedanta. Non-duality teaches us that there is no inherent separation between ourselves and the world around us. It is the recognition that we are one with all of creation, and that the external experiences we encounter are a reflection of our own inner state.

When we approach life with receptivity, we embrace every experience as an opportunity for growth and self-discovery. We let go of resistance and judgment, allowing life to unfold as it does, without trying to impose our desires or expectations upon it. This receptive attitude enables us to fully immerse ourselves in the present moment and to see the inherent beauty and wisdom in every experience, even in the face of challenges.

Receptivity does not imply passivity or indifference. It is an active state of awareness, where we observe and engage with life fully, but without clinging or aversion. It is a state of surrender, where we release the need to control outcomes and instead trust in the divine intelligence that guides the universe.

Through the practice of receptivity, we cultivate a deep sense of peace and equanimity. We no longer react impulsively to situations or allow external circumstances to dictate our inner state. We become like a calm lake, reflecting the world around us without being disturbed by its waves.

Amma's quote reminds us that true spirituality is not about seeking happiness or avoiding suffering, but it is in recognizing the fullness within and embracing all experiences with an open heart and mind. It is about recognizing the oneness of all beings and surrendering to the divine flow of life.

As we cultivate receptivity, we become more attuned to the subtle messages and teachings that life offers us. We learn to see beyond the surface level of events and circumstances, and to discern the deeper wisdom and lessons they hold. In this way, every experience becomes a catalyst for our spiritual growth and evolution.

Story

There lived a wise and esteemed minister who served a righteous King named Arjun. The minister was known for his profound wisdom, impeccable judgment, and unwavering loyalty to the king.

The king was a compassionate ruler who had a deep desire to bring prosperity and harmony to his kingdom. He sought the counsel of his wise minister on matters of governance and spirituality, knowing that the minister possessed great insight and understanding of the human heart.

One day, as the king and the minister were sitting in the royal court, discussing the affairs of the kingdom, the topic of spirituality arose. King Arjun expressed his longing to deepen his spiritual understanding and asked the minister for guidance.

The wise minister listened attentively to the king's words and then spoke with gentle wisdom. He said, "Your Majesty, true spirituality lies not only in rituals and worship but also in the way we lead our lives and govern our kingdom. It is through the embodiment of compassion, fairness, and righteousness that we can truly elevate ourselves and our kingdom."

The minister then shared a story with the king to illustrate his point:

"In a distant land, there was a great sage who possessed immense knowledge and spiritual wisdom. People from far and wide sought his guidance and sought to learn from him. One day, a young prince from a neighboring kingdom arrived at the sage's hermitage, seeking answers to his deepest questions about life and purpose.

The sage welcomed the prince and listened patiently to his inquiries. The prince asked, 'O wise sage, how can I attain true spirituality and lead a meaningful life?'

The sage smiled and replied, 'My dear prince, true spirituality is not confined to secluded hermitages or temples. It is found in the midst of the world, in the interactions and responsibilities of everyday life. It is through your actions, thoughts, and decisions that you can manifest the highest spiritual ideals.'

The prince was puzzled and asked, 'But how can I do that, revered sage?'

The sage explained, 'As a prince, you have the power to influence the lives of your subjects. Rule with fairness and justice, and let compassion guide your decisions. Treat all beings with kindness and respect, and serve the welfare of your people selflessly. By doing so, you will not only uplift your own consciousness but also create a ripple effect of positive transformation in your kingdom.'

The young prince was inspired by the sage's words and returned to his kingdom with a renewed sense of purpose. He dedicated himself to serving his people with compassion and fairness, ensuring that the needs of the less fortunate were met and justice prevailed throughout the land. Under his wise and just rule, the kingdom thrived, and its people lived in peace and prosperity."

ॐ

God

5. *"If you want to be closer to God, try to be like a child."* - Amma

The quote by Amma highlights a profound spiritual truth that lies at the core of Advaita Vedanta philosophy. Where the individual personality exists, the presence of God is veiled. Just as a child simply exists, full of innocence and without ego, Amma here invites us to approach the divine with the innocence and purity of a child.

To further understand this quote, let us explore the concept of God and the significance of childlike qualities. In Advaita Vedanta, God is not seen as an external entity but as the ultimate reality, the source of all existence. It is the essence that permeates everything, the divine presence within and beyond the manifested world.

janmādyasya yataḥ - Brahma Sutra 1.1.2.

That (is Brahman) from which (are derived) the birth etc., of this (universe).

The goal of spiritual seekers is to realize their inherent oneness with this divine essence, to experience the divinity within themselves and in all beings.

To be like a child in the context of spirituality means to approach the divine with an open heart, free from preconceived notions, doubts, and limitations that accompany our egos and personalities. A child's mind is naturally curious, innocent, and full of wonder. It is devoid of the complexities and conditioning that often burden adults. Similarly, in our spiritual journey, we are encouraged to cultivate childlike qualities such as innocence, trust, and an attitude of surrender. Purity in heart and an unwavering mind which comes from selfless actions with an attitude of being the non-doer and non-enjoyer.

The innocence of a child represents a state of openness and receptivity, where the barriers of judgment and skepticism are absent. It is a state of pure acceptance, where one is willing to explore and discover the divine without imposing limitations or expectations. Just as a child wholeheartedly embraces life's experiences, we are encouraged to approach the divine with a sense of wonder, awe, and unconditional love.

In the Bhagavad Gita, Lord Krishna emphasizes the significance of childlike qualities in attaining spiritual realization. In Chapter 9, verse 22, he states:

ananyāśh chintayanto māṁ ye janāḥ paryupāsate

To those who are constantly devoted and who worship Me with love, I give the understanding by which they can come to Me.

Such love and devotion brings our minds in alignment with the divine without wavering. By cultivating childlike devotion and surrendering to the divine with love, we can attain a deeper understanding of our connection with God.

By being like a child in our spiritual quest, we let go of the ego's need for control, knowledge, and intellectual understanding. We embrace a state of humility, recognizing our limited understanding and surrendering to the divine will. In this surrender, we open ourselves to the divine grace and guidance that flows through us, leading us closer to God-realization.

The childlike qualities of innocence, trust, and surrender allow us to transcend the limitations of the ego and connect with the divine essence within us. We become receptive vessels through which the divine can manifest and work through us. It is in this state of childlike openness and surrender that we experience the divine presence in every aspect of our lives.

In conclusion, the quote by Amma reminds us that to be closer to God, we need to cultivate the qualities of a child—innocence, trust, and surrender. By approaching the divine with an open heart and a childlike spirit, we can experience the oneness and divine presence that permeates all of creation. Through the practice of devotion, love, and surrender, we can realize our inherent connection with the divine and embark on a journey of self-discovery and spiritual growth.

Story
One day, the king, burdened by the responsibilities of his kingdom, felt a deep longing to connect with a higher purpose and find inner peace. He had heard of a monk's wisdom and decided to seek his counsel.

Upon meeting the monk, the king humbly bowed before him and expressed his desire to understand the true nature of spirituality and how to cultivate a deeper connection with the divine. The monk smiled and invited the king to join him in meditation.

As they sat in silence, the monk began to speak, "Your Majesty, spirituality is not confined to temples or rituals alone. It is a path that leads to Self-realization and inner transformation. To be closer to God, one must embrace the qualities of a child—innocence, simplicity, and a heart full of love."

The king listened intently, eager to learn more. The monk continued, "Just as a child trusts and surrenders to the care of its parents, we must trust and surrender to the divine. Let go of the burdens of your kingdom, the worries and anxieties, and open your heart to the presence of the divine within you and all around you."

The king pondered the monk's words and realized that his relentless pursuit of power and control had distanced him from his own inner essence and the divine presence. He yearned to reconnect with that childlike innocence and sense of wonder.

As the king embraced the qualities of a child, his heart opened to love and compassion. He treated his subjects with kindness and fairness, spreading joy and harmony throughout the kingdom. His actions became an inspiration to others, and soon, people started following his example, cultivating their own spiritual paths and seeking inner peace.

And so, the wise monk's teachings lived on, touching the hearts of countless individuals who sought to be closer to God by embracing the innocence, trust, and love that lie within the depths of their being, just like a child.

ॐ

6. *"See God in everyone, even if it is difficult, don't be discouraged. There is one truth that shines through all of creation. God is the pure consciousness that dwells in everything. Never forget that you are never alone on this journey. God is always with you. Allow Him to take your hand. " - Amma*

In the vast tapestry of creation, there is an underlying Truth that connects all beings. It is the presence of God, the pure consciousness that resides within every being. Amma reminds us to see God in everyone and everything, even when it may be challenging to do so. She also points out that when we make that attempt to recognize the divinity present in everyone, God takes our hands and brings us closer to always feeling the presence of God within.

eṣa sarveśvaraḥ eṣa sarvajña eṣo'ntaryāmyeṣa yoniḥ
sarvasya prabhavāpyayau hi bhūtānām

> – Mandukya Upanishad 6

This is the Lord of all; this is the knower of all; this is the
controller within; this is the source of all; and this is that
from which all things originate and in which they finally
disappear.

The All-Pervading Nature of the Lord

Introduction

In commenting on this Upanishadic mantra, Sri Sankaracharya
expounds on the concept of the all-pervading Lord. It delves
into the understanding of the Lord as the controller, knower,
source, and ultimate reality from which all things originate and
in which they eventually dissolve. The commentary highlights
the interconnectedness of the Lord with the universe and the
nature of His omniscience.

I. The Lord as the Sovereign of All:

Identifying the Lord as the ruler of the entire physical and
super-physical universe: The Lord, in His natural state, encompasses and governs all aspects of existence. The divine is not a
separate entity from the universe but is inseparable from it. The
Upanishadic mantra proclaims and emphasizes that the Lord is
the binding force within all beings.

II. The Lord's Omniscience:

Understanding the Lord as the knower of all beings: The Lord
possesses omniscience, having comprehensive knowledge of the
various conditions and states of all entities.

Recognition of the Lord's role as the Antaryāmin: The Lord is
the inner controller who permeates all beings and guides their
actions from within.

The interconnectedness between the Lord's omniscience and His all-pervading nature: The Lord's knowledge is intrinsically linked to His presence within all beings, enabling a deep understanding of their diverse experiences.

III. The Lord as the Source and Destiny of All:

Acknowledging the Lord as the origin of the universe: The Lord serves as the ultimate source from which the entire cosmos, characterized by its inherent diversity, emerges.

Recognizing the Lord as the ultimate dissolution of all things: All entities eventually return to the Lord, dissolving back into their source.

Emphasizing the Lord's encompassing nature: The Lord is that which all things proceed from and merge into, representing the encompassing reality underlying existence.

Conclusion

This mantra explores the Lord as the all-pervading entity who serves as the sovereign ruler, the knower of all beings, the inner controller, and the ultimate source and destiny of the universe. This understanding challenges the notion of separation between the Lord and the universe, emphasizing their inherent interconnectedness. The Lord's omniscience stems from His presence within all beings, enabling a profound understanding of their diverse conditions.

Recognizing the Lord's role as the origin and dissolution of all things provides a broader perspective on the interconnected nature of existence and the ultimate reality that underlies it. As we learn to live in awareness of the underlying unity, we begin to treat all beings with reverence and compassion.

Beyond the transient world of appearances, existence stands as the eternal substratum, unchanging and unconditioned. Embracing this teaching deepens our understanding of reality and opens the door to profound Self-realization.

The journey of spirituality is often accompanied by hurdles and obstacles that test our faith and understanding. It is easy to get discouraged when faced with difficult situations or when encountering people who seem different from us. However, Amma encourages us not to lose hope, for beneath the surface of diverse forms lies the unifying essence of God.

When we truly recognize the divinity within ourselves, we naturally extend that recognition to others. It is in this awareness that we can see God in everyone, irrespective of their external appearances or beliefs. This realization brings forth a sense of unity, compassion, and connectedness with all of creation.

Amma's words also remind us that we are never alone on this journey. God is always with us, holding our hand and guiding us through life's ups and downs. Just as a loving parent extends a hand to their child, God extends His divine presence to us, offering solace, guidance, and unconditional love.

Story

Once upon a time, a wise and revered sage lived in a hermitage on the edge of a jungle. His reputation for profound knowledge and spiritual insight had spread far and wide, attracting seekers from all walks of life.

One day, news reached the teacher that the king of the neighboring kingdom was seeking guidance on matters of governance and spirituality. The teacher, known for his ability to impart wisdom in a simple yet profound manner, decided to visit the king and offer his guidance.

As the teacher arrived at the royal palace, he was greeted with great honor and respect. The king, a wise and just ruler, welcomed the teacher with open arms and expressed his deep desire to understand the deeper aspects of life and leadership.

Over the course of several days, the teacher engaged in profound discussions with the king, addressing various aspects of spirituality, morality, and the nature of governance. The king listened attentively, soaking in the wisdom imparted by the teacher.

During one particular conversation, the teacher spoke about the importance of seeing God in everyone, including the subjects of the kingdom. He emphasized that true leadership comes from recognizing the divine presence in all beings and treating them with love, compassion, and fairness.

The teacher imparted a profound teaching, saying, "O King, true greatness lies not in the grandeur of your throne or the power you wield, but in your ability to see the divine presence in every soul that crosses your path. Nurture the seed of divinity within yourself and others, and you shall inspire greatness in all."

The teaching to heart and embarked on a personal journey of self-discovery and spiritual growth. He learned to see the inherent divinity in every person he encountered, regardless of their social status or background. This perspective transformed his leadership and enabled him to govern with fairness, compassion, and wisdom. From that day forward, the king embraced the teachings of the wise teacher, incorporating them into his rule and personal life.

ॐ

7. *"For Amma everything is divine. The Creator and Creation are one."* - Amma

In the realm of spirituality, the understanding of the non-dual nature of existence is a profound realization. It is the recognition that the Creator and Creation are not separate entities but rather a manifestation of the same divine essence. This profound Truth lies at the heart of Amma's teachings.

God

Amma, with her deep spiritual insight, reminds us that everything in this universe, from the grandeur of nature to the smallest blade of grass, is imbued with divinity. The Creator is not limited to a separate entity residing outside of creation, but rather permeates every aspect of it. The divine essence is present in all beings and all things.

Amma's words here align with the principles of Advaita Vedanta, which emphasize the unity of all existence.

In the Taittariya Upanishad we find:

tatsrishtva tadevanupravishat

– Taittariya Upanishad, Brahmanda Valli.

That Supreme Self, created the entirety of the manifested universe. Having created it, it entered into it.

Introduction

The Taittiriya Upanishad's Brahmananda Valli delves into the essence of Brahman – the ultimate reality that pervades all existence. This mantra declares Brahman as the source of all creation and the nature of its manifestation.

I. The Nature of Brahman:

a) According to the Upanishad, Brahman is the ultimate reality, the one being that transcends all dualities.

b) It is beyond the realm of perception and Imagination, beyond the limitations of time, space, and causality.

c) Brahman is both the manifested and the unmanifested, encompassing all that is real and unreal, defined and undefined.

II. The Creative Power of Brahman:

a) The Upanishad describes Brahman's desire to become many and to be born, leading to the creation of the universe.

b) Through austerities and divine intention, Brahman brought forth all that exists.

c) Brahman entered into creation, becoming the underlying support and intelligence behind every aspect of manifestation.

III. The Manifestation of Brahman:

a) Brahman encompasses both the tangible and intangible aspects of reality. It is the source of both the physical and non-physical realms, supporting and animating all beings.

b) The Upanishad highlights Brahman as the ultimate reality, which the wise refer to as the True (Satya).

IV. The Importance of Knowing Brahman:

a) The Upanishad emphasizes the significance of knowing Brahman, for it determines the nature of one's existence.

b) Those who perceive Brahman as non-existent become enveloped in a sense of non-existence themselves.

c) Conversely, those who recognize Brahman as existent align themselves with the eternal Truth and experience the fullness of Being.

V. Attainment of the World Beyond:

a) The disciple raises the question of whether those who do not know Brahman can attain the world beyond upon departing from this life.

b) The Upanishad affirms that it is the knowledge and realization of Brahman that leads to attaining the ultimate realm.

c) Those who possess the knowledge of Brahman transcend the cycle of birth and death, reaching the eternal abode.

VI. The Ultimate Reality:

a) The Upanishad presents Brahman as the ultimate reality that underlies all existence. It is the source from which all beings arise and dissolve, the substratum upon which the entire universe rests.

c) By recognizing Brahman as the True, seekers of wisdom come to realize the eternal essence within themselves and all creation.

Conclusion

The Taittiriya Upanishad's Brahmananda Valli provides profound insights into the nature of Brahman – the one being and the source of all creation. It elucidates Brahman's creative power, its manifestation in both the tangible and intangible realms, and the significance of realizing Brahman as the ultimate reality. By knowing Brahman, one transcends the limitations of existence and attains the world beyond, experiencing the eternal Truth that permeates all existence. Embracing the teachings of Brahman allows individuals to discover their intrinsic connection to the divine and navigate the journey of Self-realization.

The essence of this teaching is that the divine consciousness is the underlying reality of all existence. The Creator, in His unmanifest form, pervades the entire universe, and all beings are essentially manifestations of that divine consciousness. This realization brings about a profound shift in our perception of the world and our relationship with it.

When we recognize the divinity inherent in all things, we begin to see the sacredness in every moment and every encounter. Our interactions become an opportunity to experience the divine presence, whether it is through acts of kindness, compassion, or simply being fully present in the present moment.

Amma's teachings invite us to expand our awareness beyond the boundaries of the limited self and embrace the oneness of all creation. When we realize that the Creator and Creation are one, we transcend the illusion of separateness and embrace a deep sense of interconnectedness.

Story

Eager to learn from a wise teacher, the king sent a messenger to invite him to the palace. The teacher graciously accepted the invitation and arrived at the royal court with his disciples. The king received them with great respect and humility, recognizing the teacher's wisdom and spiritual presence. During their meeting, the king expressed his longing for deeper understanding of the spiritual path and his desire to lead his kingdom with wisdom and compassion. The teacher, with his gentle yet powerful presence, listened attentively to the king's words and understood the sincerity in his quest for spiritual growth.

In response, the wise teacher began to share profound insights and teachings on the nature of the Self, the path to Self-realization, and the essence of divine wisdom. He spoke of the eternal Truth that lies beyond the transient nature of the material world, and how the true power and fulfillment lie in connecting with the divine within. The king, deeply touched by the teacher's words, felt a profound resonance within his heart. He realized that his role as a ruler went beyond worldly affairs; it was an opportunity to serve his subjects with compassion and wisdom. He understood that his actions as a king could create a ripple effect of positive change in the lives of his people.

ॐ

Values

8. *"Spiritual values are like the GPS of our life. They go deep into our conscience and help us to avoid wrong turns, and we always then travel along the right path."* - *Amma*

In the vast journey of life, it is essential to have a guiding compass that directs us towards the right path. Amma beautifully compares spiritual values to a GPS system that helps us navigate the complexities of existence. Just as a GPS guides us through unfamiliar territory, spiritual values guide us through the intricacies of our thoughts, actions, and decisions, ensuring that we remain on the right course.

These spiritual values, deeply embedded in our conscience, act as beacons of light, illuminating our path and helping us make choices aligned with higher wisdom. They serve as reminders of our true nature and assist us in avoiding the wrong turns that may lead to suffering and spiritual stagnation. When we internalize these values, they become an integral part of our being, guiding us towards righteousness, compassion, and Self-realization.

The Bhagavad Gita, also emphasizes the importance of spiritual values. In Chapter 13, verse 8, Lord Krishna declares:

Amanitvam adambhitvam ahimsa kshantir arjavam |
Acaryopasanam saucam sthairyam atma-vinigrahah ||

Humility, an absence of pride, nonviolence,
tolerance,simplicity, approaching a bonafide spiritual
master, cleanliness, steadiness, and self-control.

These values mentioned by Lord Krishna are the very foundation of a spiritual life. They guide us in our interactions with others, cultivating humility, kindness, and nonviolence. They teach us to be tolerant, patient, and forgiving, allowing us to maintain harmony in relationships. Simplicity and cleanliness bring clarity and purity to our thoughts and actions. The practice of approaching a spiritual master helps us gain wisdom and guidance on our spiritual journey. And above all, steadfastness (sthairyam) and self-control ensure that we stay focused and disciplined in our pursuit of Truth.

When we uphold and live by these spiritual values, they become an intrinsic part of our consciousness. They shape our character, govern our choices, and inspire us to lead a life of integrity and purpose. They guide us towards selflessness, love, and the realization of our true nature as divine beings.

By aligning our lives with these spiritual values, we become instruments of positive change in the world. Our actions, infused with love and compassion, ripple outward, touching the lives of others and creating a harmonious and peaceful society. We become beacons of light, illuminating the path for others and inspiring them to embrace these values in their own lives.

In conclusion, spiritual values are indeed the GPS of our lives, guiding us towards the right path of truth, love, and Self-realization. They help us navigate the complexities of life with clarity, purpose, and integrity. By embracing these values and embodying them in our thoughts, words, and actions, we not only enhance our own well-being but also contribute to the upliftment of humanity as a whole. Let us heed the wisdom of Amma's words and let spiritual values be our guiding light on the journey of self-discovery and transcendence.

Story
In a kingdom, there was a wise and renowned teacher who was revered for his wisdom and spiritual insight. The king of the kingdom was intrigued by the teacher's reputation and desired to meet him. He believed that the teacher's guidance would help

him become a better ruler and lead his kingdom with wisdom and integrity.

The king approached the wise teacher and humbly sought his guidance. He expressed his desire to become a more compassionate and just ruler and asked the teacher to enlighten him on the path of righteousness. The teacher listened attentively to the king's request and agreed to mentor him on his spiritual journey.

Over the course of several meetings, the wise teacher imparted profound wisdom and spiritual teachings to the king. He emphasized the importance of moral values, such as honesty, integrity, and compassion, in the governance of the kingdom. The teacher guided the king in understanding the interconnectedness of all beings and the significance of treating every individual with respect and kindness.

As the king imbibed the teachings of the wise teacher, he began to implement them in his rule. He initiated reforms that aimed to uplift the lives of his subjects, ensuring fair and equal treatment for all. He established institutions that promoted education and healthcare for the less privileged. The king's governance became a shining example of justice and compassion, inspiring neighboring kingdoms and earning him respect and admiration from his people.

The minister of the kingdom, who had also witnessed the transformation of the king, was deeply moved by the teacher's wisdom and the positive changes in the kingdom. He approached the wise teacher and expressed his heartfelt gratitude for the teachings that had not only impacted the king but also influenced his own perspective on leadership.

The wise teacher recognized the sincerity and eagerness of the minister to learn and grow. He agreed to guide the minister on his own spiritual journey, sharing with him the principles of integrity, selflessness, and wisdom. The minister embraced the teachings wholeheartedly and dedicated himself to serving the kingdom and its people with utmost dedication and compassion.

ॐ

Obedience

9. "Progress is not possible without discipline. A nation, institution, family, or individual can advance only by heeding the words of those who deserve respect and by obeying the appropriate rules and regulations. Obedience is not a weakness. Obedience with humility leads to discipline." –Amma

Discipline is an essential aspect of spiritual and personal growth. It is the foundation upon which progress is built, enabling individuals, families, institutions, and nations to thrive and prosper. In the pursuit of spiritual evolution, discipline becomes even more crucial as it helps individuals stay focused, maintain self-control, and adhere to the teachings of wisdom.

Amma's quote emphasizes the importance of discipline in all aspects of life. Whether it is the obedience to the principles of spirituality or the adherence to societal norms and regulations, discipline acts as a guiding force that leads to personal and collective development. It is through discipline that individuals learn to cultivate virtues such as patience, perseverance, and self-restraint, which are essential on the path of Self-realization.

Due to the conditioning from many lifetimes, our minds often rebel when one attempts to follow a disciplined way of living. This is observed even in the pursuit of material well-being. We struggle to exercise, control excessive eating, put aside entertainment in order to do well in an exam, and so on. Such friction with the lower mind similarly exists when one attempts to follow spiritual disciplines. The mind tries to rebel. During such times, the love and guidance of a spiritual master and obedience to their instructions is the only way to move forward.

In the Bhagavad Gita, Lord Krishna imparts valuable insights on the significance of discipline. In Chapter 16, verse 5, He states, "The Divine qualities lead to liberation, whereas the demonic qualities result in bondage. Do not worry, Arjuna, for you are born with divine qualities." This verse highlights that the cultivation of divine qualities, which includes discipline, is essential for liberation and spiritual growth.

Discipline is about aligning one's thoughts, words, and actions with higher values and principles. It is about willingly surrendering to the guidance of wise teachers, scriptures, and spiritual practices.

To illustrate the importance of discipline in the pursuit of spiritual growth, let us consider the story of a wise sage and his disciples.

Story

A sage had dedicated his life to the path of Self-realization and had attained profound wisdom through years of rigorous spiritual practices. He had gathered a group of disciples who were eager to learn from him.

The sage recognized the potential in his disciples and understood that discipline was crucial for their spiritual progress. He taught them the importance of regular meditation, self-inquiry, and adherence to moral values. He emphasized the need to cultivate virtues such as compassion, truthfulness, and humility. The sage guided his disciples in developing a daily routine that included study, reflection, and service to others.

Under the sage's guidance, the disciples embraced discipline wholeheartedly. They woke up before sunrise to engage in their spiritual practices, maintained a simple and pure lifestyle, and remained committed to their spiritual growth. They realized that discipline was not a restriction but a means to unlock their inner potential and connect with their true nature. Through such obedience, they found inner peace and fulfillment.

In conclusion, discipline is an indispensable aspect of spiritual growth and personal development. As Amma states, obedience with humility leads to discipline. By heeding the words of wise teachers, scriptures, and spiritual practices, individuals can cultivate the virtues and qualities necessary for their spiritual evolution. Through discipline, one can embark on a transformative journey of self-discovery, Self-realization, and ultimately, liberation.

ॐ

Selfless Service

10. Don't miss the opportunities you come across to perform unselfish actions. You will then gradually gain mental purity and devotion. As you proceed with diligence, you will attain more clarity of mind and a deeper understanding. This will finally lead you to the state of perfection, the state of Self-realization." –Amma

On the path of spirituality, one of the fundamental principles is that of selfless service. Amma, in her profound wisdom, emphasizes the importance of embracing opportunities for unselfish actions. Why is this so? This is because the ego is the only obstacle to the realization of our True Self. Through selfless service, which means, performing actions that benefit others, instead of oneself, one can purify the mind, cultivate devotion, and ultimately attain the state of Self-realization.

From another perspective, selfless service is an expression of love and compassion towards others. It involves going beyond our personal desires and preferences to serve the needs of others without expecting anything in return. By engaging in acts of kindness, generosity, and service, we tap into the essence of our true nature, which is love itself.

Amma's teaching aligns with the wisdom imparted in the Bhagavad Gita. In Chapter 2, verse 47, Lord Krishna advises Arjuna:

karmaṇy-evādhikāras te mā phaleṣhu kadāchana
mā karma-phala-hetur bhūr mā te saṅgo 'stvakarmaṇi

– Bhagavad Gita 2:47

Your right is to perform your prescribed duty only, but never to lay claim to its results. Do not be motivated by the fruits of action, and never develop an attachment to inaction.

This verse emphasizes the significance of performing action without attachment to the outcome. It also warns the aspirant that just because one is on the spiritual path, it does not warrant the giving up of actions. What needs to be given up is the attitude of doer-ship, and of acting solely for one's own benefit.

When we engage in selfless service, we expand our consciousness and develop a deep sense of Being-Awareness (Sat-Chit). We recognize that we are part of a larger whole, and our actions have a ripple effect on the world around us. By offering our time, skills, resources, and love to uplift others, we contribute to the betterment of society and create a positive impact.

Selfless service is not limited to grand gestures or extraordinary acts. It is also the practice of non-doer and non-enjoyer attitude in actions. It can be as simple as lending a listening ear to someone in need, offering a helping hand to a stranger, or volunteering in community service projects. The key is to perform these acts with a genuine intention to alleviate suffering and bring joy to others keeping practice of non-doer and non-enjoyer attitude in actions.

Amma's guidance urges us to seize every opportunity for selfless action that comes our way. By doing so, we gradually purify our minds, develop clarity of thought, and deepen our understanding of the oneness of all beings. Selfless service becomes a transformative practice that leads us on the path of spiritual evolution by purifying mind and distractions by maintaining Self notion.

In conclusion, as we engage in selfless service, we learn to cultivate qualities such as humility, patience, compassion, and gratitude. We become more aware of the needs and struggles of others, and our hearts naturally expand with empathy and love. Through consistent practice, our self-centered tendencies gradually dissolve, making way for a greater alignment with our true nature.

Let us heed Amma's teachings and seize every opportunity to serve with love, compassion, and humility, thereby contributing to the collective upliftment of humanity.

Story
There lived a wise and revered monk known for his spiritual wisdom and profound teachings. People from all walks of life sought his guidance to find peace, purpose, and enlightenment. The king and his trusted minister were among those who held the monk in high regard and frequently sought his counsel.

One day, the minister approached the wise monk with a heavy heart. The kingdom was facing numerous challenges - social unrest, economic turmoil, and a growing divide among the people. The minister sought the monk's guidance on how to restore harmony and bring about positive change in the kingdom.

The wise monk listened attentively to the minister's concerns and took a moment to reflect. With a serene smile, he imparted his wisdom. He explained that the key to restoring harmony and bringing about positive change lay in the hearts of the king and his minister themselves.

The monk advised the minister to cultivate a deep sense of compassion and empathy within oneself. He encouraged the minister to lead by example, showing kindness, understanding, and respect to all individuals, regardless of their status or background. By embodying these qualities, the minister would inspire others to do the same, fostering an environment of unity and cooperation.

Furthermore, the monk emphasized the importance of selflessness and service to others. He explained that true leadership lies not in the pursuit of personal gain or power but in selflessly working for the welfare of the kingdom and its people.

The minister was encouraged to engage in acts of compassion and service, addressing the needs of the less fortunate and marginalized sections of society.

Inspired by the monk's words, the minister embraced his role as a servant-leader. He dedicated himself to implementing policies that would uplift the lives of the people, promote equality, and ensure justice for all. He worked tirelessly to bridge the gaps between different communities, fostering a sense of inclusivity and harmony.

ॐ

11. *"If we have love and compassion in our hearts, then we will wholeheartedly serve those who suffer from lack of food, clothing and shelter." -Amma*

Amidst the complexities of life, it is love and compassion that serve as guiding lights, leading us towards a path of selflessness and service. Amma's profound words remind us of the significance of extending our hearts and hands to those in need. When love and compassion reside within us, we become conduits of divine grace, embracing the opportunity to alleviate the suffering of our fellow beings.

In the philosophy of Advaita Vedanta, love and compassion are considered innate qualities of our true nature. They are not bound by boundaries or limited to specific individuals; instead, they emanate from the recognition that we are all One, the same universal consciousness. This understanding guides us towards a selfless approach to life, where we view the well-being of others as inseparable from our own.

Amma's words here emphasize the profound connection between love, compassion, and selfless service. It reflects the core teachings of Vedanta philosophy, which emphasize the unity and love for all beings. When we cultivate love and compassion within ourselves, we naturally feel compelled to extend our support and care to those who are in need, particularly those who suffer from a lack of basic necessities like food, clothing, and shelter.

Love and compassion are not just transient emotions; they are transformative qualities that have the power to transcend personal boundaries and expand our awareness to include the well-being of others. When we approach life with a heart full of love and compassion, we recognize the inherent dignity and worth of every individual, regardless of their circumstances. When we serve those who suffer, we are serving a part of ourselves, as we are all interconnected in the tapestry of existence. This understanding compels us to take action and serve others selflessly, without expecting anything in return.

The story of a wise teacher provides a beautiful illustration of love and compassion in action.

Story
In a small village, there lived a revered teacher known for his wisdom and kind-heartedness. He had devoted disciples who had imbibed his teachings and aspired to follow his example. One day, news reached the teacher of a nearby community suffering from extreme poverty and deprivation. Without hesitation, the teacher and his disciples set out to offer their assistance.

Upon reaching the impoverished community, they were greeted with gratitude and hope. The teacher and his disciples spent their days tirelessly working to provide food, clothing, and shelter to those in need. They not only addressed the immediate physical needs but also offered solace and emotional support to the suffering individuals. The teacher's love and compassion were contagious, spreading warmth and healing to every corner of the community.

As days turned into weeks, the teacher and his disciples continued their selfless service, extending love and compassion to all. They realized that true service went beyond material provisions; it meant recognizing the inherent dignity and worth of every individual. They listened attentively to the stories of the people, offering words of encouragement and hope. Through their acts of kindness, the teacher and his disciples not only provided immediate relief but also instilled a sense of empowerment and resilience within the community.

Witnessing the profound impact of their service, the disciples marveled at the transformative power of love and compassion. They understood that their teacher's teachings were not mere words but a living embodiment of divine love. They realized that serving others selflessly was not only an act of generosity but also an act of recognizing the inherent divinity in every being.

As the teacher and his disciples continued their service, the community gradually began to heal and rebuild. The seeds of love and compassion sown by the teacher blossomed into a community bound by unity, empathy, and resilience. The once downtrodden individuals became empowered, finding strength within themselves to create a better future.

Through their journey, the wise teacher and his disciples taught an invaluable lesson - that love and compassion have the power to transform lives. When we approach our actions with love and compassion, we become instruments of positive change, healing not only the external wounds of the world but also the inner wounds of the heart.

Amma's words remind us that love and compassion are not abstract concepts but tangible forces that have the ability to uplift and transform lives. When we embrace the spirit of selfless service, we create a ripple effect of love and compassion, nurturing a more compassionate and inclusive world. By wholeheartedly serving those who suffer from lack of food, clothing and shelter is the way to see compassion in action.

ॐ

12. *"Pray: O lord, entrust me with your work: please do not let me sit idle." -Amma*

In Advaita Vedanta, there exists a profound understanding that each individual is an instrument of the divine, entrusted with a unique purpose and role in the grand tapestry of creation. It is through the recognition of this divine calling and the heartfelt prayer for guidance that one embarks on a journey of selfless service and spiritual growth.

Amidst the hustle and bustle of daily life, it is easy for one to become absorbed in the superficialities of worldly pursuits, losing sight of their true purpose. From the grace of the divine, when one heeds the higher call that beckons them beyond the boundaries of the mundane, they start performing spiritual practices.

Yet, there is often a commonly observed phenomenon in such aspirants, especially those who renounce the worldly way of life and become full-time renunciates. They look to give up all actions and fall prey to idleness.

So here, Amma reminds us of the importance of surrendering to the divine will and entrusting ourselves to the work that is meant for us. In her words, "Pray: O lord, entrust me with your work: please do not let me sit idle," she encapsulates the essence of the Advaita Vedanta way, where the ego dissolves and the individual becomes a humble instrument for divine service.

The prayer itself holds a deep significance. It is not a plea for personal gain or worldly success, but rather a plea to be of service to humanity, to be a vessel for divine love and compassion. It is a surrender of the egoic desires and a recognition that the true fulfillment lies in aligning oneself with the divine purpose.

In the Advaita Vedanta way, the belief is that the divine permeates all aspects of existence. It is present in every moment, in every person, and in every circumstance. By offering oneself as an instrument, one opens the door to the divine unfolding through them, allowing love, wisdom, and grace to flow effortlessly.

This surrender and trust in the divine work does not imply passivity or idleness. On the contrary, it ignites a flame of devotion and inspiration, propelling the individual to actively engage in the service of humanity. It is a call to action, to be fully present and committed to making a positive impact in the world.

The path of Advaita Vedanta is not limited to renunciation or seclusion from society. It is about finding divinity within the realm of daily life and serving others with love and compassion. It is about recognizing that every interaction, every task, and every moment is an opportunity to express the divine qualities inherent within.

Just as a lamp illuminates a dark room, the individual who earnestly prays and surrenders to the divine work becomes a radiant source of light and inspiration. Their actions become a testament to the transformative power of selfless service and a reflection of the divine love that flows through them.

In the Bhagavad Gita, Lord Krishna imparts the wisdom that one should offer all of their actions and their very being to the divine. In Chapter 9, verse 27,

yat karoṣhi yad aśhnāsi yaj juhoṣhi dadāsi yat
yat tapasyasi kaunteya tat kuruṣhva mad-arpaṇam

– Bhagavad Gita 9:27

"Whatever you do, whatever you eat, whatever you offer in sacrifice, whatever you give, whatever austerity you practice—do it as an offering to Me."

This verse encapsulates the very essence of being free from the bondage of Karma, where every action, no matter how small or seemingly insignificant, becomes an offering to the divine.

The prayer of Amma serves as a powerful reminder for us to embrace our role as instruments of the divine, to dedicate our actions to the service of humanity, and to cultivate a deep trust in the divine guidance that flows through us. It is an invitation to live a life of purpose, meaning, and fulfillment by actively participating in the divine work that unfolds in each and every moment.

So let us heed the wisdom of Amma and offer our heartfelt prayer, "O lord, entrust me with your work: please do not let me sit idle."

Story

There once lived a sage who was known far and wide for his deep wisdom and unwavering devotion to the divine. People from far and near would flock to seek his guidance and blessings, and he would generously share his profound insights with all who came to him.

One day, a young man, filled with curiosity and a yearning for spiritual wisdom, embarked on a journey to meet the sage. He had heard stories of the sage's extraordinary teachings and the transformative impact they had on people's lives. With great anticipation, this young man made his way to the humble abode of the sage.

He asked the sage about the purpose of life and the path to spiritual realization. The sage listened attentively, his eyes filled with profound wisdom.

The sage began, "the purpose of life is to realize our true nature, to awaken to the divinity that resides within us and all of creation. It is through Self-realization that we discover the eternal source of peace, love, and bliss that exists beyond the realm of the transient and ever-changing world."

"The path to Self-realization requires steadfast dedication and a sincere longing for Truth. It is a journey of self-discovery, where one must cultivate self-discipline, practice self-inquiry, and embrace the virtues of love, compassion, and humility. By turning inward and quieting the mind, one can connect with the divine essence that pervades all of existence."

The young man played his part in the grand symphony of life, spreading love, compassion, and wisdom wherever he went. His life became a living testament to the transformative power of spirituality and the profound impact that a dedicated and wise teacher can have on the lives of others. Through his selfless service and unwavering commitment to the path of Self-realization, he exemplified the essence of the Advaita Vedanta.

ॐ

13. *"Remember to set apart at least one hour every day to do some service for others. While the food we eat nurtures our bodies, it is what we give in charity that nurtures our souls. If time is not available daily, reserve at least a few hours every week for some worthwhile act of charity." -Amma*

In the realm of selfless service, there lies a profound opportunity to help others, but also to tremendously benefit our spiritual growth. This is the paradox of selfless service, by forgetting one's own self-interest and helping others, we are tremendously benefited. Amma, with her infinite wisdom, reveals to her children this profound secret, and reminds us of the importance of dedicating time to serve those in need.

From reflecting on the teachings of Advaita Vedanta, we come to understand that our true nature is one with the entire universe. We are not separate entities, but rather the divine cosmic fabric that weaves all beings together. From this realization, the concept of selfless service emerges as a natural expression of our inherent unity and compassion.

Amma's quote serves as a gentle reminder to set aside time each day for acts of service. Just as we nourish our physical bodies with sustenance, it is equally essential to nourish our minds and hearts through acts of service. By engaging in selfless service, we not only offer our support and assistance to those in need but also cultivate a sense of inner fulfillment and spiritual growth.

The importance of dedicating regular time to serve others cannot be overstated. Amma encourages us to reserve at least one hour every day for acts of charity. This dedicated hour allows us to step outside of our own self-centered concerns and focus on the well-being of others. It provides an opportunity to extend a helping hand, lend a listening ear, or offer a kind word to those who may be struggling or in need of support.

However, Amma acknowledges that our daily schedules may not always permit an hour of service. In such cases, she advises us to reserve a few hours each week for acts of charity. This flexibility ensures that we continue to prioritize selfless acts even when faced with time constraints. It is a reminder that every effort, no matter how small, contributes to the greater good and helps nurture our souls.

In the Bhagavad Gita, Lord Krishna emphasizes the significance of selfless action and how great leaders inspired all doing in Chapter 3, verse 20,21

karmaṇaiva hi sansiddhim āsthitā janakādayaḥ
loka-saṅgraham evāpi sampaśhyan kartum arhasi
yad yad ācharati śhreṣhṭhas tat tad evetaro janaḥ
sa yat pramāṇaṁ kurute lokas tad anuvartate

– Bhagavad Gita 3:20-21

By performing their prescribed duties without self-interest, King Janaka and others attained perfection. You should also perform your duties to set an example for the good of the world. Whatever actions great persons perform, common people follow. Whatever standards they set, all the world pursues.

The story of a wise teacher and their disciples beautifully illustrates the essence of Amma's teaching.

Story
In a remote village, there lived a revered teacher who had devoted their life to the upliftment and welfare of the community. They had gathered a group of dedicated disciples who shared their vision of selfless service.

Each day, the disciples would gather around their teacher, eager to receive guidance and wisdom. The teacher would impart lessons on the importance of selfless action, emphasizing that true fulfillment and spiritual growth arise from serving others. They would recount stories of their own experiences in serving the community, inspiring the disciples to follow in their footsteps.

Encouraged by their teacher's words, the disciples made a commitment to set aside a few hours every week for acts of charity. They started by visiting the elderly in the village, offering companionship and assistance with daily tasks. They spent time at local shelters, serving meals to the homeless and engaging in heartfelt conversations. They volunteered at orphanages, bringing joy to the children through games, storytelling, and acts of kindness.

As the disciples immersed themselves in selfless service, they experienced a profound transformation within themselves. The walls of self-centeredness began to crumble, replaced by a deep sense of interconnectedness and compassion. They realized that their own happiness and fulfillment were intricately tied to the well-being of others.

Through their acts of charity, the disciple witnessed the power of love and compassion to uplift and heal. They saw how a kind word or a helping hand could bring light to someone's darkest moments. They learned that true fulfillment was not found in personal gain, but in the selfless expression of love towards others.

The teacher, observing the disciple's growth, guided them further on the path of selfless service. They emphasized the importance of humility, reminding the disciple that their actions were not meant to be driven by ego or recognition. True service comes from a place of genuine care and a desire to alleviate the suffering of others.

With each passing day, the disciple's commitment to service deepened. They became an inspiration to others, their presence radiating kindness and compassion. The impact of their selfless acts rippled throughout the community, touching the lives of many.

The story of the wise teacher and their disciple teaches us that selfless service is not bound by time or circumstances. It is a state of mind and a way of being in the world. By setting aside dedicated time for acts of charity, we align ourselves with the divine principles of love, compassion, and unity.

As we embrace Amma's teachings and commit ourselves to selfless service, let us remember that even the smallest acts of kindness can create a ripple effect of love and compassion. By offering our time, energy, and resources to uplift those in need, we contribute to the betterment of society and nurture our own spiritual growth.

ॐ

14. *"Instead of doing Pada Puja, what makes Amma happy is Her children serving the poor and needy." -Amma*

In the Guru-disciple relationship, the act of worship holds significant importance. People often engage in various rituals and practices to express their love and devotion and seek blessings. However, Amma reminds us that true devotion lies not in elaborate ceremonies but in serving the poor and needy.

Amma's teaching emphasizes the essence of selfless service as the ultimate form of worship. She states that instead of performing traditional rituals like Pāda Puja, the greatest joy and fulfillment for her come from witnessing her children actively engaged in serving those who are less fortunate.

This teaching aligns perfectly with the Advaita Vedanta philosophy, which emphasizes the oneness of all beings. It recognizes that the divine resides within each and every individual, regardless of their social status, economic background, or external appearances. Therefore, when we serve those in need, we are in fact serving the divine presence within them.

Our actions also have the power to create a positive impact on others. By extending our love, compassion, and support to those who are struggling, we not only alleviate their suffering but also contribute to the upliftment of society as a whole.

Amma's teaching echoes the timeless wisdom of the Bhagavad Gita, which emphasizes the importance of selfless action. In Chapter 3, verse 8, Lord Krishna states,

niyataṁ kuru karma tvaṁ karma jyāyo hyakarmaṇaḥ

–Bhagavad Gita 3:8

Perform your prescribed duty, for action is better than inaction.

This verse reminds us that engaging in righteous actions, driven by love and compassion, is an essential part of our spiritual journey.

The story of Amma's children around the world serving the poor and needy is a testament to the transformative power of selfless service. Inspired by Amma's teachings, they come together to address the needs of the underprivileged. People devote their time, skills, and resources to provide food, clothing, shelter, and education to those who lack these basic necessities.

These individuals, driven by the desire to serve and uplift others, experience a profound inner transformation. They transcend their ego-centric desires and develop a deep sense of empathy and compassion. They see the divine presence in the eyes of every person they serve, realizing that in helping others, they are ultimately serving the divinity within themselves.

Through their selfless service, they have become living embodiments of Amma's teachings. They radiate love, kindness, and humility, touching the lives of countless individuals and inspiring others to join in the noble cause. Their actions become a testament to the power of genuine devotion and the transformative potential of serving the poor and needy.

The practice of serving the poor and needy not only benefits the recipients but also nourishes our own spiritual growth. It purifies our hearts, expands our consciousness, and deepens our connection with the divine. It teaches us humility, gratitude, and the value of selflessness.

In the Advaita Vedanta way, the act of serving the poor and needy becomes a sacred ritual, a true form of worship. It is an expression of our love and devotion to the divine presence that resides within all beings. Through selfless service, we transcend the limitations of the ego and merge into the vast ocean of love and unity.

As we embrace Amma's teaching and immerse ourselves in serving the poor and needy, let us remember that every act of kindness and compassion is a step closer to our own spiritual evolution. By becoming instruments of love and service, we embody the essence of Amma's message and contribute to creating a world filled with love, compassion, and unity.

Story
The wise teacher emphasizes the importance of serving the poor and needy to his disciples. He teaches them that true spirituality is not confined to rituals and worship alone but is expressed through acts of kindness and compassion towards those in need.

The teacher and his disciples, eager to put these teachings into practice, venture out into the community with the intention of serving the poor and needy. They visit orphanages, shelters, and impoverished neighborhoods, offering their assistance and support to those who require it the most.

Through their selfless service, the disciples learn valuable lessons about humility, empathy, and the interconnectedness of all beings. They begin to see the divinity present in every person they encounter, irrespective of their circumstances. They realize that by serving others, they are serving the divine within themselves.

As the disciples continue their journey of service, they encounter individuals who have lost hope, who are burdened by poverty, and who yearn for a better life. With love and compassion, the disciples extend a helping hand, offering not only material support but also a sense of dignity and hope.

The impact of their actions spreads throughout the community, inspiring others to join their noble cause. People from all walks of life come forward to contribute their time, resources, and expertise, creating a network of support and compassion that uplifts the entire community.

ॐ

Compassion

15. "God is within us, but today that presence is only in seed form. What is needed for the seed to sprout is the water of compassion." -Amma

Compassion is the divine quality that connects us to the essence of our being, to the presence of God within us. It is the water that nourishes the seed of divinity and allows it to sprout and grow. Amma's profound words remind us of the transformative power of compassion and its essential role in our spiritual journey.

In the Advaita Vedanta way, compassion is not just an emotion or a feeling; it is a state of being, a recognition of the inherent interconnectedness of all beings. It is the understanding that we are all expressions of the same divine consciousness, and by extending love and kindness to others, we are essentially nurturing the divine spark within ourselves.

When we cultivate compassion, we tap into the limitless reservoir of love that resides within us. It is through acts of kindness, selflessness, and empathy that we manifest the divine qualities that are inherent in our true nature. Compassion breaks down the barriers of separation and fosters a deep sense of unity and oneness with all of creation.

The story of a wise sage beautifully illustrates the transformative power of compassion.

Story
This sage, deeply immersed in spiritual practice, radiated love and compassion to all those who crossed his path. His presence alone brought solace to the troubled hearts and uplifted the spirits of those in need.

One day, a young boy named Ravi came to the sage seeking guidance. This boy was burdened by the sorrows and challenges of his life, feeling lost and disconnected from the world around him. The sage, with his eyes filled with compassion, listened attentively to Ravi's story, understanding the depth of his pain.

The sage gently guided the young boy, teaching him the importance of compassion and how it can transform his life. He shared stories of great beings who had embodied compassion and the profound impact they had on the world. Through these teachings, Ravi began to realize that compassion was not just an external gesture; it was a way of being, a way to connect with the divine within himself and others.

Inspired by the sage's wisdom, he decided to put compassion into practice. He started by showing kindness to his family and friends, offering a listening ear, and providing support when needed. He extended his acts of compassion to strangers, lending a helping hand to those in need and offering words of encouragement to uplift their spirits.

As Ravi continued to cultivate compassion in his life, he noticed a remarkable transformation within himself. The more he gave love and kindness to others, the more he experienced a deep sense of fulfillment and joy. He realized that compassion was not just about alleviating the suffering of others, but also about recognizing the divinity within himself and nurturing his own spiritual growth.

Through his acts of compassion, Ravi became a beacon of light in his community. His actions inspired others to embrace compassion as a way of life, creating a ripple effect of love and kindness that spread far and wide. The collective presence of compassionate beings brought about a positive change in the world, fostering harmony, understanding, and a deep sense of interconnectedness.

In the Bhagavad Gita, Lord Krishna teaches the importance of compassion, stating,

Compassion

yo māṁ paśhyati sarvatra sarvaṁ cha mayi paśhyati
tasyāhaṁ na praṇaśhyāmi sa cha me na praṇaśhyati

– Bhagavad Gita 6:30

He who sees Me in all things and all things in Me, I am never lost to him, nor is he ever lost to Me.

This verse encapsulates the essence of Advaita Vedanta, highlighting the unity and interconnectedness of all existence. When we cultivate compassion, we recognize the divine presence in all beings, and in turn, we become more connected to our own true nature.

In conclusion, compassion is not just a virtue; it is the very essence of our being. When we cultivate compassion, we awaken the dormant divinity within us and experience a deep sense of connection to all of creation. It is through acts of kindness, empathy, and selflessness that we bring forth the full potential of our humanity and realize our true purpose in life.

Amma's words remind us of the importance of nurturing compassion in our hearts and actively expressing it in our thoughts, words, and actions. The practice of compassion begins with recognizing the inherent worth and dignity of every being, regardless of their background, status, or beliefs. It is a humble acknowledgment that we are all interconnected and share a common essence.

When we live with compassion, we go beyond our individual concerns and extend our care to others. We become a source of support, solace, and inspiration to those who are suffering or in need. It is through acts of service and kindness that we alleviate the pain and bring healing to the world around us.

So, the cultivation of compassion is a profound and transformative practice that leads us to the realization of our interconnectedness with all of creation. It is through compassion that we awaken to our true nature, recognizing the divine spark within ourselves and others.

Amma's quote reminds us that true compassion goes beyond superficial acts of charity. It is a state of being, a way of perceiving and interacting with the world from a place of love and understanding. When we cultivate compassion, we develop the ability to see beyond external differences and connect with the essence that unites us all.

ॐ

16. *"Keep a constant awareness and a conscious effort to say a kind word, a compassionate glance, perform good actions, and to practice patience and compassion. All these can bring light into the lives of others and into ours, as well." -Amma*

On the journey of Self-realization, Amma reminds us of the power of our words, actions, and intentions. Her quote emphasizes the importance of keeping a constant awareness and making a conscious effort to bring kindness, compassion, and goodness into the world.

The practice of mindfulness, as encouraged by Amma, involves being present in each moment, observing our thoughts and actions, and consciously choosing to act with kindness and compassion. By cultivating this awareness, we become more attuned to the impact of our words and actions on others and ourselves.

A kind word has the power to uplift someone's spirits, to offer comfort and support, and to create a sense of connection and belonging. It is a simple act, yet it can bring immense joy and light into someone's life. By choosing our words carefully, speaking with love and compassion, we can make a positive difference in the lives of those around us.

Similarly, a compassionate glance, a gentle smile, or a reassuring touch can convey understanding, empathy, and acceptance. These small gestures have the ability to create a safe and nurturing environment where others feel seen, heard, and valued. Through our presence and genuine care, we can bring light and warmth into the lives of others.

But it is not just about our external actions. Amma reminds us to practice patience and compassion within ourselves as well. The journey of Self-realization requires self-compassion and self-acceptance. It is about treating ourselves with kindness, forgiveness, and understanding. When we cultivate patience and compassion towards ourselves, we create a foundation for extending the same to others.

The teachings of the Advaita Vedanta emphasize the importance of these qualities. They remind us that our thoughts, words, and actions have a profound impact on our own spiritual growth and the well-being of those around us. Krishna teaches that

rāga-dveṣha-viyuktais tu viṣhayān indriyaiśh charan
ātma-vaśhyair-vidheyātmā prasādam adhigachchhati

— Bhagavad Gita2:64.

Being free from attachment and aversion, even while interacting with the objects of the senses, the self-controlled person attains the Grace of God.

One who is able to control his senses, mind, and intellect is known as a sage or wise person, cultivating awareness and consciously choosing to act with kindness and compassion, we cultivate the qualities of a wise person.

In Advaita Vedanta, the path to Self-realization is not separate from our interactions with others. It is through our interactions and relationships that we have the opportunity to express and embody the divine qualities of love, kindness, and compassion. By bringing light into the lives of others, we also illuminate our own path towards Self-realization.

In conclusion, Amma's quote reminds us of the power we hold to bring light and positivity into the world through our words, actions, and intentions. By keeping a constant awareness and making a conscious effort to be kind, compassionate, patient, and understanding, we create an environment of love and healing for ourselves and others. Let us embrace these practices in our daily lives and become beacons of light, spreading love and compassion to all those we encounter.

Story
One day, a young man came to Guru seeking his counsel. This young man was burdened with the weight of his past actions and was desperately seeking a way to find peace within himself. As he poured out his heart to Guru, tears streaming down his face, the wise teacher listened intently, his eyes filled with deep empathy.

Guru gently placed a hand on the young man's shoulder and spoke with a soothing voice, "my child, I understand your pain. But remember, the path to inner peace lies in the power of compassion."

Young man looked up, his eyes filled with curiosity. "Compassion, Guru? How can that help me find peace within?"

Guru smiled warmly and began to tell a story. He spoke of a time when the village faced a severe drought, and the crops withered, leaving the people in despair. In the midst of this crisis, a young woman came forward with an idea. She suggested that everyone set aside at least one hour each day to serve those in need. She believed that by sharing their resources and showing compassion to others, they could uplift the entire community.

Inspired by the young woman's words, the villagers followed her lead. They spent their time feeding the hungry, clothing the poor, and providing shelter to those without homes. Through their acts of kindness, the villagers not only nourished the bodies of the less fortunate but also nurtured their own souls. They discovered that true happiness and inner peace blossomed when they extended their love and compassion to others.

As Guru finished the story, he turned to the young man and said, "Young man, the same principle applies to your journey of finding inner peace. When you open your heart to compassion, when you extend love and kindness to others, you not only alleviate their suffering but also heal your own wounds. Compassion has the power to transform your life and bring you the peace you seek."

Young man pondered these words of the Guru, a newfound hope flickering in his eyes. He realized that true healing and peace could only come from within, through acts of selfless service and the cultivation of a compassionate heart.

ॐ

17. *"True compassion is the ability to see what is beyond body and mind. only then can you offer real help and uplift others." -Amma*

Compassion is often seen as an emotion, a feeling of empathy and concern for others. But from the perspective of Advaita Vedanta, it goes beyond mere sentimentality. It becomes a profound understanding and recognition of the oneness of all beings, transcending the boundaries of body and mind.

In the teachings of Amma, we find the wisdom that true compassion requires us to look beyond the superficial aspects of a person and recognize the essence that lies within. It is the ability to see beyond the physical appearance, the external circumstances, and even the mental states of individuals. True compassion is rooted in the understanding that at the core, we are all connected, all expressions of the same divine consciousness.

To offer real help and uplift others, we must first cultivate this deep awareness. We must transcend our limited identification with the physical form and the fluctuations of the mind. As Amma beautifully states, true compassion is the ability to see what is beyond body and mind. It is the recognition that the true essence of every being is divine, untouched by the transient nature of the material world.

When we operate from this level of awareness, our actions are no longer driven by personal preferences or attachments. We are guided by a higher purpose, a universal love that encompasses all beings. We see the suffering of others as our own, and their joys and successes as a reflection of the divine within us.

In the Bhagavad Gita, Lord Krishna teaches the path of selfless action and devotion. He encourages us to see ourselves in all beings, to treat others with love and respect, and to perform our duties without attachment to the fruits of our actions. Listing the qualities of those who are steeped in divine consciousness, Lord Krishna states:

abhayaṁ sattva-sanśhuddhir jñāna-yoga-vyavasthitiḥ
dānaṁ damaśh cha yajñaśh cha svādhyāyas tapa ārjavam
ahinsā satyam akrodhas tyāgaḥ śhāntir apaiśhunam
dayā bhūteṣhv aloluptvaṁ mārdavaṁ hrīr achāpalam
tejaḥ kṣhamā dhṛitiḥ śhaucham adroho nāti-mānitā
bhavanti sampadaṁ daivīm abhijātasya bhārata

– Bhagavad Gita 16:1-3

Fearlessness, purity of heart, steadfastness in knowledge and yoga, charity, self-control, sacrifice, study of scriptures, austerity, simplicity, non-violence, truthfulness, absence of anger, renunciation, serenity, absence of calumny, compassion for all creatures, absence of greed, gentleness, modesty, absence of fickleness, vigor, forgiveness, fortitude, purity, freedom from malice—these, O scion of the Bharata dynasty, are the endowments of one born destined to have the divine nature.

To embody true compassion, we must cultivate these divine qualities within ourselves. We must strive for fearlessness, purity of heart, and steadfastness in knowledge and yoga. We must practice charity, self-control, and sacrifice. We must engage in the study of scriptures, embrace austerity and simplicity, and cultivate non-violence and truthfulness in our thoughts, words, and actions.

But above all, we must cultivate compassion for all creatures through the recognition of the underlying divinity that is common to all. We must understand that in uplifting others, we uplift ourselves, for we are all threads woven into the grand tapestry of existence.

As we walk the path of freedom, let us strive to develop true compassion, seeing beyond the limitations of body and mind. Let us offer real help and uplift others by embodying the divine qualities and teachings of love, kindness, and selflessness. In doing so, we not only transform ourselves but also contribute to the collective awakening of humanity, where compassion becomes the guiding force in our interactions, and the world becomes a more harmonious and loving place for all.

Story
Once upon a time, in a small village nestled amidst lush green hills, there lived a wise sage. People from far and wide would

seek his guidance and solace, as his words carried the wisdom of the ages and his presence radiated an indescribable aura of compassion.

One day, three travelers arrived in the village. They were weary and downtrodden, having faced numerous hardships on their journey. Hearing of the sage's wisdom and compassion, they decided to seek his counsel.

"My dear friends," the sage said, "true compassion is not just an emotion, but a deep understanding that connects us all. It is the ability to see beyond the physical form and the fleeting nature of the mind. Compassion arises when we recognize the divine essence within every being."

"But how can we truly uplift others and offer real help?" one asked, his voice filled with sincerity.

The sage smiled and replied, "It starts with cultivating a constant awareness and a conscious effort to say a kind word, to perform good actions, and to practice patience and compassion. Each small act of kindness has the power to bring light into the lives of others and into our own."

"But sometimes, it feels overwhelming. How can we make a difference in a world filled with suffering?" he asked.

"Remember," sage said, "even the smallest acts of service and kindness can create ripples of love and healing. Start with setting apart at least one hour every day to do some service for others. And if time is not available daily, reserve at least a few hours every week for some worthwhile act of charity." The sage nodded and shared, "Pray. Pray with a sincere heart and surrender to the divine will. Pray, 'O Lord, entrust me with your work: please do not let me sit idle.' Trust that when you offer yourself as a vessel for divine service, you will be guided and empowered to make a difference."

ॐ

18. "In times of tragedies, our duty is to lend a helping hand to those in grief and thus light lamps of kindness and compassion." -Amma

In the realm of the Advaita Vedanta, the teachings of Amma echo the profound truth that our true duty in times of tragedies is to extend a helping hand to those who are grieving. It is during these challenging moments that our capacity for kindness and compassion can shine brightly, illuminating the path of healing and solace for those in need.

Tragedies often leave individuals and communities in a state of despair and sorrow. They create an atmosphere of darkness that can be overwhelming and disheartening. However, it is precisely in these moments that the light of compassion becomes even more essential. It is through acts of kindness, empathy, and support that we can offer a glimmer of hope and provide a comforting presence to those who are suffering.

When we extend a helping hand to those in grief, we not only offer practical assistance but also demonstrate our genuine care and concern. We become beacons of light in the midst of darkness, symbolizing the power of compassion to heal and uplift. By engaging in acts of kindness, whether it is offering a listening ear, providing material support, or simply offering a comforting presence, we become instrumental in kindling the lamps of kindness and compassion.

adveṣhṭā sarva-bhūtānāṁ maitraḥ karuṇa eva cha
nirmamo nirahankāraḥ sama-duḥkha-sukhaḥ kṣhamī
santuṣhṭaḥ satataṁ yogī yatātmā dṛiḍha-niśhchayaḥ
mayy arpita-mano-buddhir yo mad-bhaktaḥ sa me priyaḥ

– Bhagavad Gita 12:13-14

Those devotees are very dear to Me who are free from malice toward all living beings, who are friendly, and compassionate. They are free from attachment to possessions and egotism, equipoised in happiness and distress, and ever-forgiving. They are ever-content, steadily united with Me in devotion, self-controlled, of firm resolve, and dedicated to Me in mind and intellect.

In the Advaita Vedanta philosophy, the concept of unity and oneness is of utmost importance. It teaches us that we are all connected at the deepest level of existence, and that the suffering of one is the suffering of all. By recognizing this profound truth, we awaken to the realization that extending a helping hand to those in grief is not only a duty but also an opportunity for self-transformation.

When we lend a helping hand to others, we transcend our own self-centeredness and ego-driven desires. We embrace the essence of non-duality, understanding that our well-being is intrinsically linked to the well-being of others. In lighting the lamps of kindness and compassion, we not only bring solace to those in need, but we also nourish our own souls and cultivate a sense of interconnectedness and unity with the world around us.

In conclusion, Amma's profound teaching reminds us that in times of tragedies, our duty is not only to offer practical help, but also to be the bearers of kindness and compassion. By lighting lamps of love and support, we can alleviate the burden of grief and bring solace to those who are suffering. In doing so, we not only serve others but also embark on a transformative journey of selflessness and unity. May we all embrace the call to lend a helping hand and become beacons of light, illuminating the world with kindness and compassion.

Story

One day, as the King was attending to matters of the kingdom in his grand court, his trusted minister approached him with a concerned expression on his face. Sensing his minister's unease, the king invited him to speak openly.

"Your Majesty," "I have been pondering upon the recent tragedies that have befallen our kingdom. Many of our people are suffering, especially those who have lost their homes and loved ones. Their grief is overwhelming, and they are in dire need of assistance."

King nodded, his eyes filled with empathy. He understood the immense challenges faced by his people and the responsibility that fell upon his shoulders as their ruler. He knew that it was his duty to extend a helping hand in their time of need.

"Minister," said the king with determination, "it is our duty to lend a helping hand to those in grief. We must strive to bring light into their lives and alleviate their suffering. Let us gather our resources and devise a plan to provide food, clothing, and shelter to those in need."

Inspired by the king's words, Minister quickly set to work, mobilizing the kingdom's resources and organizing relief efforts. Together, they established shelters for the displaced, distributed food and clothing, and ensured that medical aid was provided to those injured.

As news of the king's compassionate actions spread throughout the kingdom, the people were filled with gratitude and admiration for their wise ruler. They witnessed firsthand the power of love and compassion in action, and their faith in the kingdom and its leadership was strengthened.

King embodied this profound truth by treating every individual as an extension of himself. His actions were guided by the understanding that the suffering of one was the suffering of all, and that true happiness could only be achieved when every citizen was cared for and uplifted.

ॐ

19. *"Spirituality begins and ends with Compassion. Try to see good in everything, like a bee focusing only on the flowers' nectar. " -Amma*

In the realm of spirituality, compassion serves as the foundational principle that guides our journey towards Self-realization and inner awakening. It is the essence of our connection with the world around us and the key to unlocking the depths of our own being. Amma beautifully captures this truth with her words: "Spirituality begins and ends with Compassion."

Compassion, in its purest form, is the ability to see the inherent goodness in all things, to recognize the divine spark that exists within every being and every situation. It is the recognition that we are all interconnected, part of a vast cosmic tapestry, and that our actions and intentions ripple through this interconnected web of existence.

Just as a bee focuses only on the nectar of flowers, seeking the sweetness and beauty in each one, so too must we train ourselves to see the good in everything. This requires a shift in perspective, a shift from judgment and criticism to understanding and empathy. It is a conscious choice to cultivate a compassionate heart that sees beyond appearances and embraces the underlying unity of all life.

The Chandogya Upanishad 6-9-2,

1. Yatha, saumya, madhu madhukrto nistishthanti, nanatyayanam vrkshanam rasan samavaharam katam rasam gamaynti.

2. Te yatha tatra na vivekam labhante, amushyaham vrkshasya raso'smi, amushyaham vrkshasya rasosmiti, evam eva khalu, saumya, imah sarvah prajah sati sampadya na viduh, sati sampadyamahaiti.

A profound analogy is presented to explain the significance of awareness in beings regarding their merging with the ultimate Existence. The analogy compares the bees' process of making honey to the beings' merging into Existence without conscious effort. Let's explore this analogy and its implications further.

Bees Making Honey: The Upanishad begins by drawing a parallel between bees and creatures. Just as bees diligently collect the essences of various trees standing in different quarters to make honey, creatures also merge into Existence without distinct ideas or awareness.

Essence Collection: Bees gather the essences of different trees and reduce them into a homogeneous whole, turning them into honey. Similarly, beings merge into Existence, transcending their individual identities and experiencing a sense of unity.

Absence of Distinctive Ideas: In the analogy, the Upanishad highlights that the collected essences, once transformed into honey, no longer retain distinctive characteristics. The sweetness of honey cannot be attributed to any specific tree's juice. Similarly, when beings merge into Existence, they lose their individual identities and cannot distinguish themselves from the unified Existence.

Lack of Awareness: The Upanishad states that just as bees do not have the idea, "I am the juice of this tree," beings, after merging into Existence, do not understand or realize their merging. They are unaware of their oneness with Existence during deep sleep, death, and even during the dissolution of the universe.

Merging into Existence: The analogy suggests that beings continuously merge into Existence, day after day, but remain unaware of this merging. They fail to recognize their inherent unity with the ultimate reality.

The underlying message of this passage is that beings, in their state of deep sleep, death, and dissolution, merge into the ultimate Existence without conscious effort. Just as bees collect essences and create honey without distinct ideas, beings merge into Existence without recognizing their oneness. This lack of awareness stems from the dissolution of individual identity and the experience of unity beyond dualities.

The Upanishad invites seekers to inquire into their true nature, to awaken from the state of unconscious merging, and to realize their inherent oneness with Existence. It encourages individuals to transcend limited perspectives and experience the unity that underlies all existence.

By understanding this analogy, seekers are prompted to delve deeper into their spiritual journey, to explore their true nature, and to cultivate awareness of the eternal unity that permeates all aspects of existence. The analogy serves as a reminder that the ultimate goal is to realize our inherent unity and merge consciously with the source of all being – the ultimate Existence.

In the teachings of Advaita Vedanta, the truth of oneness is emphasized. We are reminded that behind the illusion of separateness, there exists a fundamental unity that binds us all. When we embrace this truth, our hearts expand with love and compassion, transcending the limitations of the ego and embracing the divine essence within ourselves and others.

Compassion is not limited to mere sentiment or sympathy; it is a dynamic force that compels us to act for the benefit of others. It moves us to alleviate suffering, to uplift those in need, and to promote peace and harmony in the world. It is through compassionate action that we embody the highest spiritual ideals and bring about positive change in our lives and the lives of others.

The journey of spirituality, then, is not a solitary pursuit but a path of service and compassion. As we open our hearts to the suffering of others and extend a helping hand, we become conduits for divine love and grace. We realize that true spiritual growth is not measured by personal achievements or external accomplishments, but by the depth of our compassion and our capacity to make a positive difference in the world.

Amma's wisdom reminds us that compassion is not an isolated virtue; it is the very essence of our spiritual journey. It is through compassionate acts that we transcend the limitations of the ego and align ourselves with the universal flow of love and harmony. When we see the world through the lens of compassion, our perception shifts, and we begin to recognize the inherent divinity that permeates all of creation.

In conclusion, let us heed the words of Amma and embrace compassion as the guiding principle of our spiritual path. Let us cultivate a heart that sees the good in everything, just as a bee seeks the nectar in every flower. Through acts of kindness, service, and unconditional love, we can become beacons of compassion, bringing light and healing to a world in need. May our journey be one of self-transformation and service, for in the spirit of compassion, we find our true selves and realize the interconnectedness of all beings.

Story

One day, as King was addressing his council of ministers, he spoke about the importance of compassion and its integral role in spirituality. He emphasized that spirituality begins and ends with compassion, and encouraged his ministers to embrace this virtue in their own lives.

Among the ministers, known for his intellect and administrative skills. He was respected for his ability to make wise decisions and guide the kingdom in times of need. Inspired by the king's words, the minister decided to delve deeper into the practice of compassion.

Minister sought the guidance of a revered sage who lived in the outskirts of the kingdom. The sage was renowned for his profound understanding of spirituality and his embodiment of compassion. Minister approached Sage and expressed his desire to learn more about compassion and its connection to spirituality.

Sage explained that compassion is the essence of spirituality, as it connects us with the inherent divinity within ourselves and others. Over the course of several months, the minister dedicated himself to learning from Sage. He studied ancient scriptures, practiced meditation, and engaged in self-reflection to deepen his understanding of compassion. With each passing day, Raman's heart expanded, and he became more attuned to the suffering and needs of those around him.

One day, a devastating flood struck a nearby village, leaving its inhabitants stranded and in desperate need of help. Minister approached the King and shared the plight of the villagers. The king, always responsive to the needs of his people, immediately organized a relief effort to provide food, clothing, and shelter to the affected villagers.

Minister played a pivotal role in coordinating the relief efforts. He rallied the kingdom's resources, mobilized volunteers, and ensured that the necessary supplies reached the villagers promptly. Inspired by the teachings of Sage, minister approached this task with a heart full of compassion, offering solace and support to those in distress.

ॐ

Love

20. "Our selfless, innocent love is the greatest offering that we can give to the Lord." - Amma

Love is the essence of our being, the very fabric of our existence. It is not merely an emotion or a fleeting sentiment, but a profound expression of our True nature. In the teachings of Advaita Vedanta, love is regarded as the highest form of devotion and the ultimate offering to the Divine.

Amma's words remind us that our love, when offered selflessly and innocently, becomes the greatest gift we can present to the Lord. It is through love that we connect with the divine presence that permeates every aspect of creation. Love bridges the gap between the individual self and the universal Self, dissolving the illusion of separation and revealing the inherent unity that exists within all beings.

The journey of love begins with selflessness. When we cultivate an attitude of selflessness, we transcend our ego-driven desires and preferences. We learn to prioritize the well-being and happiness of others above our own. It is in this selflessness that love blossoms, expanding our hearts and allowing us to experience the divinity within ourselves and others.

Love is not limited by boundaries or conditions. It is inclusive and all-encompassing. It extends beyond caste, creed, race, or nationality. It embraces the entire creation, recognizing the interconnectedness of all beings. When we love selflessly, we see the divine in every person and every form of life. We treat others with kindness, respect, and compassion, knowing that they too are a reflection of the divine presence.

Through the practice of Advaita Vedanta, we come to understand that love is not an external force that we seek outside of ourselves. It is the very essence of our being, the core of our existence. Love is not something we acquire or attain; it is what we are at our deepest level. When we realize this truth, our love becomes boundless and unconditional, radiating outwards to touch the lives of others and bring joy and healing to the world. Yajnavalkya says that

atmanas-tu kamaya sarvam priyam bhavati

Atman and the Unity of Love

– Brihadaranyaka Upanishad 2-4-7

Insights from Brihadaranyaka Upanishad

The Brihadaranyaka Upanishad, delves into the profound concepts of the Self (Atman) and its relationship with love and desire. So, the teachings of Yajnavalkya from the Upanishad's Madhu-Kanda (Chapter II), emphasizing the unity of love and the role of ignorance in distorting its true essence.

Atman: The Infinite Self

Atman is described as the Infinite Self, the underlying essence that pervades all beings and phenomena. It is the eternal, unchanging aspect of our existence, beyond the limitations of the body and mind. Recognizing the true nature of Atman is fundamental to understanding the unity and oneness of all things.

Desire and Perceived Desirability

Yajnavalkya emphasizes that when one desires the Infinite, which is the Self, everything appears to be desirable. This suggests that the source of true desire lies in recognizing the infinite nature within oneself. When the Infinite Self is perceived in all external objects and individuals, the boundaries between the perceiver and the perceived, subject and object, begin to dissolve.

Love and Oneness
The Upanishad states that objects of love, such as a husband, wife, son, or wealth, hold significance because they are connected to the Self. The love we feel towards them is rooted in the realization of their inherent oneness and identity with the Self. In this profound love, subject-object distinctions fade away, and the essential unity of the Self is comprehended.

The Source of Attraction
Yajnavalkya points out that the real attraction of things lies in the Spirit or Brahman, the underlying essence that permeates all existence. The Spirit is the indwelling presence within every being and phenomenon. It is the source of true love and attraction, transcending superficial appearances and connecting everything in a profound unity.

Ignorance and Selfish Love
Unfortunately, many individuals remain ignorant of the true source of attraction and love. Ignorance leads them to misunderstand the nature of love, turning it into selfish attachments and conditional affection. Ignorant individuals fail to recognize the infinite aspect within themselves and others, leading to division, separation, and a distorted perception of love.

So, remind us of the essential unity underlying all existence. Love, when rooted in the understanding of Atman, transcends the limitations of subject-object distinctions. It is a love that arises from recognizing the oneness and interconnectedness of all beings. However, ignorance clouds this understanding, leading to selfish love based on external appearances. By cultivating self-awareness, seeking the true source of attraction within the Spirit or Brahman, and transcending ignorance, we can embrace a love that embodies the unity and harmony inherent in the Infinite Self.

Story

In a secluded mountain monastery, nestled amidst serene surroundings, lived a wise and compassionate monk. His days were spent in deep contemplation and meditation, seeking the ultimate Truth that lies beyond the realm of the ordinary world. The monk's heart was filled with boundless love and his every action was guided by the principles of selflessness and kindness. People from far and wide would come to seek the monk's guidance and experience his profound presence. One day, a young man arrived at the monastery, carrying a heavy burden in his heart. This young man was consumed by anger, bitterness, and a sense of deep despair. He had lost his way in the chaotic world and sought solace in the monk's teachings.

With humility and reverence, the young man approached the wise monk and poured out his troubled soul. He spoke of his struggles, his broken relationships, and the emptiness that seemed to engulf him. The monk listened attentively, his eyes filled with compassion and understanding.

The monk spoke softly, his words carrying the essence of love and wisdom. He explained that the root cause of the young man suffering was his detachment from love, both for himself and for others. He emphasized that true happiness and fulfillment can only be found in cultivating a heart filled with love, compassion, and selflessness.

The monk shared stories of his own journey, the challenges he faced, and the transformative power of love that had guided him along the path. He reminded the young man that love is not an external force to be sought outside of oneself, but rather an inherent quality within each being. It is the key to unlocking the doors of happiness and inner peace.

Inspired by the monk's teachings, the young man committed himself to the practice of love and compassion. He immersed himself in acts of selfless service, reaching out to those in need and offering his support and kindness. Through his actions, he began to experience a profound shift within himself. The heaviness in his heart gradually dissipated, replaced by a deep sense of joy and fulfillment.

ॐ

21. "Understand this great Truth: the happiness that comes from the pleasures of the world is a minute reflection of the infinite bliss that comes from within your own Self." -Amma

Deep within the heart of every being lies an eternal source of bliss and happiness. It is a profound truth that often eludes us in our pursuit of external pleasures and material possessions. The wisdom of Amma's words reminds us to turn our gaze inward, to explore the depths of our own being, where true and lasting happiness resides.

In the Upanishads, the nature of the Self is described as limitless and blissful. This explores the concept of Bliss, or ananda, and its significance in our self-experience. It delves into the seeking for limitlessness, the erroneous conclusions we draw about ourselves, and the recognition of our true nature as limitless consciousness.

Seeking Limitlessness:

As human beings, we are constantly seeking limitlessness in various aspects of our lives. We desire continuity, security, and the experience of being beyond the limitations of time and mortality. This seeking arises from our innate recognition that our true nature is limitless and blissful.

Mistaken Conclusions:
Despite our inherent limitlessness, we often fall into the trap of perceiving ourselves as limited beings. We conclude that we are ignorant, mortal, and subject to time. These conclusions are erroneous and veils our true nature of limitless consciousness. The seeking for knowledge and security stems from this mistaken self-perception.

The Nature of Consciousness:
Consciousness is the underlying essence that illuminates both knowledge and ignorance. It is the foundation upon which our entire existence rests. Ignorance and knowledge are mere manifestations of consciousness, and the recognition of this truth helps us realize our true nature as limitless consciousness.

Recognition of Ananda:
Ananda, or bliss, is an inherent quality of our true nature. It is not dependent on external objects or circumstances but arises from within ourselves. The happiness derived from worldly pleasures is a fleeting reflection of the infinite bliss that is our essence. Recognizing and experiencing this limitless bliss is the ultimate goal of our spiritual journey.

Insecurity and the Need for Love:
Our erroneous self-conclusions create a sense of insecurity within us. We seek love and security from external objects, relationships, and achievements. We become attached to these objects of love, clinging to them tightly in an attempt to fill the void caused by our mistaken self-perception. However, true security and happiness can only be found by realizing our own limitless nature.

Unity of Subject and Object:
The Upanishads reveal the unity between the subject and object. The distinction between the perceiver and the perceived, the lover and the loved, disappears when we recognize our true

nature as limitless consciousness. The love we experience for objects is a reflection of our innate connection to everything and everyone, as they all derive their existence from the same consciousness.

Embracing our True Nature:

To experience the fullness of limitlessness and bliss, we must let go of the mistaken conclusions about our limited selves. Through spiritual practices, self-inquiry, and the cultivation of self-awareness, we can transcend the illusions of ignorance and recognize our true nature as limitless consciousness. By embracing our inherent limitlessness, we live a life filled with joy, love, and fulfillment.

Conclusion

The Upanishads teach us that our True nature is one of limitless consciousness and bliss. The seeking for happiness and security in the external world is a reflection of our innate recognition of this limitlessness. By recognizing and realizing our true nature, we transcend the limitations of the ego-driven mind and experience the infinite bliss that is our birthright. Embracing our limitlessness, we live a life of profound fulfillment and love.

In the world, we often seek happiness through external means. We chase after worldly pleasures, believing that they hold the key to our contentment. Yet, time and again, we find that these pleasures are fleeting and transient, leaving us wanting more. We become trapped in a cycle of desire and attachment, always seeking the next source of temporary gratification.

Amma, in her profound wisdom, reminds us of the deeper Truth. She invites us to recognize that the happiness derived from worldly pleasures is merely a fraction, a small reflection of the infinite bliss that resides within our own selves. This infinite bliss is not dependent on external circumstances or material possessions. It is the very essence of our being, untouched by the ever-changing nature of the external world.

To access this infinite bliss, we must embark on an inward journey. We must turn our attention away from the external distractions and immerse ourselves in self-discovery. Through practices such as meditation, self-inquiry, and contemplation, we can begin to peel away the layers of conditioning and false identification that veil our true nature.

As we delve deeper into our own selves, we come to realize that the source of true happiness lies beyond the realm of the senses. It is found in the realm of pure consciousness, where the mind merges with the eternal Self, and the little self or ego is forgotten. In this state of union, we experience a profound sense of peace, contentment, and bliss that surpasses any fleeting pleasure the world has to offer.

Story

Once upon a time, in a serene monastery nestled amidst lush green mountains, there lived a wise and compassionate monk. He was known for his deep spiritual insights and his unwavering commitment to the path of Self-realization. People from far and wide sought his guidance, eager to learn from his profound wisdom.

One day, a young man arrived at the monastery seeking answers to the existential questions that had been troubling him. Young man was restless, constantly searching for happiness and fulfillment in the external world. He had tried indulging in worldly pleasures, accumulating wealth, and pursuing various paths of success, but nothing seemed to bring him lasting satisfaction.

In the presence of the serene monastery and the wise monk, the young man felt a sense of peace and calm he had never experienced before. He approached the monk with humility and openness, expressing his desire to find true happiness and meaning in life.

The wise monk then began to share his own journey of self-discovery. He spoke of his own search for happiness and how he, too, had once been caught in the illusion of external pursuits. He recounted the moment of awakening when he realized that true happiness could not be found in the transient nature of the world, but rather in the depths of his own being.

Monk explained to the young man that the key to finding lasting happiness and fulfillment lay in recognizing one's true nature, beyond the limitations of the mind and the senses. He spoke of the infinite bliss that resides within each being, waiting to be realized through inner exploration and self-inquiry.

ॐ

22. *"Logic cuts and divides, Love joins and unites everything." –Amma*

In the realm of duality, the human mind often seeks to dissect and analyze, to separate and categorize. It is through this process that we understand the world around us, applying logic and reasoning to make sense of our experiences. But in the pursuit of knowledge and understanding, we must not forget the power of love, the force that unifies and connects all aspects of existence.

Amma's profound words remind us that while logic may be necessary for our intellectual growth, it is love that transcends boundaries and bridges the gaps between individuals, communities, and even nations. Love is the unifying force that recognizes the inherent oneness of all beings, breaking down the barriers of separation and division.

When we approach life with love, we embrace the interconnectedness of all things. We recognize that the same divine essence resides within each and every being, and that our actions and intentions ripple through the collective consciousness. Love becomes the thread that weaves together the fabric of existence, uniting us in a tapestry of shared experiences.

Logic has its place in our quest for knowledge, but it is love that brings depth and meaning to our interactions. Logic may win arguments, but it is love that truly wins over hearts. Love opens our hearts to empathy, compassion, and understanding. It allows us to see beyond superficial differences and appreciate the inherent worth and beauty of every individual.

In Advaita Vedanta, love is not merely an emotion or a fleeting sentiment. It is the recognition of our interconnectedness and the expression of our true nature. Love is the essence of the divine within us, and when we tap into that essence, we align ourselves with the greater cosmic flow.

Love is inclusive, all-encompassing, and all-embracing. When we operate from a place of love, our actions become imbued with kindness, compassion, and selflessness. We prioritize the well-being and happiness of others, recognizing that their joy is intricately linked to our own. Love becomes the guiding principle of our lives, shaping our interactions, decisions, and choices.

Amma's words remind us that love is not just a lofty ideal; it is a practical and transformative force. It has the power to heal wounds, bridge divides, and create harmony. Love has the ability to dissolve the ego's need for separation and awaken us to the truth of our interconnectedness.

In the Bhagavad Gita, Lord Krishna emphasizes the importance of love in chapter 10, verse 20,

aham ātmā guḍākeśha sarva-bhūtāśhaya-sthitaḥ
aham ādiśh cha madhyaṁ cha bhūtānām anta eva cha

– Bhagavad Gita 10:20

I am the Self, O Gudakesha, seated in the hearts of all creatures. I am the beginning, the middle, and the end of all beings.

This verse reinforces that One divine being alone that resides in all beings, love is not limited to personal relationships but extends to all beings, for the divine resides within each of us.

Amma's message reminds us to cultivate love as a guiding principle in our lives. It calls us to transcend the limitations of logic and embrace the unifying power of love. When we approach life with love, we foster understanding, compassion, and harmony. Love becomes the transformative force that brings people together, dissolves divisions, and paves the way for a more inclusive and compassionate world.

Story

One day, as the king was walking through the bustling streets of his capital, he noticed a humble monk sitting under a tree, surrounded by curious onlookers. Intrigued, the king approached the gathering and sat down humbly at the feet of the monk.

The monk radiated an aura of tranquility and wisdom. His teachings touched the hearts of all who listened, and he spoke of love, compassion, and the eternal nature of the soul. The king was captivated by the words of the monk and felt a deep resonance with his teachings.

After the discourse, the king approached Swami with reverence and said, "Great sage, your words have touched my soul. I am grateful for the wisdom you have shared. I am the king of this land, and I have been entrusted with the well-being of my people. But sometimes, I feel overwhelmed by the burdens of my position. How can I find peace and guidance amidst my responsibilities?"

The wise monk smiled warmly and replied, "Dear king, the path to peace and guidance lies within your own heart. It is through inner reflection and self-awareness that you will find the answers you seek. Embrace the qualities of love, compassion, and selflessness, and let them guide your actions as a king."

Inspired by the monk's words, King spent several days in deep contemplation and introspection. He realized that true leadership is not about power and control, but about serving others with love and compassion. He recognized that his position as a king was an opportunity to make a positive difference in the lives of his subjects.

ॐ

23. *"Love is our true essence. Love has no limitations of caste, religion, race, or nationality. We are all beads strung together on the same thread of love. To awaken this unity and to spread to others the love that is our inherent nature - is the true goal of human life." -Amma*

Love is the essence that resides within each and every one of us. It is the thread that connects us all, transcending the boundaries of caste, religion, race, and nationality. Love is the purest expression of our inherent nature, a divine spark that unifies us in the tapestry of life. Amma, the embodiment of love and compassion, reminds us of the profound truth that love is not limited by any external boundaries; it is a force that flows through us all.

Advaita Vedanta emphasizes the oneness of all Existence. It recognizes that at the core of our being, we are all interconnected and inseparable. Love is the unifying force that dissolves the illusion of separation and reveals the fundamental truth of our interconnectedness. When we awaken to this unity, we tap into the boundless reservoir of love that resides within us, and we become conduits for its expression.

The true goal of human life, as Amma beautifully expresses, is to awaken this unity and spread love to others. It is through love that we find fulfillment and purpose. Love has the power to heal, transform, and uplift. When we recognize the divine essence in ourselves and in others, we naturally embrace compassion, kindness, and empathy. Love becomes our guiding light, illuminating our path and inspiring us to serve humanity.

mattaḥ parataraṁ nānyat kiñchid asti dhanañjaya
mayi sarvam idaṁ protaṁ sūtre maṇi-gaṇā iva

– Bhagavad Gita 7:7

O Dhananjaya, there is nothing else whatsoever higher than Myself. All this is strung on Me like pearls on a string.

The Supreme God as the Source and Support of the Universe
This verse delves into the verse that highlights the supreme nature of God and emphasizes the Truth of the beings in the entire universe being connected, like pearls on a string. God is the foundational support for all existence.

What are the qualities of such a God, who is the core of all beings and connects us all?

Omnipotence: God possesses limitless power and control over all aspects of creation.

Omniscience: The supreme God is all-knowing, having complete awareness of every aspect of the universe.

Omnipresence: God pervades all existence, being present everywhere simultaneously.

What are the Implications of this Truth? We must recognize the interconnectedness: The verse encourages individuals to acknowledge the inherent connection between themselves and the divine, fostering a sense of unity and reverence.

Seeking divine guidance: Understanding God as the ultimate source of the universe inspires seekers to seek guidance, wisdom, and support from the divine.

Cultivating trust and surrender: Recognizing the supreme God as the sustainer of the universe fosters trust and surrender in the face of life's challenges.

To add to the above, Amma instructs us that to awaken to such Love, enables us to overlook all differences between different beings, irrespective of their race, shape, color, opinions and national boundaries, and to see each other as expressions of that one divine.

To embody the essence of love, we must first cultivate self-love and self-acceptance. By nurturing our own inner wellspring of love, we become a reservoir from which love can flow abundantly to others. We must let go of judgments, prejudices, and limitations, recognizing that love transcends all barriers. Love is a state of being, a way of living, and it radiates through our thoughts, words, and actions.

This self-love and acceptance must again be grounded in the Truth. The mantra - "Om Purnamadah Purnamidam" speaks of oneness which is Love in essence. To recognize their true nature as Brahman, the embodiment of love. The teacher emphasizes that the Vedas, as a means of knowledge, reveal this Truth and that the student's preparedness and contemplation are crucial for its realization. The Teaching of "You are Brahman": The teacher declares to the student, "You are Brahman," affirming their inherent nature as the ultimate reality. This teaching is not a mere concept or intellectual understanding but a direct perception and recognition of one's true Self.

Amma's message reminds us to awaken the unity that lies within us and share the love that is our inherent nature. It invites us to embrace the diversity of humanity, celebrating our differences and seeing them as an opportunity to expand our capacity to love. Let us heed Amma's call to make love the focal point of our existence. Let us strive to be instruments of love, spreading kindness, compassion, and understanding wherever we go. By embracing the true essence of love, we contribute to the transformation of our world into a harmonious and compassionate place for all beings.

Love is the essence that binds us together as one human family. Let us embrace this truth and live our lives as an expression of love. For it is through love that we find unity, purpose, and fulfillment. It is through love that we truly discover the divine within ourselves and in all of creation.

ॐ

24. *"Pure love transcends the body. It is between hearts; it has nothing to do with bodies. When there is true love, there are no barriers and no limitations. Even though the sun is far away, the lotus flowers still bloom in its effulgence. In true love, there is no distance." -Amma*

Love, in its purest form, is a force that transcends the limitations of the physical realm. It exists in the realm of the heart, beyond the boundaries of the body. This profound Truth lies at the core of non-duality in Vedanta, where the essence of all beings is recognized as one and the same.

Amma's quote beautifully expresses the nature of true love, which knows no barriers or limitations. It is not bound by the physicality of bodies but rather flows freely between hearts. Love, in its purest form, is an expression of the divine, a reflection of the infinite love that permeates the universe. Just as the lotus flowers bloom in the effulgence of the distant sun, love blossoms and flourishes despite any perceived distance or separation.

When we tap into the depths of true love, we realize that our hearts are interconnected. Love becomes a bridge that unites us, enabling us to see beyond the illusions of separateness and embrace the inherent unity that binds us all. In this state of awareness, we recognize that the love we share with others is an expression of the divine love that flows through us.

The essence of non-duality lies in the realization that there is no inherent separation between ourselves and others. We are all interconnected, part of the same divine fabric of existence. When we operate from a place of pure love, we transcend the boundaries created by ego, nationality, race, or any other external factors. We see the essence of the other person, the divinity that resides within them, and we honor and cherish it with unconditional love.

Non-dual love is expansive, inclusive, and all-encompassing. It is not limited by proximity or physical presence. It is a deep resonance of the heart that transcends time and space. When we truly love someone, our connection with them goes beyond the confines of the physical world. We can feel their presence even when they are physically distant. Our love reaches out to them and bridges any perceived gaps or barriers.

tadetatsatyaṃ yathā sudīptātpāvakādvisphuliṅgāḥ
sahasraśaḥ prabhavante sarūpāḥ
tathākṣarādvividhāḥ somya bhāvāḥ prajāyante tatra
caivāpi yanti

– Mundaka Upanishad 2.1.1

This is true; as from the flaming fire issue forth, by thousands, sparks of the same form, so from the immortal proceed, good youth, diverse jivas and they find their way back into it.

The verse from Munduka Upanishad, specifically verse 2.1.1, speaks about the Truth of existence and the interconnectedness of all beings. It uses the analogy of sparks emanating from a flaming fire to illustrate the manifestation and return of diverse individuals from the immortal source.

The Analogy of Flaming Fire and Sparks:

The verse compares the process of manifestation and return to the phenomenon of sparks arising from a blazing fire. Just as sparks emerge from the fire, thousands of them, sharing the same form, so do diverse jivas or individual beings originate from the immortal source.

The Immortal Source:

The verse emphasizes the existence of an immortal and eternal essence from which all beings emerge. This immortal source represents the underlying reality or consciousness that pervades all existence. It signifies the ultimate Truth that transcends the limitations of individual identities.

Diversity of Jivas:

The verse acknowledges the diversity of individual beings, highlighting the varied forms and manifestations that arise from the immortal source. It recognizes that the jivas, or individual souls, are distinct and unique in their expressions, characteristics, and experiences.

Oneness and Return:

Despite the diversity of jivas, the verse emphasizes their oneness and ultimate return to the immortal source. Just as sparks, after their manifestation, eventually find their way back into the fire, the verse suggests that individual beings, after their life experiences, ultimately merge back into the immortal essence.

The Cyclical Nature of Manifestation and Dissolution:

The verse implies a cyclical pattern of manifestation and dissolution. As if Jivas emerge from the immortal source, undergo experiences and existence in the world, and eventually dissolve back into the same source. This cyclical process signifies the eternal nature of life and the continuous interplay between manifestation and dissolution.

Reflection of Universal Truth:

The verse invites contemplation on the oneness of all beings and the cyclical nature of existence. It points to a universal Truth that transcends individual identities and emphasizes the underlying unity and oneness of all life.

Spiritual Significance:

The verse holds spiritual significance by highlighting the eternal and immortal nature of the source from which all beings arise. It invites individuals to recognize their connection with this source and to seek a deeper understanding of their true nature beyond transient identities.

Conclusion: verse 2.1.1 of Munduka Upanishad serves as a reminder of the oneness and cyclical nature of existence. It invites individuals to contemplate the Truth of their origin, the diversity of their expressions, and the ultimate return to the immortal source. Through this reflection, one can gain insights into the underlying unity of all life and explore their spiritual connection with the eternal essence.

This verse encapsulates the essence of non-dual love. When we develop the ability to see the divine presence in every being, we cultivate a deep sense of oneness and compassion. We recognize that love is not confined to specific relationships or limited to certain individuals, but rather it is a universal force that flows through all of creation.

In the Advaita Vedanta way, love is not restricted by physical proximity or external factors. It is an eternal and boundless force that connects us at the level of the heart. When we open ourselves to this expansive love, we transcend the illusions of separation and experience the oneness that exists at the core of our being.

Amma's quote reminds us that pure love is a powerful transformative force. It has the capacity to dissolve barriers, heal wounds, and create a world where unity, compassion, and understanding prevail. It is a reminder that love is not limited by distance, but rather it has the ability to bridge any perceived gaps and bring us closer together.

Story

One day, as the sage and his disciples were traveling through a village, they came across a beggar sitting on the side of the road. The beggar was weak, hungry, and in desperate need of assistance. While some of the villagers walked past without paying much attention, the disciples felt a stirring within their hearts. They approached the beggar with compassion and offered him food and water. They treated him with respect and kindness, recognizing the divine presence within him.

As they continued on their journey, the disciples shared their experiences with the sage. They spoke of the profound joy and fulfillment they felt in serving the beggar, despite his impoverished condition. They realized that their act of kindness was not merely an act of charity but a manifestation of the love that flowed through their hearts. The boundaries of societal norms, economic differences, and personal preferences dissolved in that moment of selfless service.

The wise sage listened attentively to his disciples and smiled. He affirmed that their actions were indeed an embodiment of the non-dual love he had been teaching them. He explained that when love is free from the limitations of the ego and extends to all beings, it becomes a transformative force. It has the power to heal, uplift, and create a sense of unity in the world.

The sage reminded his disciples of the importance of continuing their practice, not only in meditation and self-inquiry but also in daily acts of compassion and service. He emphasized that love is not something to be confined to spiritual practices or limited to specific moments but should permeate every aspect of their lives. He encouraged them to see the divine presence in every person they encountered, to be mindful of the needs of others, and to extend a helping hand whenever possible.

As the disciples continued on their spiritual journey, they carried with them the teachings of non-dual love. They understood that love was not restricted by external circumstances but was an inner state of being. They saw the oneness of all beings and felt a deep sense of responsibility to serve and uplift others. Their acts of compassion became a source of joy and fulfillment, and they inspired others to awaken to the power of non-dual love.

In this way, the disciples of the wise sage became embodiments of love, spreading its transformative power wherever they went. They understood that love was not a finite resource to be withheld but an infinite wellspring that could be tapped into and shared with others. They experienced the truth of Amma's words - that true love transcends the boundaries of caste, religion, race, and nationality.

Through their actions, they demonstrated that love has the power to unite, to dissolve barriers, and to create a world where compassion and understanding prevail. Their journey of self-discovery and service exemplified the essence of Advaita Vedanta, where love is recognized as our true essence and the ultimate goal of human life.

In conclusion, Amma's quote reminds us that love knows no boundaries or limitations.

ॐ

25. *"Love is the only medicine that can heal the wounds of the world."*
-Amma

Love, in its purest form, has the power to heal the wounds of the world. Amma's profound statement reminds us of the transformative nature of love and its ability to bring healing and harmony to a world often plagued by pain and suffering. In the Advaita Vedanta perspective, love is not just an emotion or a romantic notion, but a powerful force that connects us to the essence of our true nature.

Love is the medicine that transcends boundaries, dissolves differences, and unites all beings. It is a universal language that speaks directly to the heart, fostering understanding, compassion, and unity. When we embrace love in its purest form, we realize that at the core of our being, we are all interconnected and inseparable.

In the teachings of non-duality, love is seen as the very fabric of existence, the essence of the divine. It is not limited to personal attachments or conditional emotions but is a fundamental aspect of our true nature. Love is not confined to romantic relationships or familial bonds; it encompasses all aspects of life, extending to every living being and the entire universe.

When we recognize the oneness of all beings, we begin to understand the profound impact of love. It is through love that we develop empathy, compassion, and the desire to alleviate the suffering of others. Love becomes a powerful force that motivates us to act selflessly and serve humanity, extending our love and care to those in need.

Amma's quote reminds us that love is not a passive sentiment but an active force that brings about healing and transformation. Love has the power to heal the wounds of the world, whether they are physical, emotional, or spiritual. It is through acts of love and compassion that we can contribute to the betterment of society and create a more harmonious world.

In the Bhagavad Gita, Lord Krishna teaches the importance of selfless love and service. In Chapter 12, verse 13, He says,

adveṣhṭā sarva-bhūtānāṁ maitraḥ karuṇa eva cha
nirmamo nirahankāraḥ sama-duḥkha-sukhaḥ kṣhamī

– Bhagavad Gita 12:13

He who hates no creature, who is friendly and compassionate to all, who is free from possessiveness and egoism, balanced in pleasure and pain, and forgiving.

This verse encapsulates the essence of love in the Advaita Vedanta way. Love is not selective or exclusive; it is all-encompassing and all-embracing. It transcends boundaries and distinctions, extending to every living being without discrimination. When we cultivate such love, we become agents of healing, radiating compassion and kindness to all those we encounter.

To illustrate the transformative power of love, let us delve into a story of a wise sage and his disciples. The sage, renowned for his deep understanding of non-dual love, lived in a village where people were divided by various conflicts and prejudices. The village was torn apart by hatred, and the wounds of discord were deeply ingrained.

Recognizing the need for healing, the sage embarked on a mission to teach the villagers the transformative power of love. He gathered a group of disciples who were eager to learn and embrace the path of nondual love. Together, they embarked on a journey of compassion and service, determined to bring healing to their community.

The sage and his disciples engaged in acts of selfless service, reaching out to those who were suffering and marginalized. They provided food to the hungry, shelter to the homeless, and care to the sick. But their greatest gift was the love they shared unconditionally.

As the villagers witnessed the actions of the sage and his disciples, they were deeply moved. The power of love began to touch their hearts, breaking down the barriers of hatred and division. Slowly, the wounds of the world started to heal, and a sense of unity and harmony blossomed within the village.

Through their acts of love, the sage and his disciples demonstrated that love is not a passive sentiment, but an active force that can transform individuals and communities. They showed that love has the power to heal the wounds of the world by fostering understanding, compassion, and unity.

As the villagers experienced the transformative power of love, they were inspired to embrace it in their own lives. They began to let go of their prejudices and animosities, recognizing that love was the key to their own personal healing and the healing of their community.

It is a selfless and unconditional offering that transcends individual differences and extends to all beings.

ॐ

26. "Children, Divine love is our true nature. It is shining in each and every one of us. When your heart is full of innocent love, you are absent; the ego is absent. In that state, only love is present; individuality disappears, and you become one with the Divine." -Amma

In the realm of Advaita Vedanta, Amma's quote beautifully captures the essence of our true nature, which is divine love. It reminds us that deep within us, beyond the layers of ego and individuality, there resides a radiant and boundless love that is our inherent essence.

The essence of divine love and bliss as our true nature is highlighted in various spiritual teachings. This explores the concept of divine love and its connection to our innate nature of bliss and consciousness. It emphasizes the absence of ego and the unification with the Divine that occurs when the heart is filled with innocent love.

Divine Love and Absence of Ego:

Divine love, which is our true nature, transcends the limitations of the ego. When the heart is filled with pure and innocent love, the ego dissolves, and the individuality disappears. In this state, only love remains, and one becomes united with the Divine. It is a state of egolessness and complete surrender to the power of love.

Unity with the Divine:

In the absence of individuality and ego, the experience of unity with the Divine arises. One recognizes their inseparable connection with the divine source and realizes that divine love is present within each and every being. It is a state of oneness, where the boundaries between the Self and the Divine dissolve, and a profound sense of unity is experienced.

The Ever-Shining Nature of Love and Bliss:

Just as the sun continues to shine despite clouds obscuring its light, the nature of love and bliss is ever-present and unaffected by external circumstances. Love is our inherent nature, and bliss is an integral aspect of consciousness. So, highlights that even amidst challenges or darkness, the light of love and bliss remains eternal and unchanging.

Awareness and Freedom:

Amma emphasizes that awareness or discernment plays a crucial role in experiencing freedom. By being aware of our true nature as love and bliss, we can transcend the limitations imposed by the mind-stuff or chitta, which may distort or stress our consciousness. Awareness brings clarity and liberation from bondage, allowing us to fully embody our innate divine nature.

Ananda as an Integral Aspect of Consciousness:

Ananda, or bliss, is not separate from consciousness but rather an intrinsic part of it. Just as sat, the sense of "I-am-ness," is an expression of consciousness, ananda is its integral nature. Amma highlights that when we refer to "I am" or "ahamasmi," it points to consciousness alone. Ananda arises from the unconditioned and pure state of consciousness, though it may be influenced or conditioned by various mediums.

Realization of True Nature:

Amma emphasizes that realizing our true nature as love, bliss, and consciousness is a transformative process. It involves recognizing the illusory nature of the ego, surrendering to divine love, and cultivating awareness to transcend the limitations of the mind. Through this realization, we can live in alignment with our innate divine nature and experience the freedom and joy it brings.

Conclusion

The understanding that divine love is our true nature, intertwined with bliss and consciousness, invites us to explore the depths of our being. By nurturing innocent love, surrendering the ego, and cultivating awareness, we can awaken to the eternal presence of love and bliss within us. This realization brings liberation, unity with the Divine, and the experience of freedom and joy in our lives.

According to the teachings of Advaita Vedanta, our true nature is not limited by the boundaries of the ego or the confines of the physical body. It is an expansive and eternal consciousness that is interconnected with the divine essence of all creation. In this state, our individuality merges with the universal consciousness, and we experience a profound sense of unity and oneness with the Divine.

Amma's quote emphasizes the significance of innocent love in realizing our true nature. When our hearts are filled with pure and selfless love, the ego dissolves, and we transcend the limitations of individual identity. In that state, there is no separation between ourselves and the Divine. Love becomes the sole presence, radiating from the core of our being.

Story
One day, Maya came across a wounded bird on the roadside. Its wings were broken, and it was unable to fly. Without hesitation, Maya gently picked up the bird and cradled it in her hands. She could feel its frail heartbeat and sensed its pain. Moved by compassion, Maya decided to take care of the bird until it healed.

Days turned into weeks, and Maya diligently nursed the bird back to health. She fed it with love, nurtured it with compassion, and provided a safe space for it to recover. As the bird regained its strength, a beautiful bond formed between Maya and the bird.

One evening, as Maya sat under a tree, she watched the bird spread its wings and take flight, soaring high into the sky. Tears of joy welled up in Maya's eyes as she witnessed the bird's freedom and newfound happiness. Her love was pure, free of any selfish desire or attachment. In that moment, Maya realized the profound truth that love has the power to heal, uplift, and set beings free.

ॐ

Real Amma

27. *"Children, You are embodiment of divine love and supreme conscious-ness. Awaken to this Truth by discriminating between the eternal and non-eternal. If you love Amma you should do so with the awareness of the Real principle. If we put in the necessary effort, the doors of divine grace will certainly open. May my children have the strength and blessings to receive that grace. May that grace bless everyone." -Amma*

In an imagined conversation between Amma and four disciples, let us expand on the above words from Amma.

"Disciple One: Amma, how can we awaken to our true nature as embodiments of divine love and supreme consciousness?

Amma: Discriminate between the eternal and non-eternal. Understand that everything in this world is impermanent and ultimately unreal. Recognize that your true nature is beyond the changing world of forms and that you are one with the eternal principle.

Disciple Two: Amma, how can we love you with the awareness of the Real principle?

Amma: Love me not as an individual, but as a manifestation of the Divine. See the Divine in everything and everyone, including me. When you love with this awareness, your love becomes a vehicle for spiritual growth and transformation.

Disciple Three: Amma, what kind of effort do we need to put in to receive divine grace?

Amma: We need to cultivate a deep desire for spiritual growth and make a sincere effort to overcome the obstacles that stand in our way. We need to practice self-inquiry, meditation, and other spiritual practices with dedication and devotion.

Disciple Four: Amma, can you bless us with your grace?

Amma: May my children have the strength and blessings to receive divine grace. May that grace bless everyone who seeks it. Remember, if we put in the necessary effort, the doors of divine grace will certainly open."

The Real Principle- Amma:

"Om saccidananda-murtaye namah"

asti bhāti priyam rūpam nāma chetyamsa pamchakam adyatrayam brahma rupam jagad rupam tato dvayam

— Drg drsya viveka.

Existence, knowledge, and bliss, form the essence of the five-fold name, "Asti, Bhāti, Priyam, Rūpam, Nāma," (Being, Knowing, Bliss, form and name,).

The first three are the Brahman or the ultimate reality, and the latter two are the world or the manifested reality. The Brahman and the manifested Reality are two different aspects of the same ultimate reality.

Let's take a flower as an example. What exactly is the flower before and after it falls? Attempting to explain that takes one away from the flower. When we label a flower as beautiful, fragrant, of glorious color, family, place of blooming, season, etc., and explain, we are creating an image in order to capture the flower. This is true either with a flower, or any other thing in our day-to-day activities. We reduce it to mental activity and various concepts. But through doing so, we lose "it". Existence is not meant for a description but recognition 'as it is.'

How do you know it is a flower?

It may be someone else or some authority told us, so we believe, and it has become our conviction now.

But if one wants to know - What exactly is it?

Then we cannot see through the interpretation of others or not even by our mind and thoughts.

The whole phenomenon is by itself complete and luminescent. The eye of the seer, earth, and the various supporting factors encompass it. It is not only a question of flower, but it is wholeness without division; it is there. It exists. Therefore, there is no second to label it other than 'Sat', the Being and 'Chit', the knowingness. The rest is our interpretation only, through mind made concepts. The Wholeness exists in the flower, and wholeness exists in the seer and everything. Any number of labels addition or subtraction from wholeness does not change it. Wholeness remains intact as it is.

The seer of the flower is not separate from the seen, the object called the flower. Why? Only 'knowingness-being,' which is 'bliss,' is there through and through as one underlying, indivisible Truth.

A flower is not a name, form, or description; it is wholeness, and so is Amma and everything. Therefore Amma is indivisible non-dual Truth, so is the one who reveres and prays at Her lotus feet. The Real Principle of Truth is That Awareness.

Amma's statement encourages us to look beyond appearances and seek deeper truths and understanding. She uses a metaphor of a reflection of a flower in a vessel filled with water to illustrate the limitation of relying solely on external appearances to understand reality. This reflection is only an image and can never be made our own. To understand the truth, we must seek out the Real principle, which lies beyond the superficial.

One insight we can gain from Amma's statement is that we should not be content with superficial understanding or attachments. By recognizing the limitations of external appearances, we can open ourselves up to a deeper level of insight and understanding. This encourages us to seek a more profound level of connection with the world around us, one that goes beyond surface-level perceptions.

Another insight we can gain is that we should not confuse the reflection with the real thing. While the reflection may be beautiful and captivating, it is not the true essence of the object. Similarly, while we may be drawn to external appearances or the image of someone like Amma, we must remember that this is not the same as understanding or connecting with the true essence of the person or object.

Overall, Amma's statement reminds us to look beyond appearances and seek deeper truths and understanding. It encourages us to be mindful of our attachments and to seek a more profound level of connection with the world around us.

Story
Once upon a time, in a land far away, there was a wise old man who lived alone in a small hut at the edge of the village. The villagers often sought his advice and guidance on various matters. One day, a young man approached the wise old man seeking his guidance.

The young man said, "I have been seeking knowledge and enlightenment for a long time, but I have not been able to find it. Can you guide me on my journey?"

The wise old man replied, "The external realized soul you see now is like the reflection of a flower in a vessel filled with water. You can never make that flower your own, because it is only an image. To realize the truth, you have to seek That which is true. Taking refuge in a reflection isn't enough; you have to refuge in the real thing. So you should do so with the awareness of the Real principle."

The young man was confused by the old man's words. He asked, "I don't understand. Can you please explain it to me in a simpler way?"

Real Amma

The wise old man smiled and said, "Let me tell you a story. Once upon a time, there was a man who saw a beautiful flower in a pond. He tried to pick it, but every time he reached for it, the flower moved away from him. He spent hours trying to pick the flower but was unsuccessful. Finally, he realized that the flower was just a reflection and not real. He looked around and saw the real flower on the other side of the pond, and he was able to pick it easily."

The young man understood the message behind the story. He thanked the wise old man and left, determined to seek the true knowledge and enlightenment.

ॐ

28. *"All of spirituality is contained in one word: Pure Awareness." The goal of human life is God-realization. We are not separate from God. A drop of this awareness is already present in us. What we need to do is expand this awareness and strengthen it. We should live every moment with awareness. If we continuously maintain attention on self awareness, we will be able to experience peace and happiness." -Amma*

Pure Awareness is the essence of spirituality, encapsulating the profound wisdom of Advaita Vedanta. It is the recognition and realization of our inherent connection to the Divine. Amma beautifully expresses that the goal of human life is God-realization, an awakening to the truth that we are not separate from God but an inseparable part of the Divine.

In the journey of spiritual evolution, we are invited to expand our awareness and deepen our understanding of this truth. It is through the cultivation of pure awareness that we unveil the divine nature within ourselves and experience a profound sense of peace and happiness.

111

The teachings of Advaita Vedanta emphasize the importance of living every moment with awareness. It is a constant remembrance of our true essence, our connection to the Divine. By maintaining attention on self-awareness, we become more attuned to the present moment, to the vastness of our being beyond the limitations of the ego-mind.

The practice of pure awareness involves bringing our attention inward, observing the thoughts, emotions, and sensations that arise within us. It is a gentle witnessing of our inner landscape without judgment or attachment. In this state of awareness, we begin to transcend the identification with our limited self and open ourselves to the expansiveness of our true nature.

The mind-stuff or chitta plays a significant role in our perception and experience of reality. This explores the concept of the mind-stuff or chitta as a veil or conditioning that restricts Pure Consciousness. It emphasizes its connection to the three gunas - sattva, rajas, and tamas, and their role in creating the illusion of duality.

Understanding the mind-Stuff or chitta:

The mind-stuff or chitta refers to the subtle aspect of the mind, encompassing thoughts, emotions, memories, and impressions. It is the medium through which Consciousness becomes conditioned and manifests as the mind. The mind-stuff or chitta is not the true nature of Consciousness but a conditioned overlay.

The Veil of Conditioning:

The mind-stuff or chitta acts as a veil that restricts Pure Consciousness. It is influenced by the three Gunas - Sattva, Rajas, and Tamas. Sattva represents purity, Rajas represents activity or restlessness, and Tamas represents inertia or darkness. These Gunas affect the quality of the mind-stuff or chitta and contribute to the conditioning that creates the illusion of duality.

Illusion of Duality:

The conditioned mind-stuff or chitta creates the illusion of duality, where there is a perceived separation between the subject and the object, the self and the world. It generates thoughts, beliefs, and judgments that reinforce the sense of individuality and separation. This illusion prevents the direct experience of Pure Consciousness.

Transcending the Veil of Conditioning:

In Advaita, the goal is to transcend the conditioning of the mind-stuff or chitta and realize the unconditioned nature of Consciousness. This is achieved through practices such as self-inquiry, meditation, and self-awareness. By investigating the nature of the mind and recognizing its limitations, one can gradually transcend the veil of conditioning and access the unconditioned Pure Consciousness.

Realizing Unconditioned Consciousness:

As the conditioning of the mind-stuff or chitta is transcended, the true nature of Consciousness is revealed. Pure Consciousness is unconditioned, limitless, and unaffected by the fluctuations of the mind-stuff. It is the essence of our being that exists beyond the illusion of duality. The realization of unconditioned Consciousness brings freedom, clarity, and a deeper connection with the true Self.

Integration and Transformation:

The process of transcending the conditioning of the mind-stuff or chitta is not about suppressing or eliminating thoughts and emotions but integrating them in the light of awareness. By hearing, reflection, contemplation till one gets conviction so that one can witness the conditioned patterns of the mind-stuff and gradually detach from their influence. This process leads to transformation and alignment with Pure Consciousness.

Conclusion

The mind-stuff or chitta acts as a veil or conditioning that restricts Pure Consciousness and creates the illusion of duality. Through Self-inquiry, meditation, and Self-awareness, it is possible to transcend this conditioning and realize the unconditioned nature of Consciousness. By recognizing the limitations of the mind-stuff, we can access the depths of our true Self and experience freedom, unity, and clarity in our lives.

Through the cultivation of pure awareness, we become attuned to the subtle movements of the Divine within and around us. We begin to recognize the Oneness of all beings and the inherent divinity that dwells within each and every one of us. This awareness allows us to experience a profound sense of unity and oneness with all of creation.

So, the path of pure awareness is a transformative journey that leads us to the realization of our true nature. It is through expanding and strengthening our awareness that we awaken to the inherent divinity within ourselves and all of creation. As we live each moment with conscious presence and attentiveness, we align ourselves with the divine flow and experience the profound peace, happiness, and unity that come from recognizing our oneness with the Divine. May we all embrace the practice of pure awareness and walk this path of Self-realization with love, devotion, and deep gratitude.

Story

A young seeker approached a sage with utmost reverence and humility, expressing his earnest desire to learn and grow on the path of Self-realization. The sage, who exudes an aura of tranquility and compassion, recognized the young seeker's sincere thirst for knowledge and agreed to become his teacher.

Under the sage's guidance, the young seeker began his spiritual journey, delving deep into the realms of meditation, self-inquiry, and contemplation. The sage taught him the importance of pure awareness - the ability to be fully present and conscious in each moment. He explained that by cultivating this awareness, the young seeker would come to recognize the underlying unity and divinity that permeates all of creation.

As days turned into weeks and weeks into months, Ravi diligently practiced the teachings imparted by his wise teacher. He would spend hours in silent meditation, observing the thoughts and emotions that arose within him, and gradually transcending the limitations of his ego-mind. With each passing day, his awareness expanded, and he began to experience glimpses of the profound peace and happiness that lie beyond the fluctuations of the external world.

In this way, the young seeker's journey and his embodiment of pure awareness and love became a guiding light for all who sought a deeper understanding of spirituality. His teachings reminded people of their innate divinity, urging them to embrace the power of awareness and love as a means to awaken their true selves and create a more compassionate and harmonious world. And as the village continued to thrive in the spirit of pure awareness and love, Ravi's legacy remained alive, forever illuminating the path for those who followed in his footsteps.

ॐ

Self Knowledge

29. "Enlightenment means the ability to recognize oneself in all living creatures. Real knowledge is to accept the world and recognize the many forms in it, while seeing the one Truth transparent in the many. The sun shines down, and its image reflects in a thousand different pots filled with water. The reflections are many, but they are each reflecting the same sun." -Amma

In the realm of self-knowledge, the journey of enlightenment begins with the recognition of our true nature. It is a profound realization that goes beyond intellectual understanding and delves into the depths of our being. Amma beautifully captures this essence in her quote, emphasizing the interconnectedness and oneness that underlies all of existence.

Enlightenment is not merely an intellectual pursuit or the accumulation of knowledge. It is the awakening of our consciousness to the truth of who we really are. It is a shift in perception that allows us to see beyond the limitations of the physical world and recognize the eternal essence that resides within us and all living beings.

To attain enlightenment, we must go beyond the external forms and appearances and dive deep into the core of our being. It is through this inner exploration that we come to realize the interconnectedness of all things. Just as the sun shines down and its reflection is seen in countless pots of water, the same divine essence dwells within each and every being, regardless of their outer form.

This recognition of oneness is not limited to human beings alone. It extends to all living creatures, embracing the entire web of life. It is the ability to see ourselves mirrored in the eyes of every living being, to recognize the same divine spark that animates us all. This realization shatters the illusion of separation and fosters a deep sense of unity, compassion, and love.

In the journey of Self-knowledge, we come to accept the world as it is, understanding that the myriad forms and expressions are but different manifestations of the same underlying reality. We transcend the limitations of judgment and prejudice, recognizing that the one Truth permeates all existence.

The path of Self-knowledge is not without challenges. It requires inner introspection, self-inquiry, and a willingness to let go of our egoic attachments and identifications. It calls for surrendering to the divine presence within us and allowing it to guide our thoughts, words, and actions.

Upanishadic Mantra:

Dvā suparṇā sayujā sakhāyā samānaṃ
vṛkṣaṃ pariṣasvajāte. Tayoranyaḥ pippalaṃ
svādvattyanaśnannanyo abhicākaśīti.

– Mundaka Upanishad 3.1.1

Introduction: The mantra from the Third Mundaka Upanishad presents a metaphorical depiction of two inseparable companions perched on the same tree. It reveals the relationship between the individual self (kshetrajna) and the universal Self (Isvara), highlighting their distinct roles and perspectives.

The Two Birds:

The mantra describes the two birds, suparna, as inseparable companions. They symbolize the individual self (kshetrajna) and the universal Self (Isvara) coexisting within the same body. Both birds share a common name, suggesting their inherent connection and manifestation.

Perched on the Tree:

The tree mentioned in the mantra represents the body, the field of manifestation (kshetra) and action. The tree metaphorically signifies the transient nature of the body, with its roots in Brahman and its branches extending into the manifested world. It serves as the platform for the experiences and actions of the individual self and the universal self.

The Eating Bird:

One of the birds, representing the individual self (kshetrajna), feeds on the delicious fruit of the tree. It symbolizes the limited self that experiences the fruits of its actions, marked by pleasure and pain. This bird is influenced by ignorance, desires, and karmic tendencies, leading to diverse and varied experiences in life.

The Non-Eating Bird:

The other bird symbolizes the universal Self (Brahman), characterized as the eternal, pure, and intelligent being. It does not partake of the fruit, representing its transcendence beyond the dualistic experiences of pleasure and pain. As the witness and director of both the eater and the food, Isvara remains unaffected by the relative experiences and acts as the guiding force.

The Subtle Body and Ignorance:

The individual self (kshetrajna) is conditioned by the subtle body, which includes ignorance, desires, and karmic tendencies. It is the subtle body that experiences the fruits of actions and undergoes the cycle of pleasure and pain. In contrast, the universal Self (Isvara) transcends these conditioning factors and remains free, pure, and untouched.

Witnessing and Direction:

The non-eating bird represents the eternal witness and director of the entire manifestation. Isvara's existence as the omniscient and pure consciousness provides guidance and direction to the individual self. His mere witnessing serves as the ultimate direction, similar to how a king's mere presence guides his kingdom.

Conclusion

The mantra highlights the oneness of the individual self (kshet-rajna) and the universal self (Isvara) through the metaphor of two birds perched on a tree. It emphasizes the distinction between the limited experiences of the individual self and the transcendence of the universal Self. Through this understanding, we gain insights into the role of conditioning, the nature of witnessing, and the guidance provided by the universal Self. The mantra invites us to contemplate the true nature of ourselves and our connection to the divine, leading us towards Self-realization and the recognition of our essential unity.

Through the practice of Self-awareness and knowledge, we cultivate a deeper understanding of our true nature. We learn to navigate the fluctuations of the mind and emotions, embracing the transient nature of the external world while anchoring ourselves in the eternal truth that resides within.

The journey of self-knowledge is a transformative one. As we delve deeper into our own being, we gain insight into the oneness of all things. We realize that we are not separate entities but interconnected threads woven into the fabric of existence. This awareness opens our hearts to a profound sense of compassion and empathy for all living beings.

Amma's quote reminds us that enlightenment is not a distant goal or a faraway destination. It is a realization that can be experienced here and now, in each and every moment. It is the recognition of our true nature as pure consciousness, beyond the limitations of time and space.

As we embark on the journey of self-knowledge, may we strive to see ourselves reflected in the diverse expressions of life. May we cultivate a deep sense of unity, compassion, and love, recognizing the same divine essence that shines within us all. And may this realization inspire us to live a life of service, spreading the light of self-knowledge and compassion to all beings we encounter on our path.

Story

One day, news reached the sage that a nearby kingdom was plagued by discord and suffering. The king, burdened by the weight of his responsibilities, had lost touch with his true nature and had become consumed by greed and power. The kingdom was in chaos, and the people were living in fear and despair.

Moved by compassion, the sage decided to visit the kingdom and offer his guidance to the troubled king. Accompanied by a few of his devoted disciples, he made the journey to the royal palace.

As the sage and his disciples entered the palace, they were met with skepticism and resistance from the king's ministers. They questioned the sage's authority and dismissed his teachings as mere philosophical ideas. Undeterred, the sage remained calm and composed, radiating an aura of peace and love.

One of the king's ministers, intrigued by the sage's presence, decided to engage in a conversation. He approached the sage with curiosity and asked, "What is the key to finding true happiness and peace in this chaotic world?"

The sage smiled gently and replied, "The key lies in self-knowledge and awareness. It is in recognizing our true nature as divine beings, interconnected with all of creation. When we understand that love is our essence and that we are all united in the fabric of existence, we can transcend the limitations of our ego and experience profound peace and joy."

The minister was deeply moved by the sage's words. He realized that he had been searching for happiness in external achievements and material possessions, but true fulfillment lay in cultivating love and compassion within himself.

Inspired by the sage's wisdom, the minister decided to share his newfound understanding with the king. He explained how the sage's teachings could transform the kingdom and bring about harmony and prosperity for all its inhabitants.

The sage looked into the king's eyes with compassion and spoke gently, "Your Majesty, true happiness and fulfillment can only be found when we embrace the path of love and self-awareness. It is by recognizing our oneness and acting with compassion that we can bring about positive change in ourselves and the world."

The king, who had been burdened by the weight of his desires and ambitions, felt a deep resonance within him. He realized that his power and wealth were meaningless if they did not bring happiness and well-being to his people.

ॐ

Awareness

30. *"Our ultimate dharma is Self-realization. Thoughts and actions that support our spiritual evolution are real dharma."* *-Amma*

> parīkṣya lokānkarmacitānbrāhmaṇo
> nirvedamāyānnāstyakṛtaḥ kṛtena |
> tadvijñānārthaṃ sa gurumevābhigacchetsamitpāṇiḥ
> śrotriyaṃ brahmaniṣṭham

> – Mundaka Upanishad 1.2.12

Let a Brahmin having examined the worlds produced by karma be free from desires, thinking, 'there is nothing eternal produced by karma"; and in order to acquire the knowledge of the eternal, let him Samid (sacrificial fuel) in hand, approach a preceptor alone, who is versed in the Vedas and centered in the Brahman.

Introduction:

The verse from the Mundaka Upanishad, "parīkṣya lokān karmacitān brāhmaṇo nirvedam āyānn asty akṛtaḥ kṛtena," emphasizes the importance of self-inquiry and seeking knowledge beyond the transient world of karma. Examining the world of actions and desires, cultivating a sense of detachment, and seeking a knowledgeable preceptor to attain the knowledge of the eternal.

Understanding the Worlds Produced by Karma: The verse encourages one to examine the worlds created by karma, referring to the various realms and experiences resulting from actions and desires. It highlights the transient nature of these worlds and the realization that they are not eternal or ultimately fulfilling. This examination prompts a seeker to question the true purpose and significance of worldly pursuits.

Cultivating Nirveda, Detachment from Desires: The verse urges the Brahmin to cultivate nirveda, which signifies a sense of detachment or dispassion towards worldly desires. By recognizing the impermanence and limitations of the objects of desire, one develops a state of inner detachment, freeing oneself from the constant pursuit of transient pleasures. This detachment allows for a shift in focus towards the pursuit of eternal knowledge.

Seeking Knowledge of the Eternal: In order to acquire the knowledge of the eternal, the verse recommends approaching a knowledgeable preceptor who is well-versed in the Vedas and centered in the Brahman. The preceptor serves as a guide and mentor in the journey of self-discovery and realization. Their wisdom and understanding help the seeker navigate the path to attain the knowledge of the eternal truth.

Samid in hand, Symbolizing Preparedness: The verse metaphorically suggests holding samvid, sacrificial fuel, in hand while approaching the preceptor. This symbolizes the readiness and preparedness of the seeker to embark on the spiritual journey. It implies a sincere intention, humility, and the willingness to learn and grow under the guidance of the preceptor.

Importance of the Preceptor: The verse emphasizes the significance of seeking a preceptor who is not only well-versed but also firmly established in the Brahman, the ultimate reality. The preceptor's profound understanding, direct experience, and alignment with the Brahman make them capable of imparting the knowledge of the eternal truth to the seeker. The term "shrotriya" signifies one who has heard and realized the scriptures, while "Brahmaniṣṭha" refers to one who is centered in the Brahman.

The Journey Towards Self-Realization: By examining the transient nature of the worlds produced by karma, cultivating detachment, and seeking the guidance of a knowledgeable preceptor, the seeker embarks on a transformative journey towards Self-realization. This journey involves self-inquiry, study of scriptures, contemplation, and assimilation of the knowledge imparted by the preceptor. It leads to the discovery of the eternal truth and the realization of one's true nature.

Conclusion

The verse from the Mundaka Upanishad emphasizes the importance of examining the transient worlds of karma, cultivating detachment, and seeking a knowledgeable preceptor to attain the knowledge of the eternal truth. Through self-inquiry, dispassion, and the guidance of an enlightened preceptor, one embarks on a transformative journey towards Self-realization and the understanding of their true nature beyond the limitations of worldly pursuits.

Story

One day, a young man named approached the sage with a heavy heart. He was torn between the demands of society and his inner yearning for spiritual growth. Young man sought clarity on the concept of dharma, the righteous path that would lead him to Self-realization.

The sage listened attentively to the young man's dilemmas and then began to share his insights. He explained that dharma, at its core, was the pursuit of Self-realization. It was not merely about following religious rituals or adhering to social norms, but rather about aligning one's thoughts and actions with the ultimate truth of existence.

The sage emphasized that thoughts and actions that supported spiritual evolution were the true dharma. It was not about external obligations, but rather an internal compass that guided individuals towards self-discovery and awakening. The sage emphasized the importance of cultivating awareness and be alert in every aspect of life, whether it be in relationships, work, or daily activities.

He spoke of the need to cultivate virtues such as compassion, truthfulness, humility, and non-attachment. These qualities were not only essential for individual growth but also for the betterment of society as a whole. The sage explained that when one embraced their ultimate dharma of Self-realization, they naturally radiated love, wisdom, and kindness, positively influencing those around them.

Thus the young man realized the truth about the importance of spirituality and became aware about one's nature as Brahman.

ॐ

31. "God realization and Self-realization are one and the same. God-realization is nothing but the ability and expansiveness of heart to love everything equally." -Amma

In the realm of spirituality, the concept of God realization and Self-realization holds profound significance. It is the realization that the ultimate truth, the divine essence, resides within us and permeates all of creation. Amma, with her wisdom and compassion, beautifully expresses this truth, stating that God realization and Self-realization are inseparable, as they both lead to the expansion of the heart and the ability to love everything equally.

God realization is not an external attainment, but a deep inner awakening. It is the recognition that the divine presence exists within us and in every aspect of existence. It is the realization that we are not separate from God, but an integral part of the divine consciousness that pervades all beings and forms.

Self-realization, on the other hand, is the direct experience and understanding of our true nature. It is the realization that we are not limited to our physical body or the conditioning of our mind, but are infinite and eternal beings of consciousness.

Self-realization is the journey of uncovering the layers of illusion and egoic identification, and awakening to the truth of our essential nature.

Amma reminds us that the path to God realization and Self-realization lies in the expansiveness of the heart, in the ability to love everything equally. Love becomes the gateway to realizing our inherent divine nature. When our hearts are open and expansive, free from judgment and discrimination, we can experience the divine presence in all beings and aspects of creation.

Advaita Vedanta teaches us that there is no separation between ourselves and the divine. Love becomes the bridge that connects us to the infinite source of love, wisdom, and compassion. It is through love that we recognize the interconnectedness of all life and embrace the oneness that underlies the diversity of forms.

upadraṣhṭānumantā cha bhartā bhoktā maheśhvaraḥ
paramātmeti chāpy ukto dehe 'smin puruṣhaḥ paraḥ

– Bhagavad Gita 13:23

Within the body also resides the Supreme Lord. He is said to be the Witness, the Permitter, the Supporter, Transcendental Enjoyer, the ultimate Controller, and the Paramātmā (Supreme Soul).

The verse elucidates the nature of the Supreme Person dwelling within the body. It reveals the roles of the Supreme Self as the Witness, Permitter, Sustainer, Experiencer, great Lord, and the transcendental Self.

The Upadrasta: The Witness

The Supreme Self is described as the Upadrasta, the Witness who remains uninvolved while observing the actions of the body and organs. Similar to a sacrifice where there is a separate observer (Brahma) who witnesses the proceedings, the Supreme Self remains distinct from the body and its functions.

The Anumanta: The Permitter

As the Anumanta, the Supreme Self grants approval and satisfaction to the body and organs in their actions. Even though not directly engaged in these activities, the Supreme Self appears favorably disposed towards and supportive of them.

The Bharta: The Sustainer

The Supreme Self is the Bharta, the Sustainer, ensuring the continuation of the body, organs, mind, and intellect in their respective states. It is through the reflection of consciousness that these entities exist, serving the purpose of the conscious Self.

The Bhokta: The Experiencer

Just as fire imparts heat, the Supreme Self, as the Bhokta, experiences the various manifestations of the intellect, such as happiness, sorrow, and delusion, in relation to external objects. The Self, being of the nature of eternal consciousness, allows for the diverse expressions of experiences.

Maheswara: The Great God

As the Maheswara, the Supreme Self is the great God who rules over all. Being the Self of all and independent, it holds supreme authority and dominion.

Paramatma: The Transcendental Self

The Supreme Self is the Paramatma, the transcendental Self, encompassing the characteristics of the supreme Witness and other divine attributes. It is the true Self beyond the mistaken identification with the body and intellect.

Conclusion

The verse elucidates the role of the Supreme Self in relation to the body and its faculties, highlighting its distinct nature and ultimate authority. Understanding and recognizing the presence of the Supreme Person within enables one to realize their true divine essence and attain spiritual liberation.

Story

One day, a young man arrived at a Sage's humble abode seeking answers to his existential questions. The young man was filled with doubts and confusion about the purpose of life and his own identity. He felt disconnected and longed for a deeper understanding of himself and the world around him.

He spoke of the oneness of all beings and the underlying unity that transcends the physical realm. Sage explained that God realization and Self-realization are not separate endeavors, but rather two facets of the same journey. He emphasized the importance of expanding one's heart and cultivating love and compassion for all.

To illustrate his point, Sage told the young man a story. He spoke of a flower garden where different types of flowers blossomed, each with its own unique beauty and fragrance. Despite their differences, the flowers lived harmoniously, sharing the same soil, sunlight, and water. They recognized their interdependence and celebrated the diversity that made the garden so vibrant.

In the story, Sage highlighted that just as the flowers in the garden recognized their inherent connection, human beings too must recognize the oneness that underlies all of existence. Love becomes the bridge that connects us to the divine and to one another.

As the young man listened attentively to the story, he felt a profound shift within himself. The teachings of Rishi resonated deep within his soul, igniting a flame of understanding and inspiration. He realized that the path to Self-realization and God realization lay in cultivating love, compassion, and unity.

ॐ

Self

32. "Children, we are the light of the Divine – the eternally free, infinite and blissful Atman (True Self). Proceed with innocence, effort and faith and you will discover the bliss of the Self within you." –Amma

In the realm of spirituality, there exists a profound understanding that transcends the limitations of the physical world. It is the realization that at the core of our being, we are not merely mortal beings defined by our bodies and minds, but rather we are the eternal, free, and blissful Atman, the True Self. This understanding forms the essence of the Advaita Vedanta philosophy, teaching us to explore the depths of our being and discover the boundless bliss that resides within.

Amma, with her divine wisdom, reminds us of this truth, especially in her quote: "Children, we are the light of the Divine – the eternally free, infinite and blissful Atman. Proceed with innocence, effort, and faith, and you will discover the bliss of the Self within you." These words resonate deep within our souls, awakening us to the inherent divinity that exists within each and every one of us.

To fully comprehend the depth of this teaching, we must embark on a journey of self-exploration and Self-realization. The path to Self-realization is not one of external seeking, but an inward journey of self-discovery. It is a journey that requires innocence, which refers to a pure and open heart, free from the burdens of conditioning and preconceived notions. By approaching life with innocence, we become receptive to the divine light that shines within us.

Effort is another key component on this path. It is through sincere effort that we undertake practices such as self-inquiry, meditation, and self-discipline. These practices help us to quiet the mind, transcend the limitations of the ego, and tap into the reservoir of infinite wisdom and bliss that resides within us. Effort is the catalyst that propels us forward on our spiritual journey, allowing us to uncover the ever-present truth of our divine nature.

Faith is the thread that weaves everything together. It is the unwavering trust and belief in our own divine essence and the higher power that guides us. With faith, we surrender our limited understanding and allow the wisdom of the universe to flow through us. It is through faith that we come to realize that we are not separate from the Divine, but rather an integral part of the cosmic tapestry.

The teachings of the Advaita Vedanta philosophy, along with Amma's guidance, remind us that the bliss of the Self is not something external to be acquired, but rather a realization of our inherent nature. It is an awakening to the truth that we are not separate from the Divine, but an embodiment of the Divine itself.

To illustrate this profound truth, let us delve into the story of a seeker. The seeker had spent her entire life searching for fulfillment and happiness in the external world. She had amassed wealth, achieved success in her career, and enjoyed the pleasures of life, but deep within, she felt a sense of emptiness and longing.

One day, the seeker came across the teachings of Advaita Vedanta and was captivated by the idea that true fulfillment lies within. Intrigued, she embarked on a journey of self-discovery, guided by the principles of innocence, effort, and faith.

The seeker immersed herself in the practices of meditation and self-inquiry, seeking to peel away the layers of conditioning and false identifications. With each moment of stillness and introspection, she began to realize that the true source of happiness and bliss was not in the external world, but within the depths of her own being.

As the seeker deepened her understanding, she experienced moments of profound clarity and connection with the divine. In these moments, she felt a sense of expansiveness, a deep knowing that she was not limited by her physical form, but rather an eternal, boundless consciousness.

In the Bhagavad Gita, Chapter 2, verse 16, Lord Krishna imparts profound wisdom to Arjuna:

"Nāsato vidyate bhāvo, nābhāvo vidyate sataḥ
Ubhayorapi dṛṣṭo 'ntas tv anayos tattva-darśibhiḥ"

There is no existence for the unreal, and the real never ceases to be; the seers of truth have concluded the same.

The Illusory Nature of the Unreal and the Eternal Reality: The verse "There is no existence for the unreal, and the real never ceases to be; the seers of truth have concluded the same" encapsulates the profound teachings of Advaita Vedanta, as expounded by the great philosopher So, the ultimate truth is the realization of the non-dual nature of reality, where the unreal is deemed transient and the real is recognized as eternal.

Distinguishing between the Unreal and the Real: Advaita philosophy asserts that the phenomenal world, characterized by constant change and impermanence, is unreal (mithya) in its nature. It is a product of Maya, the illusory power that veils the ultimate reality. The unreal is subject to birth and death, constantly changing and devoid of intrinsic existence.

The Eternal Nature of the Real: The ultimate reality, known as Brahman, is the only truly existent entity. It is beyond the limitations of time, space, and causation. Brahman is eternal, unchanging, and the substratum of all manifestations. It is the essence that pervades everything, and its nature is pure consciousness.

The Perspective of the Seers of Truth: The seers of truth, who have attained Self-realization through deep spiritual insight, have arrived at the understanding that the unreal has no inherent existence. Their profound wisdom and direct experience have led them to recognize the eternal reality of Brahman. They see beyond the illusions of the phenomenal world and abide in the truth of non-duality.

Maya: The Illusory Power: Maya, the creative power of Brahman, is responsible for the appearance of the unreal. It veils the true nature of Brahman and manifests as the multiplicity and diversity of the world. Maya is neither absolutely real nor absolutely unreal, but it is a power that deludes and binds individuals to the cycle of birth and death.

Liberation through Knowledge: Advaita emphasizes the path of knowledge (jnana) as the means to liberation (moksha). By realizing the illusory nature of the unreal and understanding the eternal reality of Brahman, one can transcend the cycle of suffering and attain spiritual liberation. Self-realization leads to the direct experience of the non-dual nature of existence.

Conclusion

This verse highlights the distinction between the unreal and the real, emphasizing the transient nature of the phenomenal world and the eternal existence of Brahman. Through deep introspection and the pursuit of self-knowledge, individuals can transcend the illusions of Maya and awaken to their true nature as the eternal and limitless Brahman. The teachings of Advaita Vedanta offer a path to liberation, inviting seekers to go beyond the apparent duality and realize the ultimate truth of non-duality.

Self

ॐ

33. "The Divine is present in everyone, in all beings, in everything. Like space, God is everywhere, all pervading, all powerful and all knowing. God is the principle of life, the inner light of consciousness, and pure bliss awareness. It is your very own Self. You can understand the secret of bliss when you contemplate the nature of the Self. When the waves of the mind subside you will see that everything you seek is already within you." - Amma

In the realm of Advaita Vedanta, the teachings of Amma beautifully encapsulate the profound understanding of the Divine presence within all beings and everything. Her words echo the timeless wisdom found in ancient scriptures and philosophies, emphasizing the inherent divinity and oneness of all existence.

Amma's quote reminds us that the Divine is not confined to a specific place or form but permeates the entire universe. Just as space is omnipresent, God is present in every atom, every living being, and every aspect of creation. This all-pervading Divinity is the life force that animates all living things and is the source of pure consciousness and eternal bliss.

By recognizing the Divine as the principle of life within us, we are encouraged to dive deep into self-contemplation. Amma suggests that through introspection and stilling the waves of the mind, we can unlock the secrets of bliss. When the restless thoughts and desires subside, we can realize that everything we seek externally already exists within us.

The essence of Advaita Vedanta lies in the understanding that the Divine is not separate from our own Self. It is not an external entity to be sought, but an intrinsic part of our being. This realization unveils the eternal truth that we are divine beings, interconnected with all of creation.

pratibodhaviditaṃ matamamṛtatvaṃ hi vindate
ātmanā vindate vīryaṃ vidyayā vindate'mṛtam

– Kena Upanishad 2.4.4

It (i.e., Brahman) is truly known when It is known as the Self of each state of consciousness because thereby one attains immortality. Since strength is acquired through one's own Self, immortality is attained through knowledge.

Pratibodha-viditam: This term refers to being known with reference to each state of intelligence or cognition.

Bodha and Cognitions Acquired Through the Intellect: Bodha refers to the cognitions or knowledge acquired through the intellect or mind.

The Self Encompasses All Ideas as Its Objects: It suggests that the Self (Brahman) is the ultimate reality that encompasses all ideas and thoughts as objects within itself.

Witness of All Cognitions: The Self is described as the witness of all cognitions. It means that it observes or is aware of all mental activities and thoughts.

Nature of Consciousness: The Self is said to be nothing but the power of consciousness itself, implying that it is the fundamental awareness behind all mental processes.

Non-different from Cognitions: The Self is described as non-different from the cognitions it witnesses. This means that the Self is inherent in all thoughts and is not separate from them.

No Other Door to Its Awareness: There is no other means or path to become aware of the Self except by recognizing it as the witness of all cognitions.

Brahman as the Innermost Self (Witness) of Cognitions: When one realizes Brahman as the innermost Self, the witnessing aspect of consciousness, then complete realization is achieved. Nature of Brahman: By accepting Brahman as the witness of all cognitions, it is established that Brahman is unchanging, eternal, pure, unconditioned, and present in all beings. Just as space (ākāśa) remains the same despite existing in various objects like pots or caves, Brahman characteristics remain the same despite its presence in all individual beings.

In conclusion, the concept of Pratibodha-viditam underscores the profound understanding that the realization of Brahman, the ultimate reality, occurs when one recognizes it as the innermost Self in every state of consciousness. This realization is not merely an intellectual pursuit but a path to immortality and inner strength. By comprehending Brahman as the eternal witness of all cognitions and as the very essence of one's being, individuals embark on a transformative journey towards spiritual enlightenment and the attainment of immortality. Thus, the wisdom conveyed through Pratibodha-viditam emphasizes the profound significance of self-awareness and the realization of the transcendent Self as the ultimate goal of human existence.

In the pursuit of Self-realization, Advaita Vedanta guides us to transcend the limitations of the ego and identify with the eternal and unchanging aspect of ourselves. It invites us to recognize the illusory nature of external pursuits and turn our gaze inward to discover the Divine reservoir of love, wisdom, and bliss that resides within.

Amma's teachings resonate with the core principles of Advaita Vedanta, emphasizing the unity of all existence and the divine nature of every individual. By contemplating the nature of the Self and realizing our inherent divinity, we can experience profound inner transformation and cultivate a deep sense of oneness, love, and compassion for all beings.

Story

One day, a young and curious seeker arrived at the ashram of Sage. Seeker had heard of the sage's wisdom and was eager to learn from him. With great humility, Seeker approached Sage and sought his guidance on the path of Self-realization.

Impressed by seekers sincerity and thirst for knowledge, Sage agreed to become his mentor. Under the sage's guidance, seeker embarked on a spiritual journey, delving into the depths of the scriptures and practicing meditation and self-inquiry.

As seekers' understanding of spiritual principles grew, he became more and more absorbed in his pursuit of Self-realization. He spent hours meditating, contemplating the nature of the Self, and seeking answers to life's profound questions.

During this time, a great war was brewing in the kingdom. The king, was faced with a difficult decision. He sought the counsel of sage, recognizing his wisdom and foresight.

Sage, with his deep insight and connection to the divine, advised the king to choose the path of righteousness and non-violence. He emphasized the importance of dharma and the preservation of moral values. His words touched the king's heart, and king resolved to lead his kingdom with integrity and compassion.

ॐ

Surrender

34. "When you surrender to a higher consciousness, you give up all your claims; you release your grip from everything that you have been holding on to. Whether you gain or lose; you don't want to be something any longer. You long to be nothing, absolutely nothing, so you dive into the river of Existence." -Amma

Surrender is a profound spiritual practice that brings us closer to the ultimate truth and leads us to experience the divine presence within us. It is an act of letting go, releasing our attachment to ego, desires, and the illusion of control. Through surrender, we open ourselves to the guidance and grace of a higher consciousness.

In the realm of Advaita Vedanta, surrender is understood as the recognition that our individual existence is a manifestation of the divine consciousness. It is the realization that we are not separate from the divine, but rather an expression of its infinite love and wisdom. Surrender is an act of aligning our will with the divine will, allowing ourselves to be guided by the higher intelligence that orchestrates the universe.

tad viddhi praṇipātena paripraśhnena sevayā
upadekṣhyanti te jñānaṁ jñāninas tattva-darśhinaḥ

– Bhagavad Gita 4:34

Learn the Truth by approaching a spiritual master. Inquire from him with reverence and render service unto him.
Such an enlightened Saint can impart knowledge unto you because he has seen the Truth.

Amma's words beautifully capture the essence of surrender. When we surrender, we let go of our identification with the limited self and merge into the river of Existence, the infinite consciousness that flows through all of creation. We release the need to be something, to possess or control, and instead embrace the state of being nothing, where the ego dissolves and the divine presence shines through. Surrender is not a passive act of resignation or defeat. It is an active surrendering of our egoic desires and attachments, allowing the divine will to unfold through us. It is a surrendering of our limited perspective, opening ourselves to the vastness and wisdom of the higher consciousness. In this surrender, we find freedom, liberation, and a deep sense of peace.

The path of surrender is beautifully illustrated in the Bhagavad Gita 18:66,

sarva-dharmān parityajya mām ekaṁ śharaṇaṁ vraja
ahaṁ tvāṁ sarva-pāpebhyo mokṣhayiṣhyāmi mā śhuchaḥ.

Abandon all varieties of religion and just surrender unto me. I shall deliver you from all sinful reactions. Do not fear.

This verse emphasizes the importance of surrendering to the divine, recognizing that true liberation and freedom from suffering come through surrendering our egoic attachments and surrendering to the divine will.

Story
One day, young man came across the teachings of a wise spiritual teacher, Guru. Guru spoke of the power of surrender and the transformation that it brings. Intrigued, young man sought out Guru for guidance.

Guru explained to young man that surrender is not a one-time event but a continuous process of letting go. He guided young man to practice surrendering his desires, fears, and expectations to the divine. Ravi struggled at first, as he was used to relying on his own efforts and control. But as he persisted in the practice of surrender, he experienced a profound shift in his consciousness.

Surrender

Through surrender, young man learned to trust in the divine's plan and wisdom. He realized that his limited perspective was a barrier to experiencing the divine presence. As he surrendered his egoic desires and attachments, he felt a deep sense of peace and interconnectedness with all of existence.

In time, young man realized that surrender was not about losing oneself but finding one's true essence. In surrendering to the divine, he discovered a deeper sense of purpose and fulfillment. He recognized that the river of Existence, the divine consciousness, was guiding him, and he was simply flowing with its currents.

Young man 's journey of surrender taught him that true freedom lies in letting go of the ego's grip and surrendering to the higher consciousness within. It allowed him to experience the grace and blessings that come when we align our will with the divine will.

In conclusion, surrender is a profound spiritual practice that brings us closer to the divine and leads us to a state of deep inner peace and fulfillment. It is an act of releasing our egoic attachments and surrendering to the divine will, recognizing that our true essence is connected to the infinite consciousness.

Through surrender, we let go of our need to control and manipulate outcomes, and instead, we trust in the divine intelligence that governs the universe. It is a surrendering of our limited perspective and opening ourselves to the wisdom and guidance of a higher power.

Amma's quote reminds us that when we surrender to a higher consciousness, we are willing to give up our claims, desires, and attachments. We no longer seek to be something in the external world, but instead, we dive into the river of Existence, merging with the infinite flow of life.

ॐ

Witness

35. "Develop the ability to stand back as a witness (sakshi bhava) to the thought process and emotions instead of being totally identified with them. The thinking process belongs to the mind; whereas, witnessing belongs to the higher Self. Witnessing is a state of consciously abiding in Pure Consciousness. Witnessing is the state of simply watching with perfect awareness. Once you learn this art of witnessing, which is your true nature, then everything becomes a beautiful and most delightful play." -Amma

The concept of being a witness, or cultivating the ability to stand back and observe our thoughts and emotions, is a profound teaching in the path of Advaita Vedanta. Amma's quote beautifully encapsulates the essence of this practice, emphasizing the importance of developing the skill of witnessing as a means to abide in Pure Consciousness.

In the Advaita Vedanta philosophy, the term "Drik-Drsya" refers to the ability to become the seer, the witness, of our own thoughts, emotions, and experiences. It is the recognition that we are not the mind or the body, but the pure awareness that is behind them. This practice helps us Disidentify from the fluctuations of the mind and enter into a state of higher awareness.

Amma encourages us to stand back as witnesses to our thought process and emotions rather than becoming completely identified with them. This means observing our thoughts without judgment or attachment, allowing them to arise and dissolve on their own. By doing so, we cultivate a sense of detachment and clarity, recognizing that the thoughts and emotions are not our true nature, but passing phenomena in the field of consciousness.

The practice of witnessing is a powerful tool for Self-realization. It helps us realize that we are not limited to the confines of our thoughts and emotions, but rather, we are the silent witness, the pure awareness that is ever-present. It allows us to disentangle ourselves from the grip of the mind and gain a deeper understanding of our true Self.

The Bhagavad Gita, a revered scripture in the Advaita Vedanta tradition, also emphasizes the importance of being a witness. In Chapter 13, verse 2,

shrī-bhagavān uvācha
idaṁ śharīraṁ kaunteya kṣhetram ity abhidhīyate
etad yo vetti taṁ prāhuḥ kṣhetra-jña iti tad-vidaḥ

O Arjun, this body is termed as kṣhetra (the field of activities), and the one who knows this body is called kṣhetrajña (the knower of the field) by the sages who discern the truth about both.

The Kshetra and the Kshetrajna: Understanding the Field of Activities and the Knower of the Field

Explores the concepts of kshetra (the field of activities, the body) and kshetrajna (the knower of the field, the self-realized individual).

The Significance of the Body as Kshetra:

The term "kshetra" refers to the human body, which serves as the field of activities for the soul. Just as a farmer cultivates a field, the body provides a platform for the soul to engage in various actions and experiences. The body is a dynamic instrument through which the soul interacts with the external world, acquires knowledge, and undergoes spiritual evolution.

Understanding the Kshetrajna:

The kshetrajna is the one who has a deep understanding of the kshetra, the body. This knower of the field is not limited to mere physical perceptions but possesses an awareness that extends beyond the material realm. The kshetrajna is the self-realized individual who recognizes their true nature and the eternal essence within.

Knowledge and Discernment:
Those who possess true knowledge and discernment understand the distinction between the kshetra and the kshetrajna. They perceive that the body is a temporary abode, subject to change and decay, while the kshetrajna, the eternal self, remains unchanging and unaffected by the fluctuations of the physical realm.

Self-Realization and Spiritual Growth:
Recognizing oneself as the kshetrajna brings about profound spiritual growth and self-awareness. By understanding the nature of the body as the kshetra and transcending identification with it, individuals can realize their true identity as immortal souls. This realization leads to liberation from the cycles of birth and death and enables one to live in alignment with their higher purpose.

Conclusion
The verse highlights the distinction between the body (kshetra) and the self-realized individual (kshetrajna). The body serves as a field of activities for the soul, while the kshetrajna is the knower of this field, possessing deep understanding and awareness. By recognizing the true nature of the body as transient and identifying with the eternal self, individuals can embark on a path of Self-realization and spiritual growth. Understanding the concepts of kshetra and kshetrajna helps one navigate life's experiences, cultivate self-awareness, and ultimately attain liberation and union with the Divine. Lord Krishna instructs Arjuna, "Even a knowledge of the nature of the field and the knower of the field should be considered knowledge in the mode of goodness. But beyond this, the soul itself, by means of meditation, should be seen as separate from the field and the knower of the field, and

as transcendentally situated." This verse teaches us that true knowledge lies not only in understanding the external world but also in recognizing our own transcendent nature. By practicing meditation and cultivating the ability to witness, we can perceive ourselves as separate from the field of experiences, including the body, mind, and senses. We realize our true identity as the eternal consciousness, untouched by the changing phenomena of the world.

Story
The story of a seeker on the spiritual path, illustrates the transformative power of becoming a witness. Initially, the seeker was completely identified with his thoughts and emotions, leading to a sense of restlessness and suffering. However, under the guidance of a wise spiritual teacher, the seeker learned to observe his thoughts without getting entangled in them. Gradually, he developed the ability to stand back as a witness, realizing the true nature of his being as pure awareness. This newfound awareness brought him peace, clarity, and a deep sense of liberation.

ॐ

36. *"To be able to put oneself in another's position, to be able to and to feel as another person does, this is the rare gift of an earnest spiritual seeker." –Amma*

In the realm of spirituality, one of the most valuable qualities we can cultivate is empathy - the ability to understand and experience the thoughts, emotions, and perspectives of others. Empathy allows us to transcend our individual identity and connect with the shared essence that binds us all. It is a profound expression of love, compassion, and unity.

Amma's quote emphasizes the significance of empathy in the spiritual journey. To put oneself in another's position and truly feel as they do is not merely an intellectual exercise; it is an act of profound humility and openness. It requires us to set aside our own preconceptions, biases, and judgments, and to enter into the sacred space of another person's experience.

In the teachings of Advaita Vedanta, the concept of empathy aligns with the principle of oneness. It reminds us that behind the apparent diversity of individuals and their experiences, there is a fundamental unity of consciousness. Just as we have our unique thoughts, emotions, and desires, so do others. By recognizing and honoring the divine presence within each person, we can foster a deep connection that transcends the boundaries of the self.

The practice of empathy is rooted in deep listening and observation. It involves actively engaging with others, being present in the moment, and giving our undivided attention. When we truly listen, we create a space for others to express themselves fully, without judgment or interruption. This act of presence allows us to connect at a heart level, to feel what the other person is experiencing, and to respond with kindness and understanding.

Empathy also extends beyond our interactions with individuals. It includes recognizing the suffering and struggles of all beings and feeling a sense of responsibility towards their well-being. It prompts us to extend our compassion and support to those in need, to work towards the alleviation of suffering in the world.

Amma's quote invites us to cultivate empathy as an essential aspect of our spiritual practice. It encourages us to step out of our own limited perspective and expand our awareness to include the experiences of others. By developing empathy, we break down the barriers of separation and cultivate a deep sense of interconnectedness.

In the Bhagavad Gita, Lord Krishna speaks of empathy and compassion in Chapter 6, verse 30:

yo māṁ paśhyati sarvatra sarvaṁ cha mayi paśhyati
tasyāhaṁ na praṇaśhyāmi sa cha me na praṇaśhyati

– Bhagavad Gita 6:30

He who sees Me in all things, and sees all things in Me, I never lose sight of him, nor does he ever lose sight of Me.

This verse reminds us that when we develop the ability to see the divine presence in all beings, we establish a profound connection with the Supreme.

Cultivating Empathy and Compassion: Seeing the Divine Presence in All Beings emphasizes the importance of perceiving the divine presence in all beings and establishing a deep connection with the Supreme.

Seeing the Divine in All:

The verse encourages us to develop a perspective that transcends superficial differences and recognizes the divine essence in every being. When we cultivate the ability to see the divine in all things and beings, we cultivate a sense of oneness and unity, fostering empathy and compassion.

The Reciprocal Relationship:

By seeing all things in the Divine and the Divine in all things, a reciprocal relationship is established. The verse emphasizes that when we maintain this awareness, the Supreme Being never loses sight of us, showering us with grace and guidance. Simultaneously, we never lose sight of the Divine, deepening our spiritual connection.

Compassion as an Expression of Divinity:

When we perceive the divine presence in others, our hearts naturally open up with empathy and compassion. Compassion becomes an expression of our recognition of the shared divine essence, motivating us to alleviate suffering, support others, and foster harmonious relationships.

Transforming Relationships and Society:

Embracing the teaching of seeing the divine presence in all beings has transformative effects on our relationships and society. It promotes inclusivity, respect, and understanding, transcending barriers of race, religion, and social status. By treating others with empathy and compassion, we contribute to building a more compassionate and harmonious world.

Conclusion

The verse from the Bhagavad Gita emphasizes the profound importance of developing empathy and compassion by recognizing the divine presence in all beings. By cultivating the ability to see the Divine in all things and beings, we establish a deep connection with the Supreme and experience the reciprocal love and grace that flow from this realization. When we live with empathy and compassion, we contribute to transforming our relationships and society, creating a world rooted in unity, understanding, and love.

ॐ

Education

37. "Our educational system needs to give equal importance to the intellect and the heart. -Amma

Education is not merely the acquisition of knowledge or the development of intellectual prowess; it is a holistic journey that nurtures both the intellect and the heart. Amma's profound statement emphasizes the need for a balanced approach in our educational system, where the cultivation of compassion, empathy, and values holds equal importance alongside academic excellence.

In the current era, education often tends to focus primarily on the accumulation of information, grades, and career prospects. While these aspects are undoubtedly important, they should not overshadow the essential development of the heart, which encompasses qualities like empathy, kindness, and moral values.

The Advaita Vedanta philosophy underscores the oneness of all beings and the inherent unity of existence. It teaches us to look beyond surface differences and recognize the divine spark within every individual. This spiritual perspective reminds us that education should not only aim at the intellectual growth of individuals but also nurture their capacity to relate to others with compassion, understanding, and respect.

When the heart is nurtured along with the intellect, education becomes a transformative process that goes beyond the boundaries of the classroom. It helps individuals develop a deep sense of social responsibility and empathy towards others. Through this integrated approach, students learn to apply their knowledge and skills for the betterment of society, fostering a culture of service, and making meaningful contributions to the world.

The teachings of the Bhagavad Gita, a profound scripture in the Vedantic tradition, also emphasize the importance of holistic education.

abhayaṁ sattva-sanśhuddhir jñāna-yoga-vyavasthitiḥ
dānaṁ damaśh cha yajñaśh cha svādhyāyas tapa ārjavam
ahinsā satyam akrodhas tyāgaḥ śhāntir apaiśhunam
dayā bhūteṣhv aloluptvaṁ mārdavaṁ hrīr achāpalam
tejaḥ kṣhamā dhṛitiḥ śhaucham adroho nāti-mānitā
bhavanti sampadaṁ daivīm abhijātasya bhārata

– Bhagavad Gita 16:1-3

O scion of Bharat, these are the saintly virtues of those endowed with a divine nature—fearlessness, purity of mind, steadfastness in spiritual knowledge, charity, control of the senses, sacrifice, study of the sacred books, austerity, and straightforwardness; non-violence, truthfulness, absence of anger, renunciation, peacefulness, restraint from fault-finding, compassion toward all living beings, absence of covetousness, gentleness, modesty, and lack of fickleness; vigor, forgiveness, fortitude, cleanliness, bearing enmity toward none, and absence of vanity.

Amma's call for an education system that integrates the intellect and the heart resonates with the ancient wisdom of Vedanta. It invites us to reimagine education as a transformative journey that not only empowers individuals with knowledge but also cultivates empathy, compassion, and moral values. It urges us to create learning environments where students are encouraged to develop their intellectual capacities while also nurturing their emotional intelligence and ethical foundations.

In such a system, teachers play a crucial role as facilitators and guides. They not only impart knowledge but also serve as mentors who inspire and model the values they teach. They create a nurturing environment that encourages students to explore their inner selves, reflect on their actions, and develop a deep sense of self-awareness and moral responsibility.

Moreover, an education system that places equal importance on the intellect and the heart fosters a sense of interconnectedness and unity among students. It helps break down barriers of prejudice, discrimination, and intolerance, creating an inclusive and harmonious learning community.

Ultimately, an education system that integrates the intellect and the heart cultivates individuals who are not only intellectually accomplished but also compassionate, ethical, and mindful of their role in society. It equips them with the tools to navigate the complexities of life with wisdom and empathy, making them agents of positive change in the world.

Story

One day, the kingdom faced a crisis when a neighboring kingdom threatened to invade. The king called upon his ministers and advisors to strategize and defend their land. The minister proposed an intellectual plan of action, analyzing the strengths and weaknesses of both kingdoms, while the teacher emphasized the importance of compassion, diplomacy, and finding peaceful solutions.

The king, being a wise leader, understood the significance of both perspectives. He recognized that intellectual prowess alone could not ensure a harmonious and prosperous kingdom. It was the integration of intellect and heart that would enable them to navigate challenges with wisdom, empathy, and fairness.

Inspired by the king's wisdom, the prince realized the importance of pursuing an education that encompassed both the intellect and the heart. He understood that academic achievements were valuable, but they needed to be balanced with qualities like compassion, empathy, and moral values.

Motivated by this realization, the prince approached Guruji with gratitude and determination. He expressed his commitment to pursuing an education that would nourish both his intellect and his heart. Guru, pleased with the prince's sincerity, became his guide and mentor, helping him explore the depths of knowledge while instilling in him the importance of empathy, compassion, and ethical values.

As the prince continued his educational journey, he witnessed the transformation within himself. He became not only a knowledgeable and skilled individual but also a compassionate and empathetic leader.

Years later, the prince ascended the throne and became a wise king like his predecessor. He implemented educational reforms that emphasized the integration of the intellect and the heart, ensuring that future generations would receive a holistic education that nurtured both their minds and their souls.

ॐ

38. *"Education for livelihood alone will never make our life full and complete." -Amma*

Education is often seen as a means to acquire knowledge and skills that enable individuals to secure a livelihood and achieve material success. While this aspect of education is undoubtedly important, it is equally essential to recognize that education encompasses much more than just vocational training. True education encompasses the holistic development of an individual, nurturing their intellectual, emotional, and spiritual dimensions. Amma, with her profound wisdom, reminds us that focusing solely on livelihood-oriented education will never fulfill the deeper aspirations of our hearts and souls.

In the Advaita Vedanta way, education is viewed as a transformative journey that leads to Self-realization and the realization of our interconnectedness with all of creation. It goes beyond the accumulation of information and seeks to awaken the inherent wisdom and potential within each individual. It is an exploration of the self, a journey of self-discovery and self-mastery.

Education in the Advaita Vedanta way encourages individuals to go beyond the confines of conventional knowledge and seek a deeper understanding of themselves and the world around them. It inspires them to question, to inquire, and to seek the truth beyond the surface level of existence. It encourages them to develop critical thinking skills, to cultivate empathy and compassion, and to embrace values that promote harmony, justice, and unity.

Amma's quote reminds us that a truly fulfilling life cannot be measured solely by material achievements or professional success. While livelihood-oriented education is necessary for practical purposes, it is equally important to nurture the spiritual and emotional aspects of our being. True fulfillment lies in the cultivation of wisdom, love, compassion, and a sense of purpose that transcends the limitations of the material world.

Education for Self-realization opens the doors to self-discovery and the realization of our divine nature. It guides us towards a deeper understanding of our oneness with all beings and the universe at large. It allows us to recognize that we are not isolated individuals but integral parts of the cosmic fabric, interconnected and interdependent.

In the Advaita Vedanta way, education is not limited to the classroom or the acquisition of degrees. It is a lifelong journey of self-exploration and growth. It is a process of continuous learning and unlearning, of expanding our consciousness and aligning our actions with higher principles and values.

Amma's profound insight reminds us that education should empower individuals to lead meaningful lives, to cultivate inner peace, and to contribute positively to the well-being of society. It is through education that we develop the capacity to make informed decisions, to contribute to the betterment of our communities, and to create a more compassionate and harmonious world.

In conclusion, education for livelihood alone can never fulfill the deeper yearnings of our hearts and souls. True education, in the Advaita Vedanta way, encompasses the holistic development of individuals, nurturing their intellectual, emotional, and spiritual dimensions. It is an exploration of self and the realization of our interconnectedness with all of creation. By embracing this comprehensive view of education, we can lead fulfilling lives, contribute to the well-being of society, and realize our highest potential as human beings.

Story
Once upon a time, in a small village nestled amidst lush green fields, there lived a wise teacher. Teacher had dedicated his life to imparting knowledge and wisdom to the young minds of the village. He firmly believed in the importance of education, not just for the acquisition of skills, but for the holistic development of individuals.

The village had a vibrant community where people from various backgrounds coexisted harmoniously. The villagers had deep respect for education and recognized the value it brought to their lives. They eagerly sent their children to Ravi's humble school to receive not only academic education but also teachings on values, ethics, and Self-realization.

Education

One day, as Teacher was delivering his lessons to a group of eager students, a young boy raised his hand and asked a question. "Sir," he said, "Why do we need to learn so many things? Can't we just focus on learning what we need to earn a living?"

Teacher smiled and replied, " Education is not just about earning a livelihood. It is about nurturing your mind, heart, and spirit. It is about discovering who you truly are and how you can contribute to the world in a meaningful way."

Intrigued by the Teacher 's response, the boy decided to delve deeper into the concept of education. He began to attend Teacher's classes with renewed curiosity, eager to explore the broader aspects of learning. Teacher guided the students through a transformative journey, encouraging them to question, think critically, and explore their own passions and interests.

The story of Teacher and his students serves as a reminder that education is not just about acquiring knowledge and skills for personal gain. It is about cultivating the intellect, nurturing the heart, and realizing our oneness with the world. True education empowers individuals to not only succeed in their chosen paths but also to make a positive impact on the lives of others. It is a powerful tool for personal growth, social transformation and spiritual evolution. Through education, individuals gain the ability to think critically, solve problems, and adapt to an ever-changing world. But beyond the acquisition of knowledge, education should also foster values such as empathy, compassion, and a sense of responsibility towards others.

ॐ

Equality

39. "In today's world, both men and women need motherhood, the nurturing motherly feeling, the feminine energy. By receiving this energy, it will make them independent and free." -Amma

In the realm of spirituality, the concept of equality transcends the limitations of gender, embracing the essence of the divine feminine energy present in all beings. Amma, in her profound wisdom, emphasizes the importance of nurturing motherhood, the feminine energy, for both men and women in today's world. She reminds us that by receiving this energy, individuals can attain independence and freedom.

Traditionally, motherhood has been associated with women, representing the nurturing and compassionate qualities that bring forth life, care, and support. However, Amma's teachings go beyond conventional gender roles, recognizing that the nurturing motherly feeling and feminine energy are essential for the holistic development of every individual, regardless of their gender.

In the Advaita Vedanta philosophy, the divine energy is perceived as both masculine and feminine, symbolizing the complementary aspects of creation. The masculine energy represents the dynamic and assertive qualities, while the feminine energy embodies the nurturing, compassionate, and receptive aspects. Both energies are necessary for the harmonious functioning of the universe.

Amma's message underscores the significance of embracing the feminine energy, not only for women but also for men. By embracing the nurturing motherly feeling, individuals cultivate qualities such as empathy, compassion, and unconditional love. These qualities enable individuals to foster harmonious relationships, create a nurturing environment, and contribute to the well-being of society as a whole.

In today's fast-paced and competitive world, the call for the nurturing motherly feeling becomes even more crucial. It is a reminder to prioritize empathy and compassion in our interactions, to extend a helping hand to those in need, and to create spaces of love and acceptance where all individuals can thrive.

By recognizing the importance of the feminine energy within ourselves, we embark on a journey of self-discovery and empowerment. Both men and women can tap into this nurturing energy, which resides in the depths of their being. By embracing and nurturing this aspect, individuals attain inner strength, balance, and a sense of freedom that goes beyond societal expectations and limitations.

The path to equality begins within each individual. It is an inner transformation that transcends external appearances and societal norms. When we cultivate the nurturing motherly feeling within ourselves, we break free from the confines of gender roles and embrace our true essence as beings of love and compassion.

Amma's teachings invite us to recognize and honor the divine feminine energy within ourselves and others. It is a call to nurture and uplift one another, fostering an environment of equality, respect, and understanding. When we embrace the feminine energy, we create a space where everyone is valued, heard, and supported in their journey of self-discovery and Self-realization.

Ultimately, the integration of the nurturing motherly feeling and feminine energy in both men and women contributes to a more harmonious and balanced society. It opens the door for the emergence of the highest human values of love, compassion, and unity. By embracing and embodying the divine feminine energy, individuals become agents of positive change, spreading love, healing, and empowerment in the world.

In this way, Amma's teachings on equality transcend societal boundaries, reminding us of the inherent value and power of the feminine energy. By embracing and nurturing this energy within ourselves and others, we contribute to the creation of a world where all beings are honored, respected, and cherished for their unique gifts and qualities. It is through the recognition of our interconnectedness and the embrace of the divine feminine energy that we pave the way for a more inclusive, compassionate, and harmonious future.

As the kingdom flourished under this new paradigm of equality and compassion, its influence spread beyond its borders. Other realms looked upon the kingdom as an example of progress and harmony, and the message of embracing the nurturing motherly feeling and feminine energy resonated with people from all walks of life.

Ravi and Maya continued their work, not only within the kingdom but also in neighboring lands, spreading the message of equality and compassion far and wide. Their efforts, along with the support of the wise king, created a ripple effect, inspiring countless individuals to embrace their nurturing qualities and contribute to a more inclusive and harmonious society.

And so, the kingdom thrived, not just in terms of material wealth and power but in its ability to honor and celebrate the inherent qualities of love, compassion, and empathy present within every individual. The wise king, Ravi, Maya, and the people of the kingdom became beacons of light, shining the way towards a future where the nurturing motherly feeling and feminine energy were cherished and celebrated by all, paving the path to a more compassionate and harmonious world.

ॐ

Nature

40. "By living in harmony with Nature one gains a healthy mind and body. Mother Earth and Nature are serving us. The sun, the moon and the stars all serve us. Each and every object in Nature teaches us something. Renunciation and selflessness are the greatest lessons to learn from Nature. It is the duty of human beings to protect all living creatures, seeing Nature as our mother." -Amma

Living in harmony with nature is not just about appreciating the beauty of the natural world or enjoying the benefits it provides. It goes much deeper than that. It is about recognizing our interconnectedness with all living beings and understanding our role as caretakers of the Earth.

Nature is not separate from us; it is an extension of our own being. Just as we have the capacity for love, compassion, and selflessness, so does nature. It is constantly serving us, providing us with the resources we need for our survival and well-being.

When we live in harmony with nature, we align ourselves with its rhythms and cycles. We begin to understand that we are part of a larger web of life, and our actions have an impact on the world around us. We realize that every object in nature, from the smallest blade of grass to the mightiest mountain, has something to teach us.

One of the greatest lessons we can learn from nature is the virtue of renunciation and selflessness. In nature, we see how trees generously provide shade and oxygen, how rivers selflessly flow to quench the thirst of all creatures, and how animals care for their young with unwavering devotion. Nature teaches us that true fulfillment comes not from amassing possessions or satisfying our selfish desires, but from giving and serving others.

As human beings, it is our duty to protect and preserve all living creatures, recognizing them as our fellow beings and seeing nature as our mother. We must nurture and care for the Earth, just as a child would care for their own mother. This means being mindful of our consumption, reducing waste, and taking actions to safeguard the environment for future generations. When we live in harmony with nature, we experience the profound interconnectedness of all things. We recognize that we are not separate entities, but rather integral parts of the intricate tapestry of life. This realization awakens a deep sense of gratitude and reverence for the natural world.

mama yonir mahad brahma tasmin garbham dadhāmy aham
sambhavaḥ sarva-bhūtānām tato bhavati bhārata
sarva-yoniṣhu kaunteya mūrtayaḥ sambhavanti yāḥ
tāsām brahma mahad yonir aham bīja-pradaḥ pitā

– Bhagavad Gita 14:3-4

My womb is the great-sustainer. In that I place the seed. From that, O scion of the Bharata dynasty, occurs the birth of all things.

Mama, My own Maya (Prakriti):
Lord Krishna refers to Prakrti, the material nature of the universe, as His own Maya. Maya represents the cosmic illusion that veils the true nature of reality. Prakrti consists of the three gunas or qualities: sattva (purity), rajas (passion), and tamas (inertia). It is the fundamental substance from which all manifestations arise.
Yonih, the womb (or cause) of all creatures:
Prakrti, belonging to Lord Krishna, is identified as the yonih, the womb or cause, from which all creatures are born. It serves

as the source and foundation of all existence. Just as a womb nurtures and gives birth to living beings, Prakrti provides the medium for creation and sustenance.

Prakrti is great and the sustainer of its own transformations: Lord Krishna highlights the significance of Prakrti by describing its greatness and role as the sustainer of its own transformations. Prakrti is vast and all-encompassing, surpassing the effects it produces. It permeates and sustains all the manifestations and changes that occur within it. Thus, Prakrti is qualified as mahat brahma, signifying its immense nature and the divine essence inherent within it. His connection to Prakrti, the material nature of the universe. Prakrti, as His own Maya, serves as the womb or cause from which all creatures are born. It is characterized by its greatness and ability to sustain its own transformations. This recognition highlights the profound relationship between the Divine and the material world, emphasizing the interconnectedness and interdependence of all beings within the cosmic order.

Tasmin, in that, the womb of the great-sustainer: Lord Krishna explains that He, as God, possesses the power to place the seed within the womb of Prakriti. Here, tasmin refers to the womb, which is the great-sustainer. It signifies the divine space where creation and sustenance take place.

Aham, I, God, possessing the power: Lord Krishna identifies Himself as the Divine, emphasizing His role in the process of creation. As the supreme consciousness, He possesses the power in the form of two aspects: the field and the Knower of the field. The field refers to the material world, while the Knower of the field represents the individual souls.

Dadhami, place, deposit; garbham, the seed: Lord Krishna states that He places the seed within the womb of Prakriti. This seed is symbolic of the birth of Hiranyagarbha, the cosmic form of the Divine, and it acts as the cause for the birth of all things in the material realm. The seed carries the potential for manifestation and growth.

Bringing the field and Knower of the field into association: Lord Krishna explains that by depositing the seed, He brings together the field (the material world) and the Knower of the field (the individual souls). This association occurs within the womb of Prakriti. The Knower of the field, representing the individual consciousness, interacts with the field through the limitations of ignorance, desire, and activity.

Tatah, from that deposition of the seed:

From the deposition of the seed within the womb of Prakriti, the process of birth and origination (sambhavah) begins. All things in the material realm, encompassing various forms of life, emerge from this birth. Lord Krishna addresses the scion of the Bharata dynasty, highlighting the universal nature of this process.

The birth of all things following the birth of Hiranyagarbha:

Lord Krishna further explains that after the birth of Hiranyagarbha, the cosmic form, the birth and origination of all things occur. Hiranyagarbha represents the divine potentiality for creation and sustenance. All manifestations and life forms manifest subsequently from this cosmic birth.

Conclusion

Verse 14.3 of the Bhagavad Gita elucidates the role of God in the process of creation and birth. Lord Krishna, as the Divine, places the seed within the womb of Prakriti, symbolizing the initiation of the cosmic birth. From this birth, the entire spectrum of life forms and manifestations emerge, illustrating the interconnectedness between the Divine, the material world, and the individual souls.

O son of Kunti, whatever forms are born from all the wombs, of them the great-sustainer is the womb; I am the father who deposits the seed.

– Bhagavad Gita 14:4

Whatever forms are born from all the wombs:

Lord Krishna addresses Arjuna as the son of Kunti and emphasizes that all forms of life, irrespective of their species or origin, are born from various wombs. This includes beings born from the wombs of gods, manes, humans, cattle, and beasts, among others.

The great-sustainer is the womb:

Among all the forms that are born, the great-sustainer (mahat brahma) is the womb or source. This indicates that the ultimate sustainer and source of all life forms is beyond individual manifestations and encompasses the entirety of creation. The great-sustainer represents the divine power that maintains the cosmic order.

Lord Krishna as the father who deposits the seed:

Lord Krishna identifies Himself as the father who deposits the seed, referring to the divine agency responsible for the process of creation. He is the source of life, symbolized by the seed, which initiates the formation and development of all living beings. As the father, He imparts the essence of life and facilitates the manifestation of diverse forms.

Conclusion

In verse 14.4 of the Bhagavad Gita, Lord Krishna explains that all forms of life are born from various wombs, and the great-sustainer represents the overarching source of all manifestations. Lord Krishna, as the divine father, is the one who deposits the seed and initiates the process of creation. This highlights the divine involvement in the birth and sustenance of all beings, reinforcing the oneness and dependence of all life forms on the divine cosmic order.

Living in harmony with nature is not a one-time action; it is a way of life. It requires a shift in consciousness, a recognition that we are custodians of the Earth and that our well-being is intimately linked to the well-being of the planet.

By cultivating a deep respect for nature, by being grateful for its gifts, and by taking actions to preserve its beauty and vitality, we not only gain a healthy mind and body but also contribute to the greater harmony and balance of the world.

Let us embrace the teachings of nature, learning from its wisdom and embodying its selflessness. Let us be mindful of our actions and choices, knowing that they have the power to either harm or heal the Earth. Together, let us honor and protect our precious Mother Earth, recognizing that in doing so, we are nurturing our own souls and ensuring a sustainable and vibrant future for generations to come.

ॐ

Religion

41. "When someone is full of Love and Compassion, he cannot draw a line between two countries, two faiths or two religions." -Amma

In the realm of spirituality, there is no room for divisions or separations based on nationality, faith, or religion. The teachings of non-duality, as embodied by the philosophy of Vedanta, remind us of the inherent oneness and unity of all beings. It is through the lens of love and compassion that we can transcend the boundaries that separate us and embrace the universal essence that connects us all.

Amma, a spiritual leader and embodiment of love and compassion, emphasizes the importance of breaking down the barriers created by religion and recognizing the common thread of humanity that runs through us all. Her words, "When someone is full of Love and Compassion, he cannot draw a line between two countries, two faiths or two religions," invite us to embrace a broader perspective and cultivate a deep sense of empathy and understanding for all.

Religion, in its essence, is a path that individuals follow to connect with the divine. While various religions may have different rituals, traditions, and beliefs, they all share a common purpose: to foster love, kindness, and spiritual growth. It is important to remember that the ultimate goal of any religious practice is to awaken the inner divinity and realize our true nature, which transcends the boundaries of any particular faith.

The teachings of non-duality, as expounded in the Vedanta philosophy, remind us that the divine is present in all beings and permeates every aspect of creation. This recognition of the divine essence within ourselves and others forms the foundation for a truly inclusive and expansive understanding of spirituality.

When we approach religion with an open heart and a willingness to seek common ground, we can transcend the differences and divisions that often arise from rigid dogmas and narrow interpretations. Instead, we can focus on the universal principles of love, compassion, and selflessness that underlie all spiritual paths.

Amma's teachings encourage us to cultivate a deep sense of love and compassion, not only towards those who share our beliefs but towards all beings. By expanding our capacity for empathy, we recognize that every person, regardless of their religious background, is seeking the same ultimate truth and longing for connection with the divine.

In the Advaita Vedanta way, the focus is on the realization of our true nature, which transcends the limitations of religious identities. It invites us to go beyond the external labels and rituals and dive into the depths of our own being, where the divine resides. Through self-inquiry and introspection, we come to realize that the essence of our being is pure consciousness, untouched by religious affiliations. Amma's message serves as a reminder that true spirituality is not about adhering to a specific religious doctrine or engaging in sectarian divisions. Instead, it is about cultivating a deep sense of love, compassion, and oneness that transcends religious boundaries. It is about recognizing the inherent divinity in ourselves and others, and treating all beings with kindness, respect, and understanding.

When we embrace the essence of Amma's teachings, we become beacons of light, radiating love and compassion in all our interactions. We become ambassadors of unity, bridging the gaps between different faiths and religions by embodying the universal principles of spirituality.

In conclusion, the teachings of non-duality in the Vedanta tradition remind us that love and compassion are the guiding principles that transcend religious divisions. When we approach spirituality with an open heart and a deep sense of empathy, we can embrace the common essence that unites us all. Let us strive to embody the inclusive spirit of Amma's teachings and spread love, understanding, and unity in a world that is yearning for such healing and harmony.

teṣhām evānukampārtham aham ajñāna-jaṁ tamaḥ
nāśhayāmyātma-bhāva-stho jñāna-dīpena bhāsvatā

– Bhagavad Gita10:11

Out of compassion for them alone, I, residing in their hearts, destroy the darkness born of ignorance with the luminous lamp of Knowledge.

Compassion for the seekers:
Lord Krishna expresses His compassion for the seekers who are striving for spiritual growth and seeking ultimate bliss. He is deeply concerned about their well-being and liberation from suffering. His actions are motivated by pure love and empathy for their spiritual journey.

Residing in their hearts:
Lord Krishna declares that He resides within the hearts of these seekers. This signifies His immanent presence within every being, guiding and nurturing their spiritual evolution. It also emphasizes the intimate and personal nature of the divine connection.

Destroying the darkness of ignorance:
Out of His compassion, Lord Krishna takes on the role of dispelling the darkness of ignorance (tamah) that arises from non-discrimination and delusion. This ignorance leads to false comprehension and hampers the realization of one's true nature.

He employs the luminous lamp of Knowledge (jñana-dipena) to illuminate the path of wisdom and understanding.

The lamp of Knowledge:

The lamp of Knowledge represents divine wisdom and spiritual enlightenment. It is fueled by the oil of divine grace, which arises from devotion and surrender to the divine. The lamp is further nourished by intense meditation on the divine and disciplined practices such as celibacy. The wick of the intellect is infused with the impressions of divine teachings and guided by a detached mind free from likes and dislikes.

Illumination through concentration and meditation:

Lord Krishna describes the process of making the lamp of Knowledge luminous through constant concentration and meditation. By withdrawing the mind from external objects and cultivating inner stillness, one can experience the full illumination of divine wisdom. This practice leads to profound spiritual realization and transformation.

Conclusion

In verse 10.11 of the Bhagavad Gita, Lord Krishna reveals His compassionate nature and His commitment to guiding seekers on their spiritual path. He resides within their hearts, destroying the darkness of ignorance with the lamp of Knowledge. Through devotion, disciplined practices, and focused meditation, one can experience the luminosity of divine wisdom and attain spiritual enlightenment. Lord Krishna's compassionate guidance empowers seekers to overcome ignorance and realize their true nature.

Story

One day, Rishi received a message from the king, inviting him to the royal palace. The king, a devout follower of a particular religion, had heard of Rishi's wisdom and sought his counsel. Upon meeting Rishi, the king expressed his concerns about the growing tensions between different religious communities in the kingdom.

Rishi listened attentively to the king's worries and spoke with great compassion. He said, "Your Majesty, the divisions that exist between different religions are merely superficial. Beyond the external practices and rituals, there lies a deeper truth that unites all beings. Love and compassion are the common threads that run through every faith."

Intrigued by Rishi's words, the king requested him to elucidate further. Rishi began to share stories and teachings from different religious traditions, highlighting the common themes of love, compassion, and unity. He explained that these principles are the essence of true spirituality and can be found at the core of every religious path.

As the king listened, his heart opened to the possibility of a harmonious coexistence among the different faiths in his kingdom. Inspired by Rishi's teachings, he decided to organize an interfaith gathering where representatives from various religions would come together to share their teachings and foster understanding.

Word spread quickly about the king's initiative, and people from all walks of life eagerly participated in the gathering. Religious leaders, scholars, and ordinary citizens gathered in a spirit of curiosity and open-mindedness. The atmosphere was filled with love and respect as each person shared their faith's teachings, rituals, and stories.

Through the sharing of wisdom and the open dialogue, a sense of unity and oneness began to emerge. People realized that beneath the external trappings of their respective religions, there was a universal Truth that transcends all boundaries. Love and compassion became the focal point of their discussions, reminding everyone of the common essence that unites humanity.

The interfaith gathering proved to be a transformative experience for all who attended. It sparked a new era of understanding and cooperation among the religious communities in the kingdom. The king, deeply moved by the profound impact of the gathering, recognized that true spirituality lies in embracing the universal principles of love and compassion, rather than fixating on religious differences.

Under the guidance of Rishi, the king implemented policies that promoted religious tolerance, respect, and the freedom to practice one's faith. Temples, mosques, churches, and other places of worship became spaces where people from different religions came together to share in their common devotion to a higher power.

ॐ

Leader

42. *"If you Become a zero, you become a hero." -Amma*

In the realm of leadership, it is often believed that one must possess extraordinary qualities and accomplishments to be considered a hero. Society tends to glorify individuals who have achieved greatness, who have risen above others and made a significant impact in their fields. However, Amma's quote challenges this notion and invites us to explore a different perspective on leadership.

Amma teaches us that true leadership lies not in the pursuit of personal recognition or power, but in the ability to transcend the ego and serve selflessly. To become a zero means to let go of the identification with the self and the attachment to personal achievements. It means emptying oneself of the ego's desires and ambitions, creating space for something greater to emerge.

In the Advaita Vedanta way, the concept of becoming a zero carries a profound meaning. It is a call to surrender the limited sense of self and to recognize the interconnectedness of all beings. It is an invitation to embody humility, compassion, and selflessness, knowing that true leadership arises from a place of deep inner connection and unity with others.

A leader who becomes a zero is not driven by personal agendas or the pursuit of external recognition. Instead, they are motivated by a genuine desire to serve and uplift others. Their actions are guided by love, compassion, and a deep sense of responsibility towards the well-being of the community they serve.

To illustrate this concept, let us explore the story of a wise leader named Raja.

Story

Raja was the ruler of a prosperous kingdom known for its justice and harmony. Despite his noble position, Raja remained humble and dedicated to the welfare of his people.

One day, a severe drought struck the kingdom, causing immense suffering and despair among the citizens. The crops withered, the rivers ran dry, and the people struggled to find food and water. Raja recognized the urgency of the situation and took immediate action.

Rather than relying solely on his own wisdom and power, Raja called upon the collective intelligence and resources of the community. He convened a council of wise elders, scholars, and representatives from different walks of life. Together, they brainstormed ideas and devised a plan to alleviate the suffering caused by the drought.

Raja understood that true leadership is not about imposing solutions from above but about empowering others to contribute their unique talents and perspectives. He encouraged collaboration, fostering a sense of unity and shared responsibility among the people. Through their collective efforts, the community implemented innovative strategies to conserve water, support sustainable agriculture, and provide relief to those most affected by the drought. The kingdom became a shining example of resilience and unity in the face of adversity.

Throughout the process, Raja remained at the forefront, leading by example and serving as a guiding light for his people. He did not seek personal glory or credit for the solutions implemented. Instead, he celebrated the collective achievements of the community, recognizing that their success was a reflection of their unity and shared vision.

Raja's leadership exemplified the essence of becoming a zero. He transcended his individual identity and embraced a larger purpose - the well-being of his people and the greater good of the kingdom. By emptying himself of ego-driven desires and embracing humility, he created space for the brilliance and creativity of others to shine through.

As a result of Raja's selfless leadership, the kingdom not only overcame the challenges of the drought but also experienced a profound transformation. The people developed a deep sense of connection and compassion for one another. They recognized that their collective efforts had not only alleviated their immediate suffering but had also strengthened the fabric of their community.

In the Advaita Vedanta way, the journey of becoming a zero is a transformative process of Self-realization. It is a shift from the limited identification with the ego to the recognition of the interconnectedness of all beings. By letting go of the attachments to personal achievements and desires, leaders can tap into a deeper sense of purpose and serve the greater good with love and compassion.

Amma's quote reminds us that true heroism lies not in the pursuit of personal glory, but in the ability to transcend the ego and become an instrument for positive change. When leaders embody the qualities of humility, selflessness, and compassion, they inspire others to follow their example and create a ripple effect of transformation and upliftment in the world.

As we reflect on Amma's profound words, let us embrace the call to become a zero and unleash the power of selfless leadership within us. May we cultivate humility, compassion, and a deep sense of interconnectedness, recognizing that our actions and decisions have the potential to impact the lives of others. Let us strive to be leaders who empower, uplift, and unite, making a positive difference in the world and bringing forth the true essence of heroism through selfless service.

ॐ

43. *"Nowadays everybody wants to become a leader. No one wants to become a servant. In reality, the world is badly in need of servants, not leaders. A real servant is a real leader."* -Amma

In today's world, the pursuit of leadership positions and titles often takes precedence over the noble qualities of service and humility. However, Amma's profound words remind us that true leadership lies in being a servant. In the Advaita Vedanta way, the concept of leadership is redefined as a path of selfless service and an embodiment of the divine qualities.

Amma's quote draws our attention to the urgent need for individuals who are willing to embrace the role of a servant-leader. A servant-leader is someone who selflessly dedicates themselves to the well-being of others, recognizing that true leadership is not about power, authority, or personal gain, but about serving the higher good and uplifting humanity.

yad yad ācharati śhreṣhṭhas tat tad evetaro janaḥ
sa yat pramāṇaṁ kurute lokas tad anuvartate

– Bhagavad Gita 3:21

Whatever a superior person does, another person does that very thing! Whatever he upholds as authority, an ordinary person follows that.

Superior person and ordinary person:
In this verse, Lord Krishna contrasts the actions and influence of a superior person (sresthah) with that of an ordinary person (janah). The superior person refers to a leader, a wise and enlightened individual who possesses higher qualities and virtues.

Imitation of actions:
Lord Krishna states that whatever actions the superior person performs, others tend to imitate and follow suit. The actions of a superior person serve as an example and inspiration for others to emulate. This highlights the influential role of leaders in shaping the behavior and conduct of society.

Upholding authority:
The superior person also upholds certain principles, values, or authorities as guidance for others. This authority can be derived from various sources, such as the Vedas or other recognized scriptures, as well as secular knowledge and ethical principles. The superior person recognizes and follows these authorities in their actions and decisions.

The ordinary person's response:
On the other hand, the ordinary person tends to follow the lead of the superior person. They look to the superior person for guidance and adopt the actions and authorities upheld by them. This reflects the tendency of individuals to seek direction and conform to the examples set by those they perceive as superior.

Observing the example of Lord Krishna:
Lord Krishna uses this verse to emphasize his own role as a superior person and a spiritual leader. He invites Arjuna to observe his actions and follow his guidance, highlighting his authority and the righteousness of his teachings. Lord Krishna encourages Arjuna to have faith in his wisdom and guidance, indicating that by following him, Arjuna will find the right path.

Conclusion
In Bhagavad Gita verse 3.21, Lord Krishna highlights the influence and responsibility of a superior person as a leader. Their actions and the authorities they uphold have a significant impact on others, who tend to imitate and follow their lead. Lord Krishna presents himself as the ultimate superior person and urges

Arjuna to observe and follow his teachings. This verse emphasizes the importance of wise and righteous leadership in guiding individuals and society towards the right path.

The Advaita Vedanta perspective teaches us that we are all oneness and part of the same divine consciousness. When we embody the qualities of a servant-leader, we not only uplift ourselves but also inspire and uplift others around us. We become channels of love, compassion, and selflessness, and our actions have a ripple effect that spreads positivity and transformation in the world.

To become a servant-leader, one must cultivate humility, empathy, and a genuine desire to serve others. It requires a shift in perspective, where the focus is shifted from personal ambition to the well-being of others. A servant-leader leads by example, inspiring others through their actions and showing them the path of selfless service.

Story
Once upon a time, in a prosperous kingdom, there ruled a wise and compassionate king. Unlike many other rulers of his time, he believed that true leadership was not about accumulating power or personal glory, but about serving his people with humility and empathy.

The king had a deep understanding of the Advaita Vedanta philosophy and recognized the interconnectedness of all beings. He believed that his role as a king was not to command and control, but to uplift and serve his subjects. He saw himself as a servant of the people and considered their welfare as his highest priority.

One day, a delegation of ministers from neighboring kingdoms arrived at the royal court seeking the king's guidance on matters of governance and leadership. They were astonished by the king's reputation as a compassionate and servant-hearted ruler and wished to learn from his wisdom.

The king warmly welcomed the ministers and began sharing his insights on leadership. He spoke about the importance of humility, empathy, and selfless service in true leadership. He emphasized that leadership should be rooted in a genuine desire to uplift and support others, rather than seeking personal gain or authority.

To illustrate his point, the king shared a story from his own life. He recounted a time when a devastating famine struck his kingdom, leaving the people in dire need of food and resources. Instead of relying solely on his ministers and officials to address the crisis, the king personally took charge of relief efforts.

He traveled to the most affected areas, comforting the suffering and ensuring that everyone received adequate assistance. The king worked alongside his subjects, distributing food, organizing shelters, and providing medical aid. He showed no distinction between himself and his people, as he considered them all as part of one unified whole.

Through his selfless actions and compassionate leadership, the king not only provided relief to those in need but also inspired others to join him in the service of humanity. People from all walks of life, including his ministers, nobles, and even ordinary citizens, were moved by his example and came forward to offer their assistance.

The neighboring ministers listened attentively to the king's story and were deeply inspired by his approach to leadership. They realized that true leadership was not about power, wealth, or personal status, but about serving others with love, compassion, and selflessness.

Upon returning to their kingdoms, the ministers implemented the lessons they learned from the wise king. They transformed their leadership styles, focusing on the welfare of their people and promoting a culture of service and compassion. As a result, their kingdoms flourished, and the bonds between the neighboring kingdoms grew stronger, fostering a sense of unity and shared purpose.

The story of the compassionate king and his transformational leadership spread far and wide, inspiring leaders from distant lands to adopt a similar approach. The ripple effect of his teachings reached far beyond his own kingdom, influencing generations of leaders to embrace the principles of servant leadership and Advaita Vedanta.

In this way, the wise and compassionate king left a lasting legacy, not only in his own kingdom but also in the hearts and minds of leaders across the realm. His example serves as a reminder that true leadership is rooted in humility, empathy, and selfless service. By embodying these qualities, leaders can make a profound impact on the lives of their people and create a more harmonious and compassionate world.

ॐ

Ego

44. "You can even move mount Himalayas but not one's ego." -Amma

Ego, the sense of individual identity and separateness, is a powerful force that often drives human behavior and shapes our perceptions of the world. It is the root cause of many conflicts, misunderstandings, and suffering in the world. The teachings of Advaita Vedanta and the wisdom found in the Bhagavad Gita offer profound insights into understanding and transcending the ego.

kṣhetra-jñaṁ chāpi māṁ viddhi sarva-kṣhetreṣhu bhārata
kṣhetra-kṣhetrajñayor jñānaṁ yat taj jñānaṁ mataṁ
mama

- Bhagavad Gita 13:3

And, O scion of the Bharata dynasty, understand Me to be the 'Knower of the field' in all the fields. In My opinion, that is Knowledge which is the knowledge of the field and the knower of the field.

Understanding the 'Knower of the field'
In Bhagavad Gita verse 13.3, Lord Krishna instructs Arjuna, the scion of the Bharata dynasty, to understand Him as the 'Knower of the field' present in all fields of existence. This instruction reveals a deeper understanding of the true nature of the Supreme Being.

The Knower of the field: Lord Krishna identifies Himself as the 'Knower of the field,' referring to the transcendental consciousness that perceives and comprehends the entire field of existence, which includes both the physical and subtle aspects of creation.

The field: The term 'field' refers to the entirety of creation, encompassing all living beings and their environments. It represents the physical and mental realms, including the body, senses, mind, and everything that can be perceived and experienced.

The knowledge of the field: Lord Krishna emphasizes that true knowledge, or jnana, lies in understanding the field and the Knower of the field. It involves recognizing the underlying reality that permeates and sustains all existence.

The significance of knowing the field: By recognizing and understanding the Knower of the field, one gains insights into the fundamental nature of reality and attains a deeper awareness of the interconnectedness of all beings. This knowledge helps in transcending the limitations of individuality and leads to spiritual growth and Self-realization.

The role of Knowledge in realizing the field and the Knower

Lord Krishna further explains that true Knowledge involves comprehending the field and the Knower of the field. This understanding is essential for spiritual growth and liberation.

The nature of true Knowledge: True Knowledge is not merely intellectual understanding but a direct realization of the underlying truth of existence. It transcends conventional knowledge and encompasses a deep insight into the nature of the field and its relationship with the Knower.

Gaining Knowledge of the field and the Knower: By cultivating spiritual practices such as self-inquiry, meditation, and devotion, one can gradually unfold this Knowledge within oneself. It requires sincere effort, introspection, and guidance from realized teachers.

The transformative power of Knowledge: True Knowledge has a transformative effect on an individual's perception, thoughts, and actions. It dispels ignorance, delusion, and attachment, leading to spiritual growth and liberation from the cycle of birth and death.

The role of the Knower of the field: Recognizing the presence of the Knower of the field within oneself brings clarity, inner peace, and a sense of connectedness with all beings. It allows one to transcend the limitations of individual identity and experience unity with the Divine.

Conclusion

Verse 13.3 of the Bhagavad Gita emphasizes the importance of understanding the Knower of the field and cultivating true Knowledge. By recognizing the underlying reality and the oneness of all beings, one can embark on a spiritual journey towards Self-realization and liberation. Through sincere practice and realization, one can attain the transformative power of true Knowledge and experience the inherent divinity within.

Amma, with her deep spiritual wisdom, reminds us that the ego is a formidable obstacle on the path of spiritual growth and Self-realization. She emphasizes that no matter how powerful or accomplished one may be in worldly matters, it is the ego that hinders the realization of our true nature, which is pure consciousness and divine love.

To illustrate the profound impact of the ego, Amma shares the analogy of trying to move Mount Himalayas. The Himalayas, with its immense size and grandeur, represents the magnitude and steadfastness of the ego. Just as it is impossible to physically move such a mighty mountain, the ego too resists efforts to subdue it or diminish its influence. It clings to our thoughts, desires, and attachments, causing suffering and keeping us trapped in a limited perception of reality.

The Advaita Vedanta way teaches us that the key to transcending the ego lies in recognizing our true nature as the eternal Self, the Atman. When we realize that we are not separate entities, but interconnected aspects of the divine consciousness, the ego begins to lose its grip on us. We understand that the ego is merely a temporary illusion, a false identity constructed by our minds.

Amma's teachings guide us towards the dissolution of the ego through practices such as self-inquiry, meditation, and selfless service. By turning our attention inward and exploring the depths of our consciousness, we can gradually detach ourselves from the ego's grip and awaken to our true essence.

Story

One day, a renowned sage arrived in the kingdom, spreading the teachings of non-duality and the importance of transcending the ego. The king, eager to deepen his own spiritual understanding, invited the sage to his court. Deva, intrigued by the sage's teachings, requested permission to attend the discourse.

As the sage spoke about the detrimental nature of the ego and its impact on human consciousness, Deva's curiosity grew. He realized that the ego was responsible for creating divisions, conflicts, and suffering in the world. Inspired by the sage's words, Deva felt a deep desire to overcome his own ego and live a life rooted in love and compassion.

After the discourse, Deva sought the sage's guidance. He expressed his yearning to transcend the ego and asked for practical steps to achieve this lofty goal. The sage, recognizing Deva's sincerity, agreed to become his spiritual guide.

Under the sage's tutelage, Deva embarked on a transformative journey. He learned to observe his thoughts and emotions without identifying with them, cultivating the practice of self-inquiry and meditation. The sage taught him that true Self-realization came from detaching oneself from the ego's grip and recognizing the eternal self within.

Deva dedicated himself to daily spiritual practices and selfless service. He visited the villages surrounding the kingdom, offering assistance to the needy, listening to their stories, and extending a helping hand. Through these acts of compassion, Deva realized that when he focused on the needs of others, his ego dissolved, and he experienced a profound connection with all beings.

As Deva's spiritual growth continued, his influence began to spread throughout the kingdom. People were inspired by his selflessness and kindness, and the king himself noticed the transformation in his son. Intrigued, the king approached Deva, seeking to understand the source of his inner radiance.

Deva humbly shared the wisdom he had gained from the sage and the practices he had embraced to transcend the ego. He explained that by shifting their focus from self-centered desires to selfless service, individuals could tap into the infinite well of love and compassion within themselves.

Deeply moved by Deva's words, the king realized the importance of overcoming his own ego and leading with compassion. He too sought the sage's guidance and began his own journey of self-discovery and self-transcendence.

Together, Deva, the king, and the sage worked tirelessly to create a kingdom based on love, compassion, and unity. They implemented policies that prioritized the welfare of the people, and they encouraged the citizens to recognize their inherent oneness.

ॐ

45. Ask yourself: Living in the midst of life's joyful celebration, why do I feel so miserable? –Amma

In the midst of life's joyful celebration, it is not uncommon for individuals to experience a sense of inner emptiness or dissatisfaction. Despite external success, material possessions, and social recognition, there may be a lingering feeling of unhappiness or discontentment. This paradoxical experience raises the question: Why do we feel miserable even when surrounded by happiness?

Amma's quote invites us to reflect upon the deeper layers of our being and explore the root cause of our discontentment. The Advaita Vedanta way teaches us that our true nature is not limited to our individual identity or the external circumstances of our lives. It reveals that we are interconnected with the entire universe and that our happiness does not solely depend on external factors, but rather on our internal state of being.

When we identify ourselves solely with our physical bodies, achievements, and possessions, we create a sense of separation from the world around us. We become attached to temporary experiences and external validations, constantly seeking fulfillment from external sources. This attachment leads to suffering because the external world is ever-changing and inherently transient.

The Vedanta way invites us to shift our focus from the external to the internal, from the temporary to the eternal. It encourages us to dive deep within ourselves to discover our true essence, beyond the limitations of the individual ego. By recognizing our oneness with all of existence, we can begin to experience a sense of wholeness and fulfillment that transcends the fleeting nature of external circumstances.

To embark on this journey of self-discovery, we must cultivate self-awareness and practice tranquility of mind. We need to pause and reflect on our thoughts, emotions, and desires, questioning their origin and the extent to which they define our happiness. By observing our experiences without judgment, we can gain insight into the patterns of our mind and begin to detach ourselves from the illusion of separateness.

manaḥ-prasādaḥ saumyatvaṁ maunam ātma-vinigrahaḥ
bhāva-sanśhuddhir ity etat tapo mānasam uchyate

– Bhagavad Gita 17:16

Tranquility of mind, gentleness, reticence, withdrawal of
the mind, purity of heart,-these are what is called mental
austerity.

Mental Austerity: Cultivating Tranquility and Inner Purity

Introduction: The verse highlights the importance of mental
austerity as a means to attain inner peace and spiritual growth.
This passage explores the various aspects of mental austerity,
emphasizing qualities such as tranquility, gentleness, reticence,
withdrawal of the mind, and purity of heart.

Manah-prasadah: Tranquility of Mind

Achieving a state of mental calmness and freedom from
anxiety. Cultivating a mind that is at peace, undisturbed by
external circumstances. Inner tranquility reflected in one's
demeanor and facial expressions.

Saumyatvam: Gentleness or Kindness of Spirit Fostering a
compassionate and kind attitude towards all beings. Avoiding
ill thoughts or harmful intentions towards others. Developing
a spirit of kindness, empathy, and goodwill.

Maunam: Reticence or Control of Speech Recognizing that
speech is influenced by the state of the mind. Control of speech
naturally follows from the control of the mind. Implying the
importance of being mindful of our words and speaking with
wisdom and restraint. Alternatively, maunam can also refer to
thinking of the Self, adopting the attitude of a meditator.

Atma-vinigrahah: Withdrawal of the Mind Engaging in the
practice of withdrawing the mind from external distractions.
Directing the mind inward, towards self-reflection and
contemplation.

Detaching oneself from the constant pull of sensory stimuli and external desires.

Bhava-samsuddhih: Purity of Heart Cultivating sincerity, honesty, and integrity in all interactions. Acting without duplicity or deceit in relationships. Nurturing an inner purity that stems from a genuine and compassionate heart.

Conclusion

Mental austerity plays a crucial role in the spiritual path, enabling individuals to cultivate inner peace, clarity, and spiritual growth. By practicing tranquility, gentleness, reticence, withdrawal of the mind, and purity of heart, one can purify the mind and establish a strong foundation for spiritual progress. These qualities not only contribute to personal well-being but also foster harmonious relationships and create a positive impact on the world around us.

Through meditation, contemplation, and self-inquiry, we can gradually unravel the layers of conditioning and egoic identification that keep us trapped in a limited perception of reality. As we let go of the attachments and expectations that bind us, we open ourselves to the infinite possibilities of the present moment.

The Advaita Vedanta way reminds us that true happiness lies in realizing our essential nature as pure consciousness, beyond the confines of the ego. It is in connecting with the unchanging, eternal aspect of ourselves that we find lasting fulfillment and inner peace. This realization allows us to navigate life's joys and sorrows with equanimity, knowing that our true essence remains untouched by external circumstances. Amma's quote serves as a gentle reminder that the key to lasting happiness lies in shifting our focus from the external to the internal, from seeking fulfillment in transient experiences to recognizing our innate divinity. By embracing the Advaita Vedanta way, we can transcend the limitations of the ego and experience the profound truth that happiness is not dependent on external factors, but rather on the realization of our interconnectedness with all of creation.

In conclusion, the Advaita Vedanta invites us to explore the root cause of our discontentment and offers a path towards lasting happiness and fulfillment. By shifting our perspective, cultivating self-awareness, and realizing our essential nature, we can experience the true joy that lies beyond the fleeting moments of life's celebration. May we all embark on this transformative journey and discover the eternal source of happiness within ourselves.

Story

One day, the king of the land, King, heard of the sage's reputation and decided to seek his guidance. He had everything a king could desire - wealth, power, and a prosperous kingdom. Yet, despite all his material achievements, he couldn't shake off a deep sense of emptiness and dissatisfaction that plagued his heart.

Upon reaching the sage's humble abode, King expressed his troubles to the sage. He spoke of his achievements and his vast kingdom, but confessed that he felt a void within him that no external success could fill. The sage listened attentively, his eyes filled with compassion.

The sage gently smiled and said, "Your Majesty, the answer to your discontentment lies not in the external realm, but within your own self. The true source of happiness is not found in material possessions or external accomplishments, but in realizing your essential nature as pure consciousness."

Intrigued, the king asked the sage to explain further. The sage shared the teachings of Advaita Vedanta, emphasizing the interconnectedness of all beings and the illusion of separateness created by the ego. He explained that the ego, with its constant desires and attachments, keeps individuals trapped in a cycle of seeking happiness outside themselves, leading to perpetual dissatisfaction.

To illustrate his point, the sage shared a story. He spoke of a merchant who traveled far and wide in search of a rare gem that would bring him eternal joy. He visited distant lands, met wise men, and acquired vast riches in his pursuit. Finally, he stumbled upon a wise sage who told him, "The gem you seek is within you. It is the pure consciousness that resides in your heart."

The merchant was astounded. He realized that he had been searching for happiness in all the wrong places. With renewed understanding, he embraced the path of Self-realization, delving deep within himself to discover the true source of joy.

As the sage finished his story, King's eyes sparkled with new-found hope. He realized that the answer to his discontentment lay not in acquiring more wealth or power, but in seeking the truth within himself. He bowed humbly to the sage, expressing his gratitude for the profound wisdom he had received.

ॐ

Mind

46. "Fundamentally what everyone needs is mental strength and confidence, to manage the mind, just as we manage the outside world. Our problem is that we identify with all the moods of the mind. When we are angry we become anger. It is the same with fear, excitement, anxiety, sorrow and happiness. We become one with that emotion, whether it is positive or negative. We identify with the mask, but in reality, none of these moods are really you. Your true nature is bliss." -Amma

In the realm of the Advaita Vedanta way, the teachings of Amma shed light on the nature of the mind and its profound influence on our overall well-being. She emphasizes the importance of developing mental strength and confidence to navigate the challenges of life and to uncover our true essence - pure bliss.

The mind is a powerful tool that shapes our perceptions, emotions, and actions. Often, we find ourselves identifying with the ever-changing moods and fluctuations of the mind, allowing them to dictate our experiences and define our sense of self. When we are angry, we become anger itself. When we are fearful, we become consumed by fear. This identification with the transient states of the mind creates a sense of separation from our true nature.

Amma reminds us that our true nature is not defined by the mind's fleeting moods and emotions. In reality, we are the pure consciousness that underlies all mental activity. The mind is like a mask that we wear, but it does not define our true essence. Our true nature is blissful and unchanging, untouched by the fluctuations of the mind.

To cultivate mental strength and confidence, we must first recognize the transient nature of the mind and its moods. We can observe the thoughts and emotions that arise without getting entangled in them. By developing the ability to witness the mind's activities, we create distance and disidentify from its fluctuations. This state of witnessing, known as sakshi bhava, allows us to tap into our true essence and experience the underlying bliss that is always present.

uddhared ātmanātmānaṁ nātmānam avasādayet
ātmaiva hyātmano bandhur ātmaiva ripur ātmanaḥ
bandhur ātmātmanas tasya yenātmaivātmanā jitaḥ
anātmanas tu śhatrutve vartetātmaiva śhatru-vat

– Bhagavad Gita 6:5-6

One should save oneself by oneself; one should not lower oneself. For oneself is verily one's own friend; oneself is verily one's own enemy.

Of him, by whom has been conquered his very self by the self, his self is the friend of his self. But, for one who has not conquered his self, his self itself acts inimically like an enemy.

Saving oneself through self-discipline

In Bhagavad Gita verses 6.5 and 6.6, Lord Krishna emphasizes the importance of self-discipline and self-mastery in spiritual practice. He elucidates the concept of oneself as both a friend and an enemy.

Uddharet: The verse begins with the instruction to uddharet, which means to save or uplift oneself. Lord Krishna highlights the responsibility of individuals to take charge of their own spiritual progress.

Being one's own friend: Lord Krishna states that oneself is one's own bandhu, meaning friend. This signifies that true liberation and spiritual progress can only be achieved through self-effort and self-discipline. No external source can bring about liberation or salvation.

Not debasing oneself: Lord Krishna advises against lowering oneself or engaging in self-destructive behaviors. By practicing self-discipline, individuals can elevate themselves and progress on the path of spiritual growth.

Conquering oneself: Verse 6.6 explains that those who have conquered their own senses and desires are their own friends. By exercising self-control and mastery over the mind and senses, one can become a friend to oneself.

Enemy-like behavior of an uncontrolled self: On the other hand, individuals who lack self-control and allow their senses and desires to dominate their actions experience their own self acting like an enemy. When the mind and senses are not under control, they hinder spiritual progress and obstruct the path to Self-realization.

The significance of self-discipline: Self-discipline plays a crucial role in spiritual practice. By cultivating self-control, individuals can align their thoughts, words, and actions with their higher spiritual aspirations. This discipline helps in calming the mind, developing concentration, and turning inward to realize one's true nature.

Conclusion

Verses 6.5 and 6.6 of the Bhagavad Gita highlight the importance of self-discipline and self-mastery in the pursuit of spiritual growth. By understanding oneself as both a friend and an enemy, individuals are encouraged to cultivate self-control, conquer their senses, and uplift themselves on the path of Self-realization. Through self-discipline, individuals can transform their lives and progress towards spiritual liberation.

Through practices such as meditation, self-inquiry, we can train the mind to become more focused, calm, and balanced. These practices help us to manage the mind rather than being controlled by it. As we cultivate mental strength and discipline, we become less reactive to external circumstances and more grounded in our true nature.

Story

One day, Siddharth heard of a wise sage who resided in a nearby forest. The sage was renowned for his deep understanding of the mind and his ability to bring clarity and peace to those who sought his guidance. Intrigued by the prospect of finding answers to his inner turmoil, Siddharth decided to visit the sage.

As Siddharth entered the forest, he was struck by its serene beauty. The air was filled with a sense of tranquility, and the leaves whispered ancient wisdom as they danced in the gentle breeze. Finally, he reached the humble abode of the sage, a small cottage surrounded by blooming flowers and tall trees.

With humility and curiosity, Siddharth approached the sage and shared his struggles. He poured out his heart, revealing the deep-seated dissatisfaction that had plagued him for years. The sage listened attentively, his eyes filled with compassion.

"My dear Siddharth," the sage began, "your unhappiness stems from your identification with the ever-changing nature of the mind. You have mistaken the fluctuations of the mind for your true essence. But I tell you, you are not the mind. You are the pure consciousness that witnesses its activities."

Siddharth was taken aback by the sage's words. It was as if a veil had been lifted, and he saw the truth in what the sage was saying. He realized that he had allowed his thoughts and emotions to define his sense of self, attaching his happiness and worth to external achievements and circumstances.

Over the following weeks, Siddharth spent his days in the presence of the sage, learning the art of witnessing the mind. Through meditation and introspection, he began to detach himself from the constant stream of thoughts and emotions that had previously consumed him. He learned to observe them with a sense of detachment, recognizing that they were transient and ever-changing.

As Siddharth delved deeper into the practice of self-inquiry and mindfulness, a profound transformation took place within him. He discovered a profound sense of peace and contentment that transcended the ups and downs of life. He realized that his true nature was not defined by the mind's fleeting moods, but by the eternal consciousness that lay beneath.

With this newfound understanding, Siddharth's perspective on life shifted. He no longer sought validation and happiness from external sources. Instead, he embraced the present moment and cultivated a deep sense of gratitude for the simple joys of life. He found fulfillment in acts of kindness and service, recognizing that true happiness came from giving rather than receiving.

Word of Siddharth's transformation spread throughout the village, and people began seeking his counsel. With humility and love, he shared the wisdom he had gained from his time with the sage. He taught others the art of witnessing the mind, helping them to discover their true nature and find peace amidst the chaos of the world.

Siddharth became known as a wise teacher, guiding others on the path of Self-realization. He emphasized the importance of managing the mind, recognizing its transient nature, and cultivating a deep connection with the eternal consciousness within. Through his teachings, he inspired countless individuals to embark on their own journeys of self-discovery and inner transformation.

ॐ

Concentration

47. *"Where there is concentration, there is harmony. True happiness is derived from concentration of the mind not from external objects. Through meditation, we can achieve everything, including bliss, health, strength, peace, intelligence and vitality."* -Amma

Concentration is a powerful tool that allows us to harness the full potential of our mind and experience a deep sense of harmony and happiness. In the pursuit of true fulfillment, Amma reminds us that the key lies not in external objects but in the cultivation of a focused and concentrated mind.

In the modern world, our attention is often scattered, pulled in multiple directions by the demands of daily life, the allure of technology, and the constant bombardment of information. Our minds become fragmented, and we lose touch with our innermost essence. It is in this state of distraction that we find ourselves chasing external sources of happiness, seeking fulfillment in possessions, achievements, and sensory pleasures.

However, Amma reminds us that true happiness is not found in these external pursuits. It is not dependent on acquiring more or achieving success in the conventional sense. True happiness, she tells us, is derived from concentration of the mind. It is a state of deep inner calm and contentment that arises when we are fully present and engaged in the present moment.

Through the practice of meditation, we can cultivate concentration and unlock the vast potential of our mind. Meditation is not about forcing the mind into a state of stillness, but rather about gently guiding our attention to a chosen focal point, such as the breath or a mantra. As we train our mind to remain anchored in the present moment, we gradually develop the ability to sustain concentration for longer periods of time.

With regular practice, the benefits of concentration become evident. We become more focused, alert, and attentive in all aspects of our lives. Our ability to complete tasks and solve problems improves, and we experience a greater sense of clarity and mental acuity. We are no longer at the mercy of external distractions and fleeting thoughts, but rather, we develop a sense of inner stability and resilience.

Beyond the practical benefits, concentration holds the key to unlocking deeper states of awareness and spiritual insight. As our mind becomes more concentrated, we are able to penetrate the layers of illusion and experience the true nature of reality. We discover a profound sense of interconnectedness, where the boundaries between self and other dissolve, and we recognize the inherent unity of all existence.

tapasvibhyo 'dhiko yogī jñānibhyo 'pi mato 'dhikaḥ
karmibhyaśh chādhiko yogī tasmād yogī bhavārjuna

– Bhagavad Gita 6:46

A yogi is higher than men of austerity; he is considered higher even than men of knowledge. The yogi is also higher than men of action. Therefore, O Arjuna, do you become a yogi?

The Superiority of a Yogi

In Bhagavad Gita verse 6.46, Lord Krishna extols the virtues and superiority of a yogi over those practicing austerity and knowledge, as well as those engaged in worldly actions. He urges Arjuna to embrace the path of yoga.

Higher than men of austerity: Lord Krishna states that a yogi is adhikah, higher than tapasvibhyah, men of austerity. Austerity refers to the practice of self-discipline, asceticism, and penance.

While austerity has its merits, the yogic path offers a deeper and more comprehensive approach to spiritual growth.

Superior to men of knowledge: Lord Krishna further declares that a yogi is matah, considered higher, than jnanibhyah, men of knowledge. Here, knowledge refers to scriptural learning and intellectual understanding. While knowledge is valuable, the yogic path transcends mere intellectual comprehension and leads to direct experiential realization of the divine.

Greater than men of action: Lord Krishna emphasizes that a yogi is also adhikah, higher, than karmibhyah, men of action. Karmibhyah refers to those engaged in worldly actions, such as rituals and duties. Although actions have their place, the yogic path goes beyond external activities and focuses on inner transformation and union with the divine.

The call to become a yogi: Based on the superiority of a yogi over individuals practicing austerity, knowledge, and action, Lord Krishna encourages Arjuna to embrace the path of yoga. By becoming a yogi, Arjuna can attain the highest spiritual realization and liberation.

The essence of yogic practice: Yoga encompasses various paths, including karma yoga (path of selfless action), bhakti yoga (path of devotion), jnana yoga (path of knowledge), and dhyana yoga (path of meditation). The yogi combines these paths, integrating action, devotion, knowledge, and meditation into a holistic practice aimed at realizing the true Self and attaining union with the divine.

The significance of embracing the yogic path: Lord Krishna's encouragement to Arjuna to become a yogi highlights the transformative power and potential of yoga. By cultivating the qualities of discipline, self-control, selflessness, devotion, knowledge, and inner contemplation, one can embark on a profound journey of self-discovery and spiritual growth.

Conclusion

Bhagavad Gita verse 6.46 emphasizes the superiority of a yogi over individuals practicing austerity, knowledge, and action. The yogic path offers a comprehensive approach to spiritual growth, surpassing external practices and intellectual understanding. Lord Krishna encourages Arjuna to embrace the path of yoga, which combines self-discipline, devotion, knowledge, and meditation to attain union with the divine. By becoming a yogi, one can embark on a transformative journey of Self-realization and spiritual liberation. The yogi, with a focused and concentrated mind, surpasses those who merely engage in external actions or accumulate intellectual knowledge.

Story

One day, while wandering through the city streets, Ram came across a serene park. Intrigued by the tranquility that emanated from the park, he decided to step inside and explore. As he walked deeper into the park, he noticed a small gathering of people gathered around a wise old sage.

Curiosity piqued, Ram approached the sage and joined the group. The sage was known for his teachings on concentration and its transformative power. He spoke about the importance of cultivating a focused mind in order to experience true happiness and fulfillment.

He approached the sage and expressed his struggles with concentration and his desire for a more focused and fulfilling life. The sage smiled warmly and offered to be his mentor.

Under the sage's guidance, Ram began a journey of self-discovery and inner transformation. He learned various techniques to train his mind, including meditation and mindfulness practices. The sage emphasized the importance of bringing awareness to the present moment, gently guiding the mind back whenever it wandered.

With time and consistent practice, Ram started to notice subtle changes within himself. He became more present in his daily activities, whether it was studying, working, or engaging in conversations. He discovered that by giving his full attention to each task at hand, he not only performed better but also experienced a deep sense of satisfaction and joy.

As Ram delved deeper into his practice, he began to experience moments of profound concentration. During meditation, his mind would settle into a calm and focused state, free from the usual distractions and chatter. In those moments, he felt a deep connection to his inner self and a profound sense of peace.

ॐ

Emotions

48. "Each action, thought, and emotion has its own vibration. Love, lust, hate, fear, compassion all are different vibrations that have the capability to affect the world around us." -Amma

Emotions are a fundamental aspect of human experience. They color our perception, influence our behavior, and shape our relationships with others and the world around us. In the Advaita Vedanta way, emotions are seen as vibrations that have the potential to impact both our personal lives and the collective consciousness.

Amma's quote highlights the power of emotions and their varying vibrations. Each emotion carries its unique energy and has the potential to create ripples in our own being and the world at large. Love, compassion, and joy emit high-frequency vibrations that uplift and connect us to others in a harmonious way. On the other hand, emotions such as lust, hate, and fear carry lower frequencies that can create disharmony and disconnection.

The practice of Advaita Vedanta encourages individuals to cultivate awareness and discernment when it comes to their emotions. Rather than being driven by the fluctuating tides of emotions, one learns to observe and understand their nature, recognizing them as temporary experiences that arise and pass.

Through self-inquiry and self-awareness, we can delve deeper into the essence of our emotions and understand the underlying motivations and beliefs that give rise to them. This self-reflection allows us to develop a greater sense of emotional intelligence and empowers us to consciously choose how we respond to our emotions.

kāma eṣha krodha eṣha rajo-guṇa-samudbhavaḥ
mahāśhano mahā-pāpmā viddhyenam iha vairiṇam

– Bhagavad Gita 3:37

The Supreme Lord said: It is lust alone, which is born of contact with the mode of passion, and later transformed into anger. Know this as the sinful, all-devouring enemy in the world.

tri-vidhaṁ narakasyedaṁ dvāraṁ nāśhanam ātmanaḥ
kāmaḥ krodhas tathā lobhas tasmād etat trayaṁ tyajet

– Bhagavad Gita 16.21

There are three gates leading to the hell of self-destruction for the soul—lust, anger, and greed. Therefore, one should abandon all three.

For example, when confronted with anger or hatred, instead of blindly reacting, we can pause, observe the arising emotion, and inquire into its root cause. By investigating our underlying beliefs and conditioning, we can begin to dissolve the patterns that perpetuate negative emotions and choose a more compassionate and loving response.

In the Advaita Vedanta way, the goal is not to suppress or deny emotions but to develop a conscious relationship with them. By embracing our emotions with compassion and non-judgment, we can transform them into opportunities for growth and self-discovery. Through this process, we become more attuned to the vibrations we emit, choosing love, compassion, and understanding as the guiding forces in our interactions with others.

Moreover, the impact of our emotions extends beyond our individual lives. The vibrations we emit through our emotions have the potential to ripple out and influence the collective consciousness. Just as a pebble creates ripples in a pond, our emotions can have a ripple effect, touching the lives of those around us and even resonating with the broader world.

Therefore, it is crucial to recognize the responsibility we hold in cultivating positive and uplifting emotions. By consciously nurturing emotions such as love, compassion, and joy, we contribute to a collective vibrational shift, fostering a more harmonious and interconnected world.

In conclusion, the Advaita Vedanta way invites us to embrace the transformative power of our emotions. Through self-inquiry, self-awareness, and conscious choice, we can harness the vibrations of love, compassion, and joy, positively influencing our own lives and the world around us. By recognizing the inherent interconnectedness of all beings, we can strive to create a more harmonious and compassionate world, one emotion at a time.

Story
The villagers admired the old woman's ability to fully embrace her emotions and express them authentically. They saw her as a beacon of light, radiating love and compassion in every interaction. People sought her out for advice, comfort, and guidance, knowing that she would listen with an open heart and offer words of wisdom that resonated deeply.

One day, an old woman encountered a young boy who was struggling with overwhelming anger and resentment. He had experienced a great loss in his life and found it challenging to navigate his emotions. Feeling drawn to help him, Maya sat down with the boy and shared stories from her own life, illustrating the transformative power of emotions.

She told him about a time when she herself had harbored anger and resentment, and how it had affected her relationships and well-being. But she also shared stories of compassion and forgiveness, explaining how these emotions had brought healing and peace to her own heart.

Old woman emphasized the importance of acknowledging and honoring all emotions, as they were a part of the human experience. She explained that emotions were like messengers, bringing valuable insights and opportunities for growth. By embracing and understanding them, one could navigate life with greater clarity and compassion.

ॐ

Anger

49. "Thoughtless words, Non-Discriminative, anger and impatience always create problems. The root cause of all these is ego. There may be many things we can fix in the world, but we can never rectify the things we do and say in anger. Those wounds will remain with people we've hurt, as well as in our own hearts." -Amma

Anger, like a raging fire, has the power to consume everything in its path. It is a powerful emotion that can cloud our judgment, impair our relationships, and cause irreparable damage. Amma, the embodiment of compassion and wisdom, teaches us the profound impact that anger can have on ourselves and others, and the importance of cultivating a non-reactive and discerning mind.

The Destructive Impact of Thoughtless Words and Non-Discriminative Actions

Thoughtless words and non-discriminative actions have significant consequences, both for ourselves and for others. When we speak without considering the impact of our words or act without discernment, we often create problems and hurt those around us. These actions stem from the root cause of ego, which fuels our impulsive behavior and clouds our judgment.

The Power of Words:

Words possess immense power. They can build bridges, inspire, and heal, but they can also destroy relationships, inflict emotional pain, and leave lasting wounds. Thoughtless words spoken in anger or without considering their consequences can cause irreparable damage. Once words are spoken, we cannot take them back, and their impact can linger in the hearts of those we've hurt.

Non-Discriminatory Actions:

Similarly, non-discriminatory actions driven by ego and impulsive behavior can have detrimental effects. When we act without thoughtfulness, consideration, or awareness of the potential consequences, we risk causing harm to ourselves and others. Our actions can create rifts in relationships, damage trust, and lead to regrets and guilt.

The Role of Anger and Impatience:

Anger and impatience often underlie thoughtless words and non-discriminative actions. When we allow these emotions to overpower us, we lose control of our rationality and act on impulse. Anger blinds us to the potential consequences of our actions, leading us to say or do things that we later regret.

The Wounds of Anger:

The wounds caused by anger and thoughtless actions can be deep and long-lasting. Not only do they affect the people we've hurt, but they also leave an imprint in our own hearts. The pain we inflict on others reverberates within us, reminding us of our shortcomings and the need for self-reflection and growth.

The Inability to Rectify:

Once the damage is done, it is often impossible to rectify the hurt caused by thoughtless words and non-discriminative actions. We may try to apologize and make amends, but the scars of our actions may persist. The wounds we inflict on others and ourselves through anger and impulsivity are challenging to heal completely.

The Importance of Ego Awareness:

To address these issues, it is crucial to cultivate ego awareness. Recognizing the role of ego in driving our thoughtless words, non-discriminatory actions, anger, and impatience allows us to take responsibility for our behavior. By nurturing humility, empathy, and mindfulness, we can learn to respond thoughtfully rather than react impulsively.

Conclusion

Thoughtless words, non-discriminatory actions, anger, and impatience have far-reaching consequences. They stem from the root cause of ego and can cause harm to ourselves and others. It is essential to cultivate self-awareness, practice discernment, and nurture qualities like empathy and mindfulness. By doing so, we can prevent the damage caused by our impulsive behavior, foster healthier relationships, and contribute to a more harmonious and compassionate world.

dhyāyato viṣhayān puṁsaḥ saṅgas teṣhūpajāyate
saṅgāt sañjāyate kāmaḥ kāmāt krodho 'bhijāyate
krodhād bhavati sammohaḥ sammohāt smṛiti-vibhramaḥ
smṛiti-bhranśhād buddhi-nāśho buddhi-nāśhāt
praṇaśhyati

– Bhagavad Gita 2:62-63

In the case of a person who dwells on objects, there arises attachment for them. From attachment grows hankering, from hankering springs anger.
From anger follows delusion; from delusion, failure of memory; from failure of memory, the loss of understanding; from the loss of understanding, he perishes.

The Consequences of Dwelling on Objects - In verses 2.62 and 2.63, Lord Krishna explains the chain of events that arise from dwelling on and becoming attached to external objects. These verses highlight the progression from attachment to anger, delusion, loss of memory, and ultimately the destruction of understanding.

Attachment and hankering: According to Lord Krishna, when a person constantly dwells on sensory objects and becomes attached to them, an emotional connection or sangah develops. This attachment leads to kamah, or hankering, a strong desire to possess and indulge in those objects.

Anger and Delusion: If the hankering for objects is obstructed or unfulfilled, it gives rise to krodhah, anger. When anger arises, it clouds the person's judgment and leads to sammohah, delusion. In a state of delusion, one loses the ability to discern between right and wrong actions.

Failure of Memory and Loss of Understanding: Delusion further results in smrti-vibhramah, the failure of memory. This failure prevents the person from recalling the teachings of scriptures and spiritual guides, hindering their ability to make wise decisions. As a consequence, buddhi-nasah, the loss of understanding, occurs.

Perishing and Ruin: When understanding is lost, one's spiritual progress and well-being are compromised. Lord Krishna states that a person perishes when their internal organ, their understanding, is destroyed. Such a person becomes unfit for the human goal, which is spiritual realization and liberation.

The Root of All Evils: Lord Krishna points out that thinking of objects and becoming attached to them is the root cause of these negative consequences. It is the attachment to external sensory experiences that leads to the chain reaction of emotions and mental disturbances.

The Path to Liberation: These verses serve as a cautionary reminder of the dangers of attachment and the importance of controlling the mind and senses. To attain spiritual growth and liberation, one must cultivate detachment and focus on the higher goal of Self-realization. By transcending attachment and maintaining equanimity, one can overcome the cycle of desires and destructive emotions.

Conclusion

Bhagavad Gita verses 2.62 and 2.63 shed light on the detrimental effects of dwelling on and becoming attached to external objects. Lord Krishna emphasizes the progression from attachment to anger, delusion, loss of memory, and the destruction of understanding. These verses serve as a reminder to cultivate detachment, control the mind and senses, and strive for spiritual growth on the path to liberation.

ॐ

50. *"There are no mistakes in God's creation. Every creature and every object that has been created by God is so utterly special. Learn to place others before yourself. Consider everyone, because they are each a doorway to your own Self." -Amma*

In the vastness of God's creation, every being and every object holds a unique and special place. From the tiniest insect to the grandest mountain, each creation is a manifestation of divine perfection. In the teachings of the Advaita Vedanta way, we are reminded to recognize the inherent value and significance of all that exists.

Amma's words resonate deeply with this understanding. She invites us to cultivate a deep sense of reverence and respect for every creature and every object in the world. By placing others before ourselves and considering everyone as a doorway to our own Self, we tap into the essence of non-duality— the recognition that we are interconnected and inseparable from the fabric of existence.

To embrace this teaching, we must first develop a sense of humility and surrender. We acknowledge that our limited human perspective may not fully grasp the intricate beauty and purpose of every creation. By surrendering our ego and opening ourselves to the wisdom of the Divine, we allow ourselves to see the perfection in all that exists.

When we recognize the divine presence in others, we naturally treat them with love, compassion, and respect. We understand that each person we encounter is a reflection of our own Self, and their joys and sorrows, strengths and weaknesses, mirror aspects of our own being. Through this realization, we deepen our capacity for empathy and understanding, creating a foundation for genuine connection and unity.

By valuing every creature and object as an integral part of God's creation, we awaken to a profound sense of interconnectedness. We begin to see the world through the lens of unity, where our actions are guided by the recognition that what we do to others, we ultimately do to ourselves. This awareness inspires us to act with kindness, compassion, and integrity, knowing that our actions ripple through the oneness web of life.

Advaita Vedanta teaches us that there are no mistakes in God's creation. Every being and every object has a purpose and contributes to the grand tapestry of existence. By embracing this truth, we let go of judgments and comparisons, and we honor the uniqueness of each individual and the gifts they bring.

In cultivating a deep appreciation for the diversity and interconnectedness of life, we expand our consciousness and open ourselves to a higher level of spiritual awakening. We move beyond the limitations of individuality and embrace the vastness of our shared existence. Our hearts become filled with love, compassion, and gratitude, as we recognize the divine essence within ourselves and others.

As we walk the path of non-duality, we learn to see beyond the superficial differences that separate us and embrace the underlying unity that binds us all. We celebrate the richness of diversity and honor the inherent worth of every creature and every object. Through this lens of love and understanding, we find joy in serving others and nurturing the oneness web of life.

Amma's wisdom reminds us that by placing others before ourselves and recognizing their sacredness, we tap into the profound truth of our oneness. As we honor and cherish every being and every object as a doorway to our own Self, we deepen our spiritual journey and awaken to the boundless love and unity that permeates all of creation.

Story

One day, while wandering through the forest, young boy stumbled upon a wounded bird. The bird's wing was injured, and it was unable to fly. Boy's heart filled with compassion as he saw the bird's struggle. Without hesitation, he carefully picked up the bird and cradled it in his hands.

As the boy held the injured bird, a deep sense of connection and empathy washed over him. He could feel the bird's pain and vulnerability, and he knew that he had to do something to help. With a gentle touch, he created a makeshift nest for the bird and placed it in a safe spot under a shady tree.

Over the following days, the boy dedicated himself to caring for the bird. He would visit it every day, bringing food and water, and tending to its injuries. The bird, sensing the boy's genuine care and love, began to recover. Its wing healed, and soon it was ready to take flight once again.

As the boy watched the bird soar into the sky, he felt an immense joy and gratitude in his heart. He realized that his act of compassion and selfless service had not only brought healing to the bird but had also transformed his own being. Through his connection with the bird, the boy had experienced the profound truth of interconnectedness and unity.

ॐ

Happiness

51. "While the momentary happiness obtained from the world ultimately pushes you into the throes of never-ending sorrow, spiritual pain uplifts you to the abode of everlasting bliss and Peace." -Amma

Happiness is a pursuit that has consumed humanity throughout the ages. We search for it in material possessions, relationships, achievements, and various external circumstances. Yet, the more we chase after fleeting moments of happiness, the more we find ourselves caught in a never-ending cycle of longing and dissatisfaction.

Amma, with her profound wisdom, reminds us that true and lasting happiness cannot be found in the external world. While worldly pleasures may offer temporary joy, they are inherently transient and subject to change. The happiness derived from material possessions and outer experiences is conditioned and impermanent, and thus it inevitably leads to disappointment and sorrow.

In the pursuit of lasting happiness, Amma guides us towards a deeper understanding of spiritual fulfillment. She reminds us that true happiness lies not in accumulating external objects or chasing after fleeting desires but in realizing our divine nature and connecting with the eternal source of bliss that resides within us.

The path to lasting happiness begins with a shift in our perspective. Instead of seeking happiness solely in external circumstances, we are invited to turn inward and discover the wellspring of joy that exists at the core of our being. This inner journey requires us to cultivate self-awareness, cultivate spiritual wisdom, and deepen our connection with the divine.

mātrā-sparśhās tu kaunteya śhītoṣhṇa-sukha-duḥkha-dāḥ
āgamāpāyino 'nityās tans-titikṣhasva bhārata
yaṁ hi na vyathayantyete puruṣhaṁ puruṣharṣhabha
sama-duḥkha-sukhaṁ dhīraṁ so 'mṛitatvāya kalpate

– Bhagavad Gita 2:14-15

But the contacts of the organs with the objects are the producers of cold and heat, happiness and sorrow. They have a beginning and an end, (and) are transient. Bear them, O descendant of Bharata.

O (Arjuna, who are) foremost among men, verily, the person whom these do not torment, the wise man to whom sorrow and happiness are the same -- he is fit for Immortality.

The Transience of Sensory Experiences: In the verse Lord Krishna explains to Arjuna the nature of sensory experiences and their impact on human life. Contacts between the organs and their corresponding objects produce sensations such as cold, heat, happiness, and sorrow. These experiences are fleeting, having a beginning and an end. It is essential to bear them without attachment or aversion, recognizing their impermanent nature.

The Transitory Nature of Sensory Experiences:

Sensory experiences, whether pleasurable or painful, are temporary in nature. The organs of perception, such as hearing and touch, come into contact with their respective objects, giving rise to sensations like cold and heat. However, these experiences are not enduring and are subject to change. They arise and subside, influenced by external circumstances and the functioning of our senses.

The Dual Nature of Cold and Heat:

Cold and heat, two sensory experiences highlighted in the Gita, can bring both pleasure and pain. They have no fixed nature and can vary depending on individual preferences and circumstances. What may be cold for one person might be comforting for another. Similarly, the perception of heat can evoke different responses in different individuals. Their dual nature reflects the inherent subjectivity of sensory experiences.

Happiness and Sorrow:

Happiness and sorrow, distinct from cold and heat, possess defined natures. They are emotions experienced in response to various life situations. While happiness brings joy and contentment, sorrow brings sadness and distress. These emotions are part of the human experience, and their intensity varies from person to person. However, they are not permanent states and arise and fade away in response to different circumstances.

Bearing Sensory Experiences:

Lord Krishna advises Arjuna to bear these sensory experiences without being swayed by them. He encourages him to cultivate equanimity and not be attached to or averse to the fluctuations of pleasure and pain. By recognizing the transient nature of these experiences, one can maintain a balanced state of mind and navigate through life's ups and downs with resilience.

The Wise One: Sama-Duhkha-Sukha:

The wise person, referred to as "sama-duhkha-sukha" by Lord Krishna, is someone who remains unaffected by the dualities of happiness and sorrow. This individual sees both pleasure and pain as temporary manifestations and does not let them disturb their inner equanimity. By realizing the eternal nature of the Self, they rise above the fleeting nature of sensory experiences.

Fit for Immortality: One who bears cold, heat, happiness, and sorrow with equanimity becomes fit for Immortality, symbolizing liberation or spiritual enlightenment. By transcending the fluctuations of sensory experiences and recognizing their impermanence, individuals attain a state of freedom from attachment and aversion. They gain a deeper understanding of the eternal Self, realizing their true nature beyond the transient world of sensory perceptions.

Conclusion

The Bhagavad Gita teaches us to bear the transience of sensory experiences with equanimity. By understanding the impermanent nature of cold, heat, happiness, and sorrow, we can cultivate resilience and avoid being swayed by the fluctuations of life. Recognizing our true nature beyond sensory perceptions, we can attain a state of inner peace and become fit for the ultimate goal of spiritual liberation.

So, the pursuit of happiness takes on a new meaning when viewed through the lens of Amma's teachings. True happiness is not found in the transitory pleasures of the world but in the awakening of our inner divinity. By turning inward, cultivating spiritual wisdom, and surrendering to a higher power, we can experience the abode of everlasting bliss and peace. May we all embark on this journey of Self-realization, discovering the unending happiness that lies within our own hearts.

Story

One day, while wandering through the city, Arun came across a wise sage who was known for his deep spiritual insights. Intrigued, Arun approached the sage and shared his inner turmoil. He expressed his longing for true happiness and asked the sage for guidance.

The sage listened attentively to Arun's words and then began to recite a verse from the Bhagavad Gita. He said, "In the material world, happiness is fleeting and transient. It is like a mirage that promises fulfillment but ultimately leaves us thirstier. True happiness lies not in the external world but in the realization of our divine nature. When one understands their eternal connection with the Supreme, they attain a state of unending bliss and peace."

The verse resonated deeply within Arun's heart. He realized that he had been searching for happiness in all the wrong places, seeking fulfillment in temporary pleasures that could never bring lasting joy. Inspired by the sage's words, Arjun decided to embark on a spiritual journey to discover his true nature and find the abode of everlasting happiness.

Arun dedicated himself to self-reflection, study, and meditation. He delved into the teachings of the Bhagavad Gita, immersing himself in its profound wisdom. He learned about the nature of the self, the importance of selflessness, and the power of devotion.

As Arjun progressed on his spiritual path, he began to experience a profound shift in his perception. He realized that true happiness resided within him, beyond the fluctuating circumstances of the external world. It was the divine spark within his own being that held the key to everlasting bliss and peace.

ॐ

52. *"The more space we create in our heart for others, the more happiness and contentment we feel. The law of the universe, and of life, is selflessness." -Amma*

The philosophy of non-duality in Vedanta teaches us that the true nature of reality is the underlying oneness that pervades everything. This oneness is not limited to external manifestations but extends to the realm of our hearts and minds. It is through selflessness and the expansion of our capacity for love and compassion that we come closer to experiencing this profound unity.

Amma, a spiritual teacher and embodiment of love and compassion, reminds us of the importance of creating space in our hearts for others. She emphasizes that selflessness is not only a moral virtue but also a fundamental law of the universe. When we embrace selflessness and extend our love and kindness to others, we not only benefit them but also experience deep happiness and contentment within ourselves.

In the non-dualistic perspective, the separation between self and others is illusory. We are interconnected, and our actions have a ripple effect that impacts the collective consciousness. When we act from a place of selflessness, we acknowledge and honor the inherent unity that binds us all. We recognize that the happiness and well-being of others are intimately linked to our own.

Selflessness is not about sacrificing our own needs or neglecting self-care. It is about cultivating a mindset of genuine concern and care for others. It is about expanding our hearts to include the joys and sorrows of others, extending a helping hand without expectation, and practicing empathy and understanding. In doing so, we move beyond the limitations of the ego and tap into the infinite wellspring of love that resides within us.

etāny api tu karmāṇi saṅgaṁ tyaktvā phalāni cha
kartavyānīti me pārtha niśhchitaṁ matam uttamam

–Bhagavad Gita 18:6

But even these actions have to be undertaken by renouncing attachment and (hankering for) results. This is My firm and best conclusion, O Partha.

Renouncing Attachment and Results:

Lord Krishna instructs that even these actions, referring to the prescribed duties and rituals mentioned in the previous verses, should be undertaken with a spirit of renunciation. One must let go of attachment to these actions and the desire for their outcomes. Renouncing attachment means performing actions selflessly, without seeking personal gain or attachment to the results. So, experience deep happiness and contentment within ourselves.

Firm and Best Conclusion:

Krishna asserts that this teaching is his firm and ultimate conclusion. It encapsulates the essence of his guidance on the path of Self-realization and liberation. By emphasizing the renunciation of attachment and results, Krishna highlights the importance of performing actions with a selfless and detached mindset, also experiencing deep happiness and contentment within ourselves.

Purification through Actions:

Previously, Lord Krishna established that sacrifices, charity, and austerity are purifiers. These actions are means for purifying the mind and elevating consciousness. However, even these purifying actions should be performed without attachment and the hankering for results. The intent is to cultivate a state of inner renunciation, experience deep happiness, contentment within ourselves and selflessness while engaging in these actions.

Relevance to Seekers of Liberation:

Lord Krishna's teaching holds particular significance for those seeking spiritual liberation. For such individuals, the focus is on transcending the cycle of birth and death and realizing the ultimate truth of one's eternal nature. By renouncing attachment and results, experience deep happiness and contentment within ourselves. So, seekers of liberation can free themselves from the bondage of actions and attain a state of higher consciousness.

Differentiating between Nityakarmas and Kamyakarmas:

Krishna's instruction to renounce attachment and results applies not only to the prescribed duties but also to actions performed for desired outcomes (kamya karma). While nitya karmas, the daily obligatory duties, have their significance and inherent results, even they should be performed with renunciation. The emphasis is on cultivating deep happiness and contentment within ourselves by selfless attitude and detachment from the fruits of all actions.

Avoiding Bondage and Seeking Liberation:

The teaching of renouncing attachment and results serves as a means to avoid bondage and move towards liberation. When actions are performed selflessly, without attachment or desire for personal gain, they become a means for spiritual growth and Self-realization. By letting go of ego-driven motives, also experiencing deep happiness and contentment plus, one can attain a state of liberation and ultimate union with the divine.

Conclusion

Lord Krishna's instruction to renounce attachment and results in performing actions highlights the importance of selflessness and detachment on the path of spiritual evolution. By cultivating a mindset of renunciation, seekers of liberation can purify their minds, experience deep happiness and contentment, free themselves from the bondage of actions, and ultimately attain Self-realization. This teaching serves as a guiding principle for leading a purposeful and selfless life, contributing to personal growth and the well-being of society.

The more we open ourselves to selflessness, the more we align ourselves with the inherent nature of the universe. We begin to see that our individual identities are transient and limited, while our connection to the universal consciousness is eternal and boundless. This recognition allows us to transcend the narrow confines of the ego and embrace the broader perspective of unity and oneness.

Selflessness is a transformative practice that leads to the expansion of our consciousness. It frees us from the limitations of selfish desires, attachments, and the incessant pursuit of personal gain. As we let go of the ego-driven mindset and shift our focus towards serving others, we tap into a deep well of joy, contentment, and fulfillment that transcends fleeting external pleasures.

Story

One sunny morning, as Ram was tending to his garden, a young boy named Arun approached him with a heavy heart. Arun was known for his selfish and materialistic nature, always seeking personal gain and rarely considering the needs of others. However, something had changed within him, and he sought Ram's guidance.

With a gentle smile, Ram welcomed Arun and listened attentively to his concerns. Arun expressed his deep dissatisfaction with life, despite having acquired wealth, possessions, and external success. He admitted to feeling an emptiness that no amount of material comfort could fill.

Ram, recognizing this as a turning point in Arun's life, began to share his wisdom. He spoke about the power of selflessness and the importance of creating space in one's heart for others. Ram explained that true happiness and contentment are not found in the pursuit of personal gain but in the act of serving others with love and compassion.

Intrigued by Ram's words, Arun asked how he could cultivate selflessness and experience the joy that comes from serving others. Ram smiled and suggested that Arun accompany him on his daily acts of service in the village.

From that day on, Arun became Ram's eager apprentice, learning the art of selflessness through firsthand experience. They visited the sick, offering them comfort and healing words. They provided food and clothing to the needy, ensuring that no one went without basic necessities. They spent time with the elderly, listening to their stories and providing companionship. Arun observed how Raman approached each act of service with genuine care and love, without any expectation of reward or recognition.

ॐ

53. *"Fill your hearts with love and gratitude. Life gives us what we need and necessarily what we want. It follows its own wisdom, which is often incomprehensible to our gross minds. We should learn to accept situations in life. This attitude of acceptance is the secret of happiness."* -Amma

In the journey of life, there are countless moments of joy and moments of hardship. We often find ourselves striving for what we want, chasing after desires and dreams, believing that happiness lies in obtaining the objects of our desires. But the truth is that life has its own plans, its own wisdom that surpasses our limited understanding.

Amma teaches us that true happiness comes from a heart filled with love and gratitude, a heart that accepts and embraces life as it unfolds. Life, with all its ups and downs, is a gift that provides us with exactly what we need, even if it may not align with what we want or expect.

When we cultivate love and gratitude in our hearts, we shift our perspective. We learn to see the beauty in every experience, even in moments of challenge or disappointment. We recognize that life's circumstances are not random or arbitrary, but rather purposeful lessons that shape and mold us into better versions of ourselves.

Gratitude is the key that unlocks the door to contentment and inner peace. When we appreciate the blessings that surround us, big or small, we shift our focus from what is lacking to what is present. We realize that there is abundance in every moment, and that every experience, whether joyful or difficult, is an opportunity for growth and learning.

Moreover, the attitude of acceptance is crucial on the path to happiness. Life unfolds according to its own divine plan, and our resistance or attachment to specific outcomes only brings suffering. By accepting what is, we surrender to the flow of life, trusting in its inherent wisdom. We let go of our desires and expectations, and instead embrace the present moment with openness and grace.

Amma reminds us that the secret of happiness lies in filling our hearts with love and gratitude, and in accepting life as it is. Through love, we connect with the divine essence within us and in all beings. Love opens our hearts, dissolves barriers, and brings us closer to the truth of our oneness.

samaḥ śhatrau cha mitre cha tathā mānāpamānayoḥ
śhītoṣhṇa-sukha-duḥkheṣhu samaḥ saṅga-vivarjitaḥ
tulya-nindā-stutir maunī santuṣhṭo yena kenachit
aniketaḥ sthira-matir bhaktimān me priyo naraḥ

– Bhagavad Gita 12:18-19

He who is the same towards friend and foe, and so also in honor and dishonor; who is the same under cold, heat, happiness and sorrow, who is free from attachment to everything.

The person to whom denunciation and praise are the same, who is silent, content with anything, homeless, steady-minded, and full of devotion is dear to Me.

Bhagavad Gita 12:18-19, these verses outline the characteristics attitude of acceptance is the secret of happiness:

Same towards friend and foe: The person who possesses spiritual maturity treats both friends and foes with equanimity.

They have transcended the duality of likes and dislikes and maintain an unbiased and impartial attitude towards others.

Same in honor and dishonor: The aspirants remain unaffected by praise or criticism. They do not seek validation or derive their self-worth from external opinions. Their self-esteem is anchored in their inner being, and they maintain equanimity in both favorable and unfavorable circumstances.

Same in pleasure and pain: This refers to the ability to remain steady and balanced amidst the fluctuations of life. The enlightened individual does not get attached to transient pleasures or overwhelmed by sorrow. They maintain inner stability and composure regardless of external circumstances.

Free from attachments: The spiritual person is detached from worldly possessions, relationships, and outcomes. They do not cling to anything or anyone, recognizing the impermanence and transient nature of the material world. Their freedom from attachment allows them to experience true inner peace with an attitude of acceptance is the secret of happiness.

Equanimity towards denunciation and praise: The enlightened person does not get swayed by either criticism or praise. They do not identify with external opinions or judgments. Their self-worth is rooted in their connection with the divine, and they remain unaffected by the opinions of others.

Silent and restrained in speech: The spiritually evolved individual practices restraint in speech. They use their words mindfully, avoiding unnecessary gossip, criticism, or harmful speech. Their silence signifies their inner stillness and the ability to refrain from engaging in idle chatter.

Contentment: The person finds contentment within themselves and is not dependent on external circumstances or material possessions for their happiness. They embrace simplicity and are satisfied with the basic necessities of life. Having an attitude of acceptance is the secret of happiness.

Attitude of acceptance is the secret of happiness: This indicates the detachment from worldly attachments, including the attachment to a specific physical dwelling. The spiritually evolved person's true home lies within their spiritual connection with the divine.

Steady-minded and devoted: The person possesses a steady and unwavering mind. Their thoughts are focused on the supreme Reality, the ultimate truth. They are devoted to the divine and engage in acts of worship and surrender, deepening their connection with the divine presence.

These qualities describe the ideal characteristics of an individual who has an attitude of acceptance which is the secret of happiness. They embody virtues such as equanimity, detachment, contentment, and devotion. By cultivating these qualities, one can progress on the path of spiritual realization and experience a deep connection with the divine.

In the teachings of Advaita Vedanta, we understand that there is a deeper reality beyond the surface appearances of life. It is the recognition that all forms, all experiences, are expressions of the same divine essence. When we cultivate love and gratitude, when we embrace acceptance and surrender, we align ourselves with this deeper reality. We tap into the infinite wellspring of joy and peace that resides within us.

So, let us fill our hearts with love and gratitude. Let us open ourselves to the wisdom of life's unfolding. Let us embrace acceptance and surrender, trusting in the divine plan. In doing so, we discover the secret of happiness, the profound truth that life's blessings are abundant, and that true fulfillment comes from within.

Story

Once an old woman's days were filled with simple joys and moments of connection. She would wake up early in the morning, greeted by the vibrant hues of the rising sun, and offer her prayers of gratitude for the gift of a new day. She would then go about her daily tasks with a sense of purpose and contentment.

One day, the old woman came across a young boy, who was known for his troubled and restless nature. The boy had lost his parents at a young age and was often consumed by a sense of bitterness and discontent.

Moved by the boy's plight, the old woman approached him with kindness and compassion. She shared her own experiences of gratitude and the power it had to transform her perspective. She encouraged Ravi to focus on the blessings in his life, no matter how small they may seem.

Intrigued by the old woman 's words, the boy decided to give it a try. He started each day by acknowledging the simple joys around him—a beautiful sunrise, the chirping of birds, the gentle breeze that brushed against his face. Slowly but surely, the boy's heart began to soften, and he started to experience moments of genuine happiness and contentment.

As the old woman continued to share her wisdom with others in the village, the community began to embrace the power of love, gratitude, and acceptance. The villagers realized that true happiness lay not in chasing after external desires, but in cultivating an attitude of appreciation for the present moment.

One day, a traveler passing through the village overheard the conversations about an old woman's teachings. Intrigued, he approached an old woman and asked her the secret to her radiant happiness. Old woman smiled warmly and replied, "It is love and gratitude that fill my heart, and acceptance that brings me peace. When we embrace the blessings that surround us and let go of resistance, we tap into the infinite wellspring of joy within."

The traveler was deeply touched by the old woman 's words and the transformation he witnessed in the village. He recognized the profound wisdom in her teachings and vowed to carry the message of love, gratitude, and acceptance to other communities.

ॐ

54. sJust like any other decision, happiness is also a decision. We should make the firm decision: Whatever may come my way, I will be happy. I am courageous and I am not alone. God is with me." -Amma

The Power of Choosing Happiness

Happiness, the elusive state of being that we all seek, is often perceived as something that is influenced by external circumstances. We believe that happiness will come to us once we achieve certain goals, acquire material possessions, or find ourselves in ideal situations. However, the wisdom shared by Amma, the embodiment of love and compassion, reminds us that happiness is not a result of external factors, but rather a conscious decision we make from within.

In the journey of life, we encounter countless challenges, uncertainties, and disappointments. Our happiness can easily be swayed by these external circumstances if we allow them to dictate our emotional state. But what if we choose to rise above the external noise and make the firm decision to be happy, regardless of the circumstances that come our way?

Amma encourages us to take charge of our own happiness by making a conscious decision to be happy. It is a shift in perspective that empowers us to find joy and contentment in every moment, even amidst challenges and difficulties. It is recognizing that happiness is not dependent on external achievements, but on our internal state of being.

Making the decision to be happy is an act of courage. It requires us to acknowledge our own inner strength and to trust in the presence of a higher power. Amma reminds us that we are never alone on this journey. God, the divine presence within us and all around us, is always there, supporting and guiding us. When we cultivate this awareness and trust in the divine, we tap into an infinite source of strength and resilience that enables us to navigate through life's ups and downs with grace and joy.

Choosing happiness does not mean denying or suppressing our true emotions. It is about acknowledging our emotions and allowing ourselves to experience them fully, but not allowing them to control our happiness. We can choose to respond to life's challenges with a positive mindset, seeking opportunities for growth, learning, and finding silver linings even in the most difficult circumstances.

This decision to be happy is rooted in the understanding that happiness is not derived from external achievements or possessions, but from within. It is a state of mind that can be cultivated through practices such as gratitude, mindfulness, and self-reflection. When we shift our focus from what is lacking to what we already have, from what is beyond our control to what we can control—our thoughts, attitudes, and actions—we awaken the dormant happiness within us.

It is not something we need to seek outside of ourselves, but a quality that already exists within us. By making the conscious decision to be happy, we align ourselves with our true essence and open the doors to experiencing boundless joy, peace, and fulfillment.

In conclusion, Amma's profound message invites us to reclaim our power to choose happiness. It is a decision that requires courage, trust, and a deep connection to our inner selves and the divine presence. By making this decision, we liberate ourselves from the constraints of external circumstances and tap into the infinite wellspring of joy that resides within us. Let us remember that happiness is not a destination but a journey, and we hold the key to unlock its abundant blessings.

Story
One day, a young man, burdened by the weight of his worries and sorrows, approached a sage seeking solace. Young man poured out his heart, sharing his struggles and the constant search for happiness that seemed elusive to him.

The sage listened attentively, his eyes filled with compassion. He smiled gently and said, "My dear friend, happiness is not something to be found outside of yourself. It is your true nature, the essence of your being. It is like a radiant sun hidden behind the clouds. The clouds may come and go, but the sun is always shining."

The young man was puzzled by the sage's words. He had always believed that happiness was something to be achieved or obtained through external means. But sage's words sparked a flicker of curiosity within him.

The sage continued, "Look within yourself, my friend. Discover the eternal source of joy that resides in your heart. It is not dependent on the circumstances of your life or the possessions you acquire. It is a choice, a decision to embrace the inherent happiness that is your birthright."

Intrigued, the young man embarked on a journey of self-discovery. He delved deep into introspection, reflecting on his thoughts, beliefs, and perceptions. With each passing day, he learned to detach himself from external influences and connect with the timeless essence within.

As the young man grew in self-awareness, he began to experience moments of pure bliss and contentment. He realized that true happiness was not derived from the fleeting pleasures of the world, but from the unwavering peace that resided in his own being.

ॐ

Humility

55. "A seed has to get buried in the soil for its real form as a plant to emerge. Only through modesty and humility can we grow. Pride and conceit will only destroy us. Live with the firm attitude, 'I am everyone's servant.' Then the whole universe will bow down to us." -Amma

In the vast expanse of the universe, there exists a profound wisdom that transcends the limitations of the human mind. It is the wisdom of humility, the transformative power of embracing a servant's heart. Amma, the embodiment of love and compassion, beautifully reminds us of this timeless truth.

Imagine a tiny seed, carrying within it the potential to grow into a magnificent tree. Before it can manifest its true form, the seed must surrender itself to the embrace of the soil. It surrenders its ego, its identity as a seed, and allows itself to be humbly buried, unseen by the world above.

In this act of surrender, the seed sets into motion a remarkable journey of transformation. It breaks through its protective shell, reaching out to the depths of the earth to anchor itself. It draws nourishment from the soil, absorbs the warmth of the sun, and dances with the rhythm of the rain. Gradually, it sprouts and grows, its slender shoot reaching towards the sky, adorned with vibrant leaves and blossoms.

The seed's transformation from a dormant state to a flourishing tree is a testament to the power of humility. It recognizes that growth and expansion are not fueled by pride and conceit, but by surrendering to the greater forces of life. Similarly, in our own journey towards Self-realization, humility plays a vital role.

Humility is the recognition that we are not separate entities, but interconnected threads woven into the tapestry of existence. It is the understanding that we are part of a greater whole, and that our purpose lies in serving the well-being of others. When we adopt the firm attitude, "I am everyone's servant," we open ourselves to the profound wisdom that resides within.

Through humility, we free ourselves from the shackles of ego and embrace the beauty of interdependence. We acknowledge that our growth and evolution are intricately linked to the growth and evolution of all beings. We become channels through which love, compassion, and kindness flow freely, nourishing the world around us.

In the realm of non-duality, Advaita, humility takes on an even deeper significance. It is the recognition that the true Self, the essence of our being, is beyond the limitations of the ego. It is the realization that in the vastness of existence, we are but expressions of the divine consciousness, oneness and inseparable.

Tam hovacha yam vai, saumya, etam animanam na nibhalayase, etasya vai, saumya, esho'nimna evam mahan nyagrodhas-tishthati srddhatsva, saumya iti

– Chandogya Upanishad 6,12-2.

Father Uddalaka said to him—'My child Svetaketu, the Subtle Essence which you do not perceive,—it is from that Subtle Essence that this large Banyan-tree grows up'.— Have faith: my son.'

The Indwelling Spirit: The Banyan Tree and its Seed
The metaphor of the Banyan tree and its seed in this teaching illustrates the profound concept of the indwelling spirit. Through the dialogue between a father and his son, the invisible essence within the seed is compared to the expansive tree, highlighting the all-pervading nature of the ultimate reality.

Fetching and Breaking the Fruit:

The father asks his son to bring a fruit from the Banyan tree, emphasizing the disparity between the tree's large size and the smallness of its fruit and seed. The son obediently brings a fruit and presents it to his father, demonstrating the tangible aspect of the tree's manifestation.

The Atomic Seed and Subtle Essence:

Upon breaking the fruit, the son discovers tiny granules, representing the atomic seeds within. The father urges his son to split one of these seeds, acknowledging the challenge due to their minuscule size. Eventually, the son succeeds and finds nothing visible inside the seed, indicating the presence of an invisible, jelly-like subtle essence.

The Miracle of Growth:

The father now unveils the deeper meaning of the analogy. He explains that the invisible essence within the seed is responsible for the remarkable phenomenon of the vast tree's growth. Although imperceptible, this subtle essence has transformed into the expansive tree, defying the limitations of physical perception. This miracle invites the son to have faith and explore the profound implications of this analogy.

The Pervading Essence:

The father further expands the analogy, highlighting that the subtle essence pervades the entire tree, despite its atomic nature. Similarly, the vast universe is permeated by the same essence that originated from a small seed. This essence is the true Self of the tree, and by extension, the entire universe. The father imparts the profound revelation, "Tat-tvam-asi, you are that," signifying the universal essence present in all beings.

Conclusion

The teaching of the Banyan tree and its seed offers a powerful contemplation on the indwelling spirit. It emphasizes that the invisible essence within the seed is responsible for the manifestation of the vast tree, mirroring the inherent divinity within all of creation. This teaching invites individuals to recognize their inherent connection to the universal essence and perceive the divine presence within themselves and the world around them. By contemplating this profound analogy, one can deepen their understanding of the indwelling spirit and realize their essential unity with the cosmos.

When we live with the attitude of a humble servant, the universe responds in kind. It bows down to us, not in a sense of hierarchical power, but in recognition of our alignment with the natural order of things. It is a bowing of reverence and gratitude, acknowledging the profound impact of our selfless service.

Amma's words remind us that humility is not a sign of weakness, but a source of strength. It is through humility that we find our true power, our true purpose. It is through humility that we cultivate deep connections with others, transcending the illusory boundaries of separation.

Story

The sage, with his gentle and compassionate demeanor, attracted seekers from far and wide. People would flock to him, seeking guidance and solace in the midst of their dualistic existence. They longed to experience the unity and interconnectedness that the sage spoke of.

Among the many who sought the sage's teachings was the humble servant. Despite his lowly position, the servant possessed a pure heart and an innate understanding that went beyond societal distinctions. He saw beyond the surface-level differences and recognized the underlying essence that connected all beings.

One day, the servant approached the sage with a question burning in his heart. "Master," he asked, "how can I truly embody the teachings of non-duality in my daily life? How can I live in a state of humility and serve others selflessly?"

The sage smiled warmly at the servant and invited him to sit beside him. "My dear friend," the sage began, "the path of non-duality is not confined to the realm of philosophy or intellectual understanding. It is a lived experience, a way of being in the world."

He continued, "To truly embody non-duality, you must recognize the illusion of separation that permeates this dualistic world. You must see beyond the veils of ego and identify with the essence that connects all beings. This essence is pure consciousness, the very fabric of existence."

The servant listened intently, his heart open to receive the sage's wisdom. He felt a deep resonance within him, as if the words were not mere concepts but truths that he had always known.

The sage continued, "Humility is the key to unlocking the doors of non-duality. It is the recognition that you are not separate from others, but an integral part of the interconnected web of existence. When you approach life with humility, you dissolve the boundaries of ego and open yourself to the flow of divine love and compassion." The servant nodded, his heart filled with a profound understanding. He realized that his role as a humble servant was not a position of subservience but an opportunity to transcend the egoic self and serve as a channel for the divine.

ॐ

56. *"Humility makes you receptive to all experiences without judging them. Thus, with humility you can go deeper and learn more."* -Amma

samaṁ paśhyan hi sarvatra samavasthitam īśhvaram
na hinasty ātmanātmānaṁ tato yāti parāṁ gatim

– Bhagavad Gita 13:29

Since by seeing equally God who is present alike
everywhere he does not injure the Self by the Self,
therefore he attains the supreme Goal.

Attaining the Supreme Goal through Equal Vision

This verse mentions the significance of perceiving God equally present everywhere and its impact on one's spiritual journey. By realizing the true nature of the Self and refraining from causing harm, one can attain the supreme Goal of liberation. This essay explores the verse and its implications.

The Significance of Equal Vision:

The verse emphasizes the importance of perceiving God equally present in all beings and entities. It calls for transcending superficial differences and recognizing the underlying divine essence in everything. By cultivating equal vision, one develops a sense of unity and interconnectedness with all of creation.

Non-Injury to the Self:

The verse states that by perceiving God equally, one does not injure the Self by the Self. This refers to the understanding that the true Self transcends the realm of actions and their consequences. It calls for refraining from causing harm to oneself and others, both physically and mentally. This non-injuring attitude arises from a deep sense of compassion, respect, and the recognition of the divine in all beings.

Overcoming Ignorance and Destruction of the Self:

The verse addresses the objection that no creature injures themselves by themselves. The response clarifies that unenlightened individuals, due to ignorance, mistakenly identify the non-Self as the Self. Through their actions, they destroy even the self they have accepted, adopting new identities repeatedly. Consequently, they remain ignorant of their true Self, which remains unrecognized and seemingly destroyed by their ignorance. Such unenlightened individuals are considered destroyers of the Self.

Attaining the Supreme Goal:
In contrast, the person who has realized the Self as described in the verse does not injure the Self either through superimposition or non-superimposition. By perceiving God equally and understanding the true nature of the Self, they overcome ignorance and destructive tendencies. Through this realization, they attain the supreme Goal, which is liberation from the cycle of birth and death. This realization brings about the experience of unity, divine grace, and ultimate spiritual fulfillment.

Conclusion

Bhagavad Gita 13:29 emphasizes the importance of perceiving God equally and refraining from causing harm. By realizing the true nature of the Self and cultivating equal vision, individuals can overcome ignorance, destructive tendencies, and attain the supreme Goal of liberation. This verse encourages unity, compassion, and spiritual growth, offering a path towards Self-realization and transcending the limitations of the material world.

Story

The story of a wise teacher and his disciples beautifully illustrates the significance of humility in the quest for Self-realization. The teacher, renowned for his wisdom, had three devoted disciples who accompanied him on his spiritual journey.

One day, as they traveled through a dense forest, they encountered a poor beggar sitting by the roadside. The beggar, dressed in tattered clothes and with a weathered face, looked up at the teacher and his disciples with eyes filled with longing.

Moved by compassion, the teacher approached the beggar and asked, "What is it that you seek?"

The beggar replied, "Master, I have heard of your wisdom and the profound teachings you impart to your disciples. I wish to learn from you and find peace in my heart."

The teacher smiled and said, "Very well, but I have a condition. Before I accept you as my disciple, you must prove your worthiness through an act of humility."

The beggar, eager to embark on the path of Self-realization, humbly agreed to the teacher's condition.

Days turned into weeks, and the beggar diligently served the teacher and his disciples, performing menial tasks and tending to their needs with utmost humility. He washed their clothes, prepared their meals, and cleaned their living quarters without a hint of resentment or expectation.

Impressed by the beggar's unwavering humility, the teacher finally called him and said, "You have passed the test of humility. From this day forward, I will be your guide on the path of Self-realization."

The beggar's heart swelled with gratitude as he realized that his sincere humility had opened the door to the spiritual teachings he so eagerly sought. From that moment on, he devoted himself wholeheartedly to the teacher's guidance, striving to cultivate humility in every aspect of his life.

Through the teacher's wise counsel and his own unwavering humility, the beggar began to experience profound shifts in his consciousness. He learned to see beyond the illusions of the ego and recognize the divine essence that resides in all beings. He understood that true wisdom comes not from asserting one's superiority but from embracing the oneness of all life.

ॐ

57. *"Thankfulness is a humble, open and prayerful attitude that helps you receive more of God's grace." -Amma*

In Advaita Vedanta, the practice of thankfulness holds immense significance. It is a humble and prayerful attitude that opens the doors for us to receive more of God's grace and deepen our understanding of our true nature.

Thankfulness, or gratitude, is a powerful tool that helps us cultivate a sense of interconnectedness with the divine and all of creation. It is an acknowledgment of the abundant blessings that surround us, both seen and unseen. By expressing gratitude, we shift our focus from what is lacking in our lives to recognizing the countless gifts and opportunities that are bestowed upon us each day.

The practice of thankfulness is rooted in the understanding that everything in existence is an expression of the divine. It reminds us that we are not separate from God, but rather an integral part of the cosmic tapestry. Through gratitude, we align ourselves with the flow of divine energy and become receptive to the grace that is constantly flowing towards us.

Thankfulness also serves as a powerful antidote to the ego, which tends to keep us trapped in a state of separation and dissatisfaction. It is through gratitude that we dissolve the illusion of lack and realize the abundance that is present in every moment. As we cultivate a grateful heart, we become aware of the infinite blessings that surround us, from the simplest joys of life to the profound experiences that shape our spiritual journey.

anapekṣhaḥ śhuchir dakṣha udāsīno gata-vyathaḥ
sarvārambha-parityāgī yo mad-bhaktaḥ sa me priyaḥ

– Bhagavad Gita 12:16

He who has no desires, who is pure, who is dextrous, who is impartial, who is free from fear, who has renounced every undertaking-he who is (such) a devotee of Mine is dear to Me.

Qualities to receive God's grace
Verse 12:16 describes the qualities of a beloved devotee who is dear to the Divine. These qualities include detachment from covetable objects, purity, dexterity, impartiality, fearlessness, and renunciation of self-centered actions. This essay explores these qualities and their significance in the spiritual path.

Detachment from Covetable Things:
The verse highlights the importance of having no desires for covetable objects such as the body, sensory organs, and their interrelationships. The beloved devotee recognizes the transient nature of material possessions and seeks spiritual fulfillment beyond worldly attachments. This detachment enables them to focus their energies on the pursuit of higher truths.

Purity: The verse emphasizes the need for external and internal purity. External purity refers to maintaining cleanliness in one's physical surroundings, while internal purity pertains to a pure heart, free from negative emotions and impure intentions. The beloved devotee strives for purity in thoughts, words, and actions, aligning themselves with divine virtues.

Dexterity:
Dexterity refers to the ability to promptly and skillfully understand and perform one's duties. The beloved devotee possesses mental agility, discernment, and efficiency in carrying out their responsibilities. They approach their duties with dedication, mindfulness, and a sense of divine service.

Impartiality:
The beloved devotee remains impartial, not favoring or aligning with any particular group or individual. They treat everyone equally, recognizing the divine presence within all beings. Impartiality fosters harmony, compassion, and unity, allowing the devotee to transcend personal biases and embrace the interconnectedness of all creation.

Fearlessness:
Fearlessness is a quality that arises from deep trust in the divine and a profound understanding of the impermanence of the material world. The beloved devotee is free from fear, knowing that their true essence is eternal and transcendent. They face challenges with courage, resilience, and unwavering faith in the divine will.

Renunciation of Self-centered Actions:
The beloved devotee renounces self-centered actions and desires for personal gain. They engage in selfless service, detached from the results of their actions. By relinquishing the ego's desires and expectations, they surrender to the divine will and dedicate their actions to the service of God and humanity.

Conclusion
Bhagavad Gita 12:16 highlights qualities include detachment from covetable objects, purity, dexterity, impartiality, fearlessness, and renunciation of self-centered actions. By cultivating these qualities, individuals can deepen their spiritual practice, strengthen their connection with the divine, and align themselves with the path of love, devotion, and selfless service.

In the non-dual perspective, thankfulness goes beyond mere external circumstances or material possessions. It is a recognition of the underlying unity and interdependence of all things. We express gratitude not only for the blessings that come our way but also for the challenges and lessons that contribute to our spiritual growth. With a thankful heart, we embrace the entirety of existence as a manifestation of divine wisdom and love.

Story

One day, a renowned sage visited the village, and the villagers flocked to seek his wisdom. Ram, filled with excitement, joined the gathering and sat attentively, eager to soak in the sage's teachings. The sage began to speak about the power of thankfulness and its ability to connect one with the divine.

Inspired by the sage's words, Ram embarked on a journey to deepen his practice of gratitude. Every morning, as the sun rose, he would offer his heartfelt thanks for the gift of a new day. He would express his gratitude for the air he breathed, the earth beneath his feet, and the beauty of nature that surrounded him.

One day, as Ram was walking through the village, he noticed an old woman sitting by the roadside, her eyes filled with tears. Concerned, Ram approached her and asked if there was anything he could do to help. The old woman shared her story of poverty and hardship, expressing her despair and hopelessness.

Moved by her plight, Ram took a moment to center himself in gratitude. He closed his eyes, took a deep breath, and silently offered his thanks for the opportunity to serve. With a heart full of compassion, he extended a helping hand to the old woman, offering her food, clothing, and a glimmer of hope.

As Ram continued his practice of thankfulness and selfless service, his actions started to have a profound impact on the village. People began to notice his unwavering gratitude and the genuine care he showed for others. Inspired by his example, the villagers, too, started to embrace a spirit of thankfulness and compassion.

ॐ

Optimism

58. "Optimism is the light of God. It is a form of grace which allows you to look at life with greater clarity. It is a great factor for eliminating suffering. When we have light within, no darkness can affect us. We should always have a positive attitude towards life." -Amma

Optimism is not just a mere outlook on life; it is a radiant light that illuminates our path and uplifts our spirit. It is a profound grace that enables us to see beyond the apparent challenges and difficulties and embrace the inherent goodness and beauty that exists in every moment.

In the realm of Advaita Vedanta, optimism is understood as an expression of our innate connection to the divine. It arises from the realization that our true nature is divine, and that divine essence is eternally blissful and perfect. When we recognize this truth, we naturally cultivate an optimistic mindset, knowing that we are an integral part of a benevolent and harmonious universe.

Optimism allows us to see life's experiences as opportunities for growth, learning, and self-discovery. It enables us to navigate through the ups and downs with resilience, knowing that every situation holds within it the potential for spiritual evolution. We understand that challenges are not obstacles to our happiness but stepping stones towards greater wisdom and Self-realization.

Just as the sun shines its light indiscriminately upon all, regardless of their circumstances, optimism teaches us to embrace a similar attitude towards life. We recognize that the divine light shines equally upon everyone, and we have the power to perceive that light in all beings and situations. It is this optimistic perspective that enables us to extend compassion, understanding, and support to others, even in the face of adversity.

antavanta ime dehā nityasyoktāḥ śharīriṇaḥ
anāśhino 'prameyasya tasmād yudhyasva bhārata

– Bhagavad Gita 2:18

These destructible bodies are said to belong to the everlasting, indestructible, indeterminable, embodied One. Therefore, O descendant of Bharata, join the battle.

The Nature of the Self: Everlasting and Indestructible

Bhagavad Gita 2:18 delves into the understanding of the Self as an everlasting and indestructible entity. The verse emphasizes the temporary and illusory nature of the physical body, drawing parallels to the fleeting reality of mirages and dreams. Discriminating individuals recognize the eternal and indeterminable nature of the Self, which remains unaffected by the destruction of the physical body. This essay explores the meaning and implications of these teachings.

Destructible Bodies and the Indestructible Self: The verse highlights the perishable nature of physical bodies, likening them to the ephemeral appearances in dreams and illusions. Just as the perception of water in a mirage vanishes upon examination, the reality of the body dissipates when scrutinized with the aid of true knowledge. In contrast, the Self is described as everlasting and indestructible, transcending the temporal existence of the physical form. This distinction emphasizes the eternal essence of the Self, which remains untouched by the transitory nature of the body.

Everlastingness and Indestructibility:

The usage of the terms "everlasting" and "indestructible" is not redundant but serves to highlight different aspects. The everlastingness refers to the Self's transcendence of both the destruction of the physical body and its transformation through afflictions like diseases. It signifies that the Self is not subject to any form of destruction. The term "indestructible" emphasizes that the Self cannot be determined or apprehended through ordinary means of knowledge, such as direct perception. It denotes the Self's inherent nature as beyond the realm of empirical observation.

Self-Knowledge and Scripture:

The Self is considered self-evident, requiring no external means for its determination. It is the very essence of the knower, and therefore, the search for means of knowledge arises from the recognition of the Self. While scriptures, including the Vedas, play a significant role in revealing the nature of the Self, their authority lies in negating superimposed qualities and misconceptions rather than unveiling something unknown. The scriptural authority rests on its faultlessness and the recognition of the eternal and immediate presence of Brahman as the innermost Self.

Joining the Battle: Overcoming Sorrow and Delusion:

The verse concludes with the instruction to Arjuna to join the battle. This instruction does not impose a duty to engage in war but rather serves as an affirmation to overcome sorrow and delusion. Arjuna's initial reluctance arises from being overwhelmed by emotions, obscuring his understanding of duty. The Gita, as a scripture, aims to alleviate sorrow and delusion inherent in the cycle of birth and death, providing guidance for Self-realization rather than prescribing specific actions.

Conclusion

Verse 2:18 sheds light on the impermanence of the physical body and the everlasting nature of the Self. By discerning the illusory nature of the body and recognizing the indeterminable essence of the Self, individuals can cultivate a deeper understanding of their eternal nature. The verse encourages seekers to transcend sorrow and delusion, embracing their true Self and fulfilling their inherent purpose on the path of Self-realization.

Optimism is not a denial of reality or a blind optimism that overlooks the pain and suffering in the world. Rather, it is an acknowledgment of the inherent goodness and divine potential that exists within every individual and every situation. It is a conscious choice to focus on the positive aspects and to approach life with faith, hope, and resilience.

When we embrace optimism, we align ourselves with the higher truth and transcend the limitations of the ego. We cultivate a deep trust in the divine order of the universe, knowing that everything unfolds according to a greater plan. This trust allows us to surrender to the flow of life, free from attachment to outcomes and grounded in the present moment.

Story

One year, a severe drought struck the village, causing despair and hardship among the farmers. Crops withered, and water sources dried up, leaving the villagers in a state of desperation. Many of the farmers lost hope and fell into a cycle of despair, unable to see a way out of their predicament.

Amidst the gloom, Ram remained steadfast in his optimism. He knew that dwelling on the negative would only exacerbate their suffering, so he decided to take a different approach. Instead of succumbing to despair, he focused on finding innovative solutions to combat the drought.

Ram gathered the farmers and shared his ideas. He proposed a rainwater harvesting system that would help conserve water during the rainy season, allowing them to sustain their crops during the dry spells. He organized workshops to teach his fellow villagers about efficient irrigation techniques and encouraged them to plant drought-resistant crops.

Despite the initial skepticism and doubts from others, Ram's unwavering optimism and belief in the power of their collective efforts inspired the villagers. They began implementing the new techniques and working together as a community to overcome the challenges posed by the drought.

As they worked hand in hand, Ram's optimism became contagious. The villagers started to see the progress they were making and the resilience they possessed as a community. They realized that their mindset had a significant impact on their ability to find solutions and adapt to challenging circumstances.

Gradually, the rains returned, and the village flourished once again. The fields that were once barren transformed into lush green landscapes. The villagers reaped a bountiful harvest, not only in terms of crops but also in the growth of their own inner strength and resilience.

Ram's unwavering optimism and belief in the abundance of life had not only saved the village from despair but had also transformed it into a beacon of hope and inspiration for neighboring communities. His story spread far and wide, reminding people of the power of optimism and the ability to see opportunities in the face of adversity.

ॐ

59. *"Don't be discouraged by your incapacity to dispel darkness from the world. Light your little candle and step forward." -Amma*

In the vast expanse of the world, where darkness may sometimes seem overwhelming, it is easy to feel disheartened and powerless. We witness countless struggles, conflicts, and suffering, and it can be daunting to imagine how one individual can make a significant impact. However, the wisdom of Amma reminds us that our own light, no matter how small, can still make a difference.

The Advaita Vedanta view teaches us that we are interconnected beings, manifestations of the same divine consciousness. We may perceive ourselves as separate entities, but at the core, we are all oneness and share a common essence. When we understand this profound truth, we realize that even the tiniest flicker of light within us has the potential to dispel darkness.

Imagine a room engulfed in complete darkness, where even the faintest glimmer of light can make a profound difference. In this analogy, each individual represents a candle, capable of illuminating their immediate surroundings. Our actions, thoughts, and intentions become the flame that radiates light into the world.

Amma's quote reminds us not to be discouraged by the enormity of the darkness we witness but to focus on the power and potential of our own light. It calls upon us to ignite our inner candle and step forward with courage and conviction. It is not about trying to eradicate darkness from the entire world but rather about illuminating our own path and those around us.

When we embrace the Advaita Vedanta perspective, we realize that our individual actions contribute to the collective consciousness. By cultivating qualities such as kindness, compassion, love, and selflessness, we ignite our inner flame and radiate light into the world. Our small acts of goodness and positivity can have a ripple effect, inspiring others to kindle their own inner light.

It is essential to remember that the impact of our light may not be immediately visible or measurable. We may never witness the full extent of its influence, but that should not discourage us. Just as a candle brings comfort and dispels darkness in a room, our actions, no matter how small, can bring solace and inspiration to those around us.

The Advaita Vedanta view invites us to recognize that the journey of dispelling darkness begins within ourselves. It calls for self-reflection and introspection, allowing us to identify and overcome our own inner shadows. As we embrace our innate goodness and cultivate qualities that bring light into our lives, we naturally radiate that light outward.

jyotiṣhām api taj jyotis tamasaḥ param uchyate
jñānaṁ jñeyaṁ jñāna-gamyaṁ hṛidi sarvasya viṣhṭhitam

– Bhagavad Gita 13:18

That is the Light even of the lights; It is spoken of as beyond darkness. It is Knowledge, the Knowable, and the Known. It exists especially in the hearts of all.

The Knowable, Knowledge, and the Qualification of Devotees Verse 13:18 explores the nature of the Knowable, Knowledge, and their relationship to the individual. The verse emphasizes that the Knowable is the source of all light, including the lights of the sun and other celestial bodies. It is described as transcending darkness and ignorance. Additionally, the verse clarifies the interplay between the Knowable, Knowledge, and the qualification of devotees. This essay delves into the significance of these concepts and their implications for spiritual seekers.

The Illuminating Light of the Knowable:

The verse highlights the relationship between the Knowable and the lights of the sun and other celestial bodies. The lights of these objects are said to shine because they are enkindled by the light of consciousness emanating from the Knowable. This understanding is derived from Upanishadic texts and corroborated by verses in the Bhagavad Gita itself. By recognizing the illuminating power of the Knowable, seekers can grasp its transcendence over darkness and ignorance.

The Knowable, Knowledge, and the Known:

The Knowable is referred to as jneyam, the object of knowledge, as well as jnanagamyam, the result of Knowledge. It encompasses the essence of that which needs to be known and the transformative effect of attaining that knowledge. Additionally, the verse mentions jnanam, which represents various qualities such as humility, knowledge, and wisdom. These qualities are associated with the path of Self-realization and are attainable through the pursuit of Knowledge.

The Existence of the Knowable, Knowledge, and Qualification:

The verse states that the Knowable, Knowledge, and the Known specially exist within the hearts and intellects of all creatures. These aspects are perceived within the individual's inner realm. This recognition emphasizes the subjective nature of spiritual realization and the need for inner discernment. The verse sets the stage for the conclusion of the discussion by summarizing the topics of the field (13:1-7), Knowledge (13:8-12), and the Knowable (13:13-17).

Qualification for Attaining the State of the Lord:

By understanding the concepts of the field, Knowledge, and the Knowable, devotees become qualified for the state of the Lord. This qualification implies the readiness and preparedness to embark on the path of Self-realization. It involves cultivating the necessary qualities, developing a deep understanding of the Knowable, and embracing the transformative power of Knowledge. Through this qualification, devotees can attain a state of unity with the Lord and experience spiritual fulfillment.

Conclusion

Verse 13:18 provides insights into the nature of the Knowable, Knowledge, and the qualification of devotees. The verse emphasizes the illuminating power of the Knowable, its transcendence over darkness, and its presence within the hearts and intellects of all beings. Understanding these concepts and cultivating the necessary qualities enables devotees to embark on the path of Self-realization and attain a state of unity with the Lord. By delving into these teachings, seekers can deepen their spiritual journey and experience the transformative power of divine knowledge.

Story
One day, a village was engulfed in darkness. A thick blanket of clouds covered the sky, obscuring the sun's rays and casting a shadow over the village. The people felt a sense of despair and hopelessness as they struggled to navigate through the gloom. But the old woman remained undeterred. She believed that even a single candle could bring hope and light.

With her candle in hand, the old woman went from house to house, offering her flame to those in need. She lit the candles of the elderly, bringing warmth and comfort to their hearts. She visited families struggling with illness, allowing the gentle glow of her candle to soothe their pain and bring solace. Old woman's optimism was infectious, and soon the entire village started to embrace her spirit of hope.

Word of the old woman's candle of light spread to neighboring villages, and people from far and wide sought her out. They came with their own candles, eager to join in the collective effort to dispel the darkness. Maya realized that her small candle had ignited a spark within others, and together they formed a united front against despair.

As more and more people gathered, their combined light illuminated the village. The darkness gradually receded, and a sense of renewed hope filled the hearts of the villagers. Old woman's belief in the power of light had proven true, and she became a symbol of resilience and optimism.

Inspired by the old woman's actions, the villagers began to recognize that they too possessed the power to make a difference. They realized that by igniting their own inner flames of kindness, compassion, and love, they could contribute to the collective brightness of their community.

With time, the village transformed into a beacon of light and positivity. The darkness that once overshadowed their lives was replaced by the radiant glow of unity and compassion. People came from afar to witness the remarkable transformation and to learn from the village's example.

ॐ

60. *"There is no use in blaming or judging others or destiny for anything and everything that happens in your life. It is all the fruit of your own actions. Destiny can be changed through austerities and spiritual practices. Be at peace and do your work in the present to make your future happy and blissful. Act properly and sincerely, and then if something goes wrong, you can consider it as your karma, destiny, or God's will. " -Amma*

In the realm of non-duality and Vedanta philosophy, the concept of personal responsibility and the understanding of the interplay between actions, destiny, and spiritual practices are crucial. Amma's quote beautifully encapsulates the essence of this understanding, urging individuals to take ownership of their lives and embrace the power to shape their own destinies.

na prahṛishyet priyaṁ prāpya nodvijet prāpya chāpriyam
sthira-buddhir asammūḍho brahma-vid brahmaṇi sthitaḥ

– Bhagavad Gita 5:20

A knower of Brahman, who is established in Brahman, should have his intellect steady and should not be deluded. He should not get delighted by getting what is desirable, nor become dejected by getting what is undesirable.

The concept of a "Brahmavit" or a knower of Brahman, a person who is established in Brahman and the attributes they should have. We will explore the qualities of a Brahmavit, the importance of a steady intellect, the concept of delusion, and the reaction to desirable and undesirable events.

Understanding the Brahmavit

A Brahmavit is a person who is established in Brahman, the ultimate reality. The Brahmavit is described as someone who has renounced all actions, signifying a state of being where actions are not driven by desires and personal will, but are aligned with the cosmic order. The Brahmavit is a person who has realized the absolute Self, beyond the physical body and personal ego.

Importance of a Steady Intellect

Steady intellect or "sthira-buddhi" is an important characteristic of a Brahmavit. This refers to a firm conviction in the existence of the same pure, taintless Self in all beings. This unwavering belief is the foundation of their wisdom and understanding, allowing them to see beyond surface differences and perceive the underlying unity of all existence.

Freedom from Delusion

A Brahmavit should be free from delusion or "asammudhah." Delusion here refers to the erroneous perception of reality, often caused by ignorance or misconceptions. By being free from delusion, the Brahmavit can perceive the true nature of reality, unclouded by personal biases or illusions.

Reaction to Desirable and Undesirable Events

The text further explains that a Brahmavit should not be overly delighted when acquiring what is desirable, nor should they be dejected when faced with what is undesirable. This is because these situations are typically sources of happiness and sorrow for those who identify the Self with the body. However, for the one who has realized the absolute Self, these situations do not cause happiness or sorrow, as their inner state is not dependent on external circumstances.

In conclusion, the verse 5:20 provides a profound insight into the nature of a Brahmavit - a person established in Brahman. A Brahmavit is characterized by a steady intellect, freedom from delusion, and an equanimous response to desirable and undesirable events. The realization of the absolute Self allows the Brahmavit to transcend personal desires and fears, experiencing a state of inner peace and stability regardless of external circumstances.

Story
A young man named, who finds himself in a state of frustration and discontent. He feels that life has dealt him a difficult hand, and he often finds himself blaming others or attributing his circumstances solely to destiny. However, one day he encounters a wise sage who imparts to him the teachings of non-duality and the profound wisdom of Self-realization.

The sage explains that every action has a consequence, and our lives are shaped by the choices we make. Blaming others or external circumstances only perpetuates a cycle of disempowerment and prevents personal growth. Instead, the sage encourages young man to take responsibility for his own actions and decisions, understanding that they are the primary factors in shaping his life's outcomes.

Inspired by these teachings, the young man embarks on a journey of self-reflection and introspection. He realizes that he has the power to change his destiny through the choices he makes and the actions he takes. With renewed determination, he begins to practice spiritual disciplines such as meditation, selfless service, and self-inquiry.

As the young man delves deeper into his spiritual practices, he gradually experiences a shift in his perspective. He realizes that true peace and fulfillment come from within, and that external circumstances are merely reflections of his inner state of being. He understands that his thoughts, words, and actions are like seeds that shape his future experiences.

Young man no longer blames others or considers himself a victim of fate. Instead, he embraces the idea that his present actions are the seeds he is sowing for his future, and that he has the power to manifest positive outcomes through his conscious choices.

Over time, the young man witnesses the transformation that comes from taking responsibility for his life. He finds greater peace, joy, and fulfillment in the present moment, irrespective of external circumstances. He realizes that when he acts with integrity, kindness, and compassion, he not only creates a positive future for himself but also contributes to the collective well-being of others.

ॐ

Smile

61. *"We all have something to give. A smile doesn't cost one cent, yet all too often we forget to give this to others." - Amma*

In the realm of non-duality and the philosophy of Vedanta, the significance of a smile goes far beyond a simple facial expression. It embodies the essence of oneness and the recognition of our inherent unity with all beings.

A smile is a gesture of love, compassion, and acceptance. It transcends language and cultural barriers, conveying a message of warmth and goodwill. When we offer a genuine smile, we acknowledge the divinity within ourselves and in others. It is an affirmation of our shared humanity and the recognition that we are all interconnected in the web of existence.

In the teachings of non-duality, we are reminded that there is a fundamental oneness that underlies all of creation. Beyond the illusion of separateness, we are interconnected at the level of consciousness. When we smile at someone, we extend our recognition of this underlying unity, honoring the divine presence within them.

A smile has the power to uplift and heal. It can brighten someone's day, dissolve tension, and create a sense of connection. In the non-dual perspective, we understand that the happiness and well-being of others are intricately linked to our own. By sharing a smile, we contribute to the collective consciousness of love and harmony.

Furthermore, a smile is an expression of our true nature. It arises from a place of inner peace and contentment, reflecting the inherent joy that resides within us. When we allow ourselves to be present in the moment, free from the entanglements of past and future, we naturally radiate the purity and serenity of our true self.

The practice of offering a smile aligns with the principle of selfless service. By sharing a smile, we give without any expectation of receiving something in return. It is a spontaneous act of kindness and a reminder that our purpose is not solely focused on personal gain but rather on uplifting and serving others.

Through the lens of non-duality, a smile serves as a gateway to Self-realization. It reminds us that the ultimate truth is beyond the limited boundaries of the ego-self. When we smile, we momentarily transcend the confines of the individual identity and tap into the infinite wellspring of divine love and compassion.

In conclusion, a smile holds profound significance in the Advaita Vedanta view. It is a potent tool for expressing our inherent unity, offering love and kindness, and awakening to our true nature. As we embrace the practice of smiling, we become agents of positive change, spreading joy and goodwill wherever we go. So let us remember to give freely the gift of a smile, for it costs nothing yet holds immeasurable value in the realm of non-duality.

Story

Once upon a time, in a small village nestled amidst lush green fields, there lived a young boy. Boy was known for his radiant smile that could light up the darkest of days. His smile was so infectious that whenever he walked through the village, the people couldn't help but feel a sense of warmth and happiness.

Young boy understood the power of a smile. He believed that it had the ability to transform not only his own mood but also the mood of those around him. He saw how a simple smile could dissolve conflicts, ease tensions, and bring people closer together. With this understanding, the young boy made it his mission to spread smiles wherever he went.

One day, as the young boy was strolling through the village, he noticed an old woman sitting by the roadside, looking sad and dejected. He approached her with a gentle smile and asked if everything was alright. The old woman sighed and shared her story with the young boy. She had been feeling lonely and isolated, as her children had moved away to the city and she rarely had visitors.

Young boy listened intently, his smile never fading. He empathized with the old woman's situation and knew that his smile could make a difference. He began to talk to her, sharing stories and jokes, and soon enough, the old woman's frown turned into a smile. In that moment, she felt a sense of connection and companionship that she had longed for.

Word of the young boy's smile-spreading abilities quickly spread throughout the village. People started seeking him out whenever they needed a pick-me-up or a reminder of the joy that exists within them. The young boy became known as the "Smiling Sage," and his presence became a source of inspiration and happiness for everyone.

As the young boy continued to share his infectious smile, the village underwent a transformation. The people started greeting each other with warm smiles, even amidst their daily struggles. The once-divided community began to unite, supporting and uplifting one another. The power of the young boy's smile had awakened a sense of oneness and love among the villagers.

ॐ

Discipline

62. "Be like the honeybee who gathers only nectar wherever it goes. Seek the goodness that is found in everyone." –Amma

Discipline play a significant role in our journey towards spiritual growth and Self-realization. They serve as guiding principles that help us navigate through life with wisdom, clarity, and compassion. Amma's quote, "Be like the honeybee who gathers only nectar wherever it goes. Seek the goodness that is found in everyone," beautifully encapsulates the essence of the disciplines that lead us towards non-duality and Self-realization.

In Advaita Vedanta, disciplines are not merely external practices, but a way of living that cultivates awareness, inner transformation, and the recognition of our interconnectedness with all of creation. These disciplines serve as the means to unveil our true nature and dissolve the illusion of separateness.

Yatha, saumya, madhu madhukrto nistishthanti, nanatyayanam vrkshanam rasan samavaharamkatam rasam gamaynti.
Te yatha tatra na vivekam labhante, amushyaham vrkshasya raso'smi, amushyaham vrkshasya rasosmiti, evam eva khalu, saumya, imah sarvah prajah sati sampadya na viduh, sati sampadyamaha iti

– Chandogya Upanishad 6-9-1 and 6-9-2

The Analogy of the Bees and Honey
The text begins with a metaphor where the bees are compared to individuals and the honey they produce to the ultimate reality, the Being. Bees collect nectar from various trees and process it to create a homogeneous substance, honey. The individual characters

of the nectar from different trees cannot be distinguished in the honey. This is compared to individuals merging into the Being.

Merging into the Being

When individuals reach or merge into the Being, they lose their individual distinctions just like the various essences of flowers in the honey. They do not cease to exist, but their individual identities, such as their names, genders, or species, vanish. Instead, they exist as part of the homogeneous essence of the pure substance that is the Being.

Loss of Individual Consciousness: Just like the essences of various flowers are present in the honey but are not individually conscious of their presence, individuals who merge into the Being lose their individual consciousness. They do not have thoughts such as "I am Mr. So-and-so" or "I am a woman." All distinctions vanish and they exist as part of the absolute reality, the Being.

The Final State of Pure Reality

The text concludes by stating that this is what happens when we reach the ultimate truth or pure Reality, the Absolute Being. Our individual consciousness and distinctions cease to exist and we merge into the homogeneous essence of the Being, just like the essences of flowers merge into the honey.

In summary, the Upanishadic text uses the analogy of bees creating honey from various trees to explain the concept of individuals merging into the Being. It emphasizes the loss of individual consciousness and distinctions upon reaching this ultimate state of reality.

One of the fundamental disciplines is the cultivation of discernment, the ability to discriminate between the transient and the eternal. It involves recognizing that the external world, with its ever-changing forms and experiences, is impermanent and fleeting. By turning our attention inward and seeking the eternal essence within ourselves and others, we shift our focus from the superficial to the essence. We start to see the underlying unity that connects all beings, transcending the limitations of physical appearances and societal labels.

Another discipline is the practice of self-inquiry, which involves exploring the nature of our own existence and questioning the beliefs, identities, and attachments that create a sense of separation. Through self-inquiry, we begin to unravel the layers of conditioning and egoic patterns that veil our true nature. We inquire into the source of our thoughts, emotions, and perceptions, realizing that they arise and dissolve within the vast expanse of consciousness.

The discipline of selfless service (seva) is also emphasized in the Advaita Vedanta path. By engaging in acts of kindness and compassion without seeking personal gain or recognition, we expand our capacity to love and serve others. This practice helps us transcend the limited ego-self and cultivate a sense of oneness and interconnectedness with all beings. We recognize that every interaction is an opportunity to serve the divine presence that dwells within each individual.

Story
The villagers would often gather around the sage, seeking his wisdom and guidance. One day, a young man approached the sage with a troubled heart. He felt lost and disconnected, unable to find meaning and purpose in his life. The sage listened attentively to the young man's story and understood the turmoil within him.

The sage gently smiled and said, "My child, the answers you seek lie within you. The disciplines of Advaita Vedanta can help you awaken to your true nature and find the unity and purpose you long for." Intrigued, the young man asked the sage to guide him on this path. The sage agreed and began teaching him the practices of discernment, self-inquiry, selfless service, and awareness.

With discernment, he learned to see beyond the illusions of the ego and recognize the underlying unity in all of creation. He began to question his thoughts and beliefs, unraveling the layers of conditioning that had kept him trapped in a limited perception of reality.

Through self-inquiry, he delved deep into the core of his being, exploring the nature of consciousness and discovering the unchanging awareness that lay beyond the fluctuations of the mind. Inspired by the teachings of the sage, the young man embraced selfless service as a way of expressing his inherent unity with others. He dedicated himself to helping those in need, offering his time, skills, and resources for the betterment of the community. In serving others, he experienced a profound sense of oneness and found fulfillment in contributing to the well-being of others.

Mantra Japa

63. *"Children, do not forget to always repeat your mantra japa wherever you are, whatever work you are doing irrespective of time and place. Mental purity will come through constant chanting of the divine name with alertness."* - Amma

In the realm of Advaita Vedanta, the practice of mantra japa holds great significance. It is a powerful tool that allows individuals to cultivate mental purity, deepen their spiritual connection, and realize the inherent unity of all things. The repetition of a sacred mantra serves as a constant reminder of the divine presence within and helps to bring about a state of focused awareness.

In the Bhagavad Gita, specifically in Chapter 12, Lord Krishna emphasizes the importance of devotion and surrender to the Supreme. He explains that those who are steadfast in their spiritual practice, constantly engaged in the repetition of the divine name, and dedicated to selfless service attain the highest state of realization.

mayy āveśhya mano ye mām nitya-yuktā upāsate
śhraddhayā parayopetās te me yuktatamā matāḥ

– Bhagavad Gita 12:2

Those who meditate on Me by fixing their minds on Me with steadfast devotion (and) being endowed with supreme faith they are considered to be the most perfect yogis according to Me.

The verse seems to be discussing the qualities of a devout practitioner of yoga, focusing on their meditative practices, devotion, faith, and their perception of the supreme being.

Devotion to the Supreme Being

The verse begins by describing those who meditate on the supreme Lord of all the masters of yoga, or Omniscient One. They are those who concentrate their minds on this being, seeing beyond the limitations caused by attachment and other defects. The practitioner is called to devote their mind to the Cosmic form of God, suggesting a form of meditation that transcends the individual self and connects with the greater cosmic order.

Steadfastness and Dedication

The practitioner's devotion is described as steadfast, or "nitya-yuktah." This suggests a consistent, ongoing commitment to their practice. This dedication isn't momentary or temporary, but a sustained effort in accordance with the teachings of yoga.

The Power of Supreme Faith

The verse emphasizes the importance of "paraya sraddhaya," or supreme faith. This faith is not just belief but a profound trust and certainty in the spiritual path one is pursuing. This kind of faith is essential in the journey of yoga, as it provides the practitioner with the strength and conviction to persist in their practice.

The Most Perfect Yogis

The verse concludes by stating that those who embody these qualities are considered the most perfect yogis. They spend their days and nights with their minds constantly fixed on the supreme being, reflecting their unwavering dedication and devotion.

In conclusion, the verse provides a rich description of the qualities of a devoted yogi. These include a deep and unwavering devotion to the supreme being, a consistent and steadfast dedication to their practice, and a supreme faith that fuels their spiritual journey. These qualities distinguish them as the most perfect yogis, devoted to their path and constantly focused on the divine.

The practice of mantra japa involves the continuous repetition of a specific mantra or divine name. It serves as a means to calm the mind, transcend the limitations of the ego, and establish a deep connection with the divine. Through the regular and disciplined repetition of the mantra, one gradually attunes their consciousness to the divine vibration and experiences a sense of oneness with the Supreme.

As individuals engage in mantra japa, they develop mental alertness and focus. The constant repetition of the sacred words helps to quiet the restless mind and bring about a state of inner stillness. It allows one to transcend the fluctuations of thoughts and emotions, enabling them to experience the pure awareness that lies beyond the mind.

Furthermore, mantra japa creates an atmosphere of divine presence and spiritual energy. The vibrations generated through the repetition of the mantra permeate one's being and the surrounding environment, creating a sacred space for inner transformation and growth. It acts as a powerful catalyst for purifying the mind, dissolving negative tendencies, and awakening the dormant spiritual potential within.

The practice of mantra japa is not limited to specific times or places. It is a continuous and integrated aspect of one's life. Whether engaged in daily chores, at work, or in solitude, the practitioner remains connected to the divine through the repetition of the sacred mantra. The mantra becomes a constant companion, guiding and uplifting the individual in every moment.

Through the regular practice of mantra japa, individuals experience a deepening of their spiritual connection and an expansion of consciousness. The repetition of the divine name becomes a source of inspiration, love, and guidance. It cultivates devotion, surrender, and an unwavering faith in the divine presence.

As Amma beautifully expresses, the practice of mantra japa is a reminder to always repeat the divine name, regardless of time or place. It is a way to infuse every aspect of life with sacredness and to align oneself with the divine presence. By constantly chanting the mantra with alertness and sincerity, one attains mental purity, deepens their spiritual understanding, and opens the door to profound experiences of unity and oneness.

So, mantra japa is a powerful practice in the realm of Advaita Vedanta. It serves as a means to cultivate mental purity, deepen spiritual connection, and realize the inherent unity of all things. Through the regular repetition of the sacred mantra, individuals transcend the limitations of the ego, attune their consciousness to the divine vibration, and experience the blissful awareness of their true nature. With each repetition, they draw closer to the divine, expanding their capacity for love, devotion, and Self-realization.

Story

A young aspirant approached the sage with great reverence and shared his longing for spiritual growth. The sage, recognizing the young aspirant's sincerity and eagerness, imparted to him the practice of mantra japa. He gave the young aspirant a sacred mantra, a divine name to repeat, and explained its significance in attaining mental purity and deepening one's spiritual connection.

With the mantra in his heart, the young aspirant returned to the village and began his daily practice of mantra japa. He would wake up before sunrise, find a quiet corner in his humble home, and immerse himself in the repetition of the divine name. With each repetition, his mind grew calmer, and he felt a deep sense of peace and contentment.

Young aspirant remarkable transformation in his presence and demeanor. His words were filled with kindness and wisdom, and his actions reflected a selfless and compassionate nature.

People were naturally drawn to his radiant energy and sought his counsel in times of need.

One day, the village faced a severe drought, and the crops withered under the scorching sun. Despair and worry filled the hearts of the villagers as they struggled to find a solution. Young aspirant, guided by his spiritual practice, realized that he had a role to play in uplifting the village.

He called upon the villagers and shared with them the power of mantra japa and the significance of surrendering to the divine will. He encouraged everyone to come together and chant the sacred mantra with sincerity and devotion, offering their collective prayers for rain and prosperity.

The villagers, inspired by the young aspirant 's words and the depth of his spiritual connection, embraced his suggestion wholeheartedly. Every day, they gathered in the village square, chanting the divine name with unwavering faith and hope. Their hearts filled with gratitude and trust in the divine plan.

ॐ

64. *"Children, Japa should be practiced constantly with each breath. It is the instrument to subside restless mind, with its unending thought waves. The impurities in the mind will disappear, without you even being aware of it. Then the mind will always remain peaceful, bestowing good health to both mind and body." -Amma*

The practice of Japa, the repetitive chanting of a sacred mantra, holds great significance in the path of Advaita Vedanta. It is a powerful tool to calm the restless mind, dissolve impurities, and awaken the innate divinity within us. Amma, with her profound wisdom, encourages us to embrace Japa as a constant companion, a practice that can transform our lives and lead us to a state of profound peace and well-being.

In the journey of Self-realization, the mind is often the biggest obstacle. It is constantly bombarded with thoughts, desires, and distractions, causing restlessness and agitation. Through the practice of Japa, we learn to subside the turbulent waves of the mind and cultivate inner stillness. By repeating the sacred mantra with each breath, we redirect the mind's energy and focus, allowing it to dwell in the sacred vibrations of the divine name.

As we engage in the constant practice of Japa, something magical begins to happen. The impurities and distractions that once clouded our minds gradually dissipate. We become more aware of the subtle shifts taking place within us, as the mind becomes clearer and more serene. The repetitive chanting of the mantra acts as a purifying agent, cleansing our thoughts, emotions, and intentions, and bringing us closer to our true nature.

Amma reminds us that the benefits of Japa extend beyond the realm of the mind. It is a practice that nourishes not only our mental well-being but also our physical and spiritual health. The harmonizing vibrations of the mantra reverberate through our entire being, creating a profound sense of balance and harmony. The mind and body become aligned, and we experience a deep sense of inner peace and tranquility.

Through constant Japa, the mind becomes a tool of self-transformation. We become more attuned to our inner world and develop a heightened sense of self-awareness. The repetitive chanting of the mantra serves as a constant reminder of our divine essence, allowing us to connect with the eternal presence that resides within us. As the mind becomes more peaceful and centered, our thoughts and actions naturally align with higher principles and values.

The practice of Japa also deepens our connection with the divine. It is a way of establishing a personal relationship with the higher power, allowing us to experience the presence of the divine in our daily lives. The mantra becomes a bridge that spans the gap between the finite and the infinite, enabling us to commune with the divine and receive its blessings and grace.

In the non-dualistic Vedanta view, the practice of Japa leads us to the realization that we are not separate from the divine. It helps us transcend the limitations of the individual self and recognize the inherent unity of all existence. Through the constant repetition of the mantra, we dissolve the illusion of separateness and merge into the boundless ocean of oneness.

Amma's guidance on the practice of constant Japa is a reminder of the profound potential that lies within each one of us. It is an invitation to embark on a sacred journey of self-discovery and transformation. Through the power of Japa, we can transcend the restless mind, purify our being, and awaken to the eternal truth of our divine nature.

Story
One day, a young man approached a sage, seeking answers to the fundamental questions of life. Young man was overwhelmed by the complexities of the world and was searching for a deeper understanding of his existence. He yearned to find true peace and happiness, free from the constant fluctuations of the mind.

With humility and sincerity, the young man approached the sage and bowed before him. The sage, with a gentle smile, welcomed him and invited him to sit down. Young man poured out his heart, expressing his desire to experience a sense of unity, love, and purpose in life. He sought guidance on how to overcome the challenges of the mind and find lasting peace.

The sage listened attentively to the young man's words, his eyes radiating a profound sense of compassion. He began to share the teachings of the Advaita Vedanta way, guiding young man towards Self-realization and liberation from the illusions of the mind.

The sage explained to the young man that the key to transcending the fluctuations of the mind lies in understanding the nature of the self. He emphasized the importance of realizing that one's true essence is beyond the limitations of the individual ego. The sage described the self as an eternal, unchanging presence that resides within every being, interconnected with the entire universe.

He shared stories and analogies to help the young man grasp the concept of non-duality, where the apparent separateness of individuals and objects is an illusion. The sage emphasized that the ultimate reality is a unified consciousness, where everything is interconnected and interdependent.

Young man listened intently, his mind gradually opening up to a new understanding of his own existence. The sage encouraged him to engage in practices such as meditation, self-inquiry, and selfless service to cultivate self-awareness and develop a deeper connection with the true self.

ॐ

Prayers

65. "Our prayers should be 'O lord let me become a Purer and purer instrument in your hands." -Amma

In the realm of Advaita Vedanta, prayers are seen as a means to cultivate a deeper connection with the divine and align oneself with the eternal Truth. It is not about seeking external fulfillment or gratification but rather a heartfelt surrender to the divine will and a yearning to become a pure instrument of divine grace.

The essence of selfless service and spiritual humility comes from pure heart, so, let's delve into the statement.

Prayer for Purity

Amma emphasizes the significance of aspiring for purity. Purity is not merely about moral rectitude but also about clarity of intention and the removal of selfish desires. It implies the willingness to align oneself with a higher purpose or divine will.

The Instrument in God's Hands

This suggests surrender, humility, and an openness to being used for a higher purpose. The metaphor implies that we are not the doers of our actions but channels through which divine will operates.

The Path of Selflessness

Here, prayer relates to the path of selflessness. As instruments in God's hands, we surrender our ego and our desires, aligning ourselves with the divine. This alignment often manifests in the form of selfless service or Seva, where actions are performed not for personal gain but for the welfare of others.

The Power of Humble Prayer

In asking to become a purer instrument, we acknowledge our imperfections and express a willingness to improve and grow. This humility opens us to divine grace, enabling personal transformation and spiritual progress.

So, Amma's quote encapsulates the essence of spiritual surrender, humility, and selfless service. It suggests that our prayers should reflect not a desire for personal gain, but a longing to be of service to the divine and, by extension, to all of creation. The Gita also says in verse 5:13 as-

sarva-karmāṇi manasā sannyasyāste sukhaṁ vaśhī
nava-dvāre pure dehī naiva kurvan na kārayan

– Bhagavad Gita 5:13

The embodied man of self-control, having given up all actions mentally, continues happily in the town of nine gates, without doing or causing (others) to do anything at all.

This verse delves into the nature of the self, its relationship to actions, and the understanding of the enlightened versus unenlightened individual. Let's break down these ideas into different sections.

Renunciation of Actions

The verse begins with a discussion of how a person can live happily by mentally giving up all actions through discriminating wisdom. This implies observing actions without identifying with them, which leads to freedom from the activities of speech, mind, and body.

The Nine-Gated Town

The body is metaphorically described as a 'town with nine gates', referring to the nine openings in the human body. It implies that the body, like a town, is inhabited by various faculties (the organs, mind, intellect, and objects) that serve its needs and are productive of various results and experiences. In this 'town', the embodied one, after renouncing all actions, resides.

Perception of the Self

The verse highlights the difference in the perception of the self between enlightened and unenlightened individuals. The unenlightened person perceives the body and organs as the Self, while the enlightened individual realizes the Self as distinct from the body and its organs. This distinction is essential for understanding the notion of 'being in the body', similar to being in a house.

Renunciation and Discriminating Wisdom: The verse underscores that it is reasonable to mentally renounce the actions of others, which have been ignorantly superimposed on the supreme Self. This is due to the discriminating wisdom, which allows the individual to stay in the body, yet distinct from it, like staying in a house.

The Self: Devoid of Direct or Indirect Agentship

The verse concludes by emphasizing that the Self, by its nature, has neither direct nor indirect agentship. It does not act, nor is it affected.

To summarize, the verse presents a deep dive into the nature of the Self, the process of mentally renouncing actions, and the distinct perceptions of the enlightened and unenlightened individuals. The ultimate emphasis is on the transcendental nature of the Self that remains unaffected by actions and their consequences.

ॐ

Meditation

66. "Meditation is the technique that allows you to shut the doors and windows of the senses, so that you can look within and see your True Self. Meditation, prayer and chanting mantra should become a spontaneous part of your life. In the morning, chant the holy name for at least ten minutes after your bath. Meditate at least for a little while. Do the same in the evening." -Amma

Meditation is a profound practice that takes us on a journey of self-discovery and inner transformation. It is a technique that allows us to quiet the mind, transcend the limitations of the ego, and connect with the deeper aspects of our being. Through meditation, we can access the realms of pure consciousness and experience the truth of our existence.

Amma, in her wisdom, emphasizes the importance of making meditation, prayer, and chanting mantra a spontaneous part of our lives. She encourages us to create a sacred space within ourselves where we can shut the doors and windows of the senses and turn our attention inward. By setting aside dedicated time for meditation, we create an opportunity to dive deep into the ocean of our own consciousness and experience the vastness and expansiveness of our true nature.

In the morning, Amma suggests chanting the holy name for at least ten minutes after our bath. This practice serves as a beautiful way to start the day, invoking a sense of devotion and opening ourselves to the divine presence within. The repetition of the sacred mantra creates a rhythm that soothes the mind and prepares us for the stillness and silence of meditation.

In the evening, Amma encourages us to once again engage in meditation. This practice helps us to unwind, let go of the day's experiences, and find inner peace and clarity before entering into the realm of sleep. By dedicating this time to meditation, we create a space for self-reflection, introspection, and connection with the divine.

In this state of deep meditation, we come to realize our true Self. We recognize that beyond the thoughts, emotions, and sensory experiences, there is a timeless and unchanging essence within us. We awaken to the eternal presence of pure consciousness, which is our true nature.

Through regular meditation, we cultivate a greater sense of inner peace, clarity, and harmony. We become aware of the divine qualities that reside within us and begin to embody them in our daily lives. It is a practice that brings us closer to the truth of who we are and helps us align our thoughts, words, and actions with that truth. It is through the regular and sincere practice of meditation that we can experience the fullness of our being and awaken to the infinite potential that lies within us.

ātmetyevopāsīta, atra hyete sarva ekam bhavanti|
tadetatpadanīyamasya sarvasya yadayamātmā, anena
hyetatsarvaṃ veda | yathā ha vai padenānuvindedevam;
kīrtiṃ ślokaṃ vindate ya evaṃ veda ||

– Brihadaranyika Upanishads 1-4-7

The Self alone is to be meditated upon or recognized upon, for all these are unified in It. Of all these, this Self alone should be realized, for one knows all these through It, just as one may get (an animal) through its footprints. He who knows It as such obtains fame and association (with his relatives).

The Purpose of Self-Realization
So, why the 'Self' should be the primary object of realization. The response uses the analogy of tracking an animal through its

footprints to illustrate the point: once you find the animal (the 'Self'), you automatically find everything else, as everything is contained within the 'Self'.

This particular verse emphasizes the nature of the ultimate reality (Brahman) and the individual soul (Atman) and the importance of recognizing and meditating upon the Self (Atman).

The Primacy of the Self

This verse says "the Self alone is to be meditated upon." This assertion underscores the primary place of the Self (Atman) in spiritual practice. It suggests that all spiritual efforts should be directed toward understanding and realizing one's true nature, which is the Self.

The Unifying Principle of the Self

Here, it says "for all these are unified in It." This statement suggests that the Self is not just the individual consciousness, but also the fundamental unity behind the diversity of existence. The Atman is the underlying principle that unifies all beings and phenomena.

The Path to Universal Knowledge

Focus on the statement "for one knows all these through It." It implies that true knowledge of the world comes through understanding the Self. By realizing the Self, one attains universal knowledge, as the Self is the essence of all that exists.

The Fruits of Self-Realization

So, the benefits of realizing the Self - "He who knows It as such obtains fame and association." Here, fame and association could be interpreted metaphorically as spiritual fulfillment and unity with the divine. This part suggests that Self-realization leads not just to intellectual understanding, but also to spiritual bliss and fulfillment. This verse from the Br.Up underscores the pivotal role of Self-realization in spiritual practice and the attainment of universal knowledge. It implies that by knowing the Self, one understands the unity underlying the multiplicity of existence and attains spiritual fulfillment.

Therefore Amma's guidance on the importance of meditation serves as a reminder that this practice is not separate from our daily lives but an integral part of it. By embracing meditation as a way of life, we open ourselves to the profound wisdom and transformation that it offers. Through meditation, we come to know ourselves deeply, experience inner peace and joy, and discover the eternal presence of the divine within us.

ॐ

Devotional Singing

67. "When a singer sings from the heart, he or she is in touch with divinity, with beyondness. Pure music is as big as space. It is the secret of allowing the pure sound of the universe to flow through you." -Amma

One can have spiritual connection through music. According to Amma, when a singer truly engages their emotions and sings from the heart, they are not just producing a melody but are tapping into a divine energy. This connection transcends the physical world, reaching into a realm of 'beyondness', a state that surpasses our typical understanding of existence.

So, pure music to the vastness of space. Just as space is boundless and infinite, pure music, created with sincere emotion and without any artificiality or pretense, is limitless in its depth and capacity to touch souls.

The act of producing pure music is a form of spiritual channeling. It's not about actively creating something but rather about allowing the 'pure sound of the universe' to flow through you. This implies a sense of surrender, of becoming a medium through which the universe expresses itself.

The profound spiritual experience that music can offer, both to the creator and the listener emphasizes the idea that when music is created with genuine emotion and openness, it becomes a divine language that transcends worldly barriers, connecting us to a realm beyond our ordinary perception. When a singer sings from the heart, the performance becomes more than just a physical act of producing sounds. It transcends into a spiritual experience where the singer connects with something greater than themselves, beyond the material world. The act of singing becomes a way to touch the divine, the ultimate reality that lies beyond our senses. It is a way to express emotions that are often difficult to put into words, to communicate on a deeper level with the audience, and to evoke a sense of awe and wonder. By singing from the heart, the performer taps into a universal language that can unite people of different cultures and backgrounds, and bring them together in a shared experience of beauty and transcendence. This is the essence of what Amma means when she says that a singer in touch with divinity is in touch with beyondness.

Amma's statement suggests that when a singer truly sings from their heart, they are able to connect with something greater than themselves, something beyond the physical world. By tapping into their emotions and expressing them through their music, the singer is able to touch a deeper, spiritual dimension, and become more attuned to the divine. Essentially, Amma is emphasizing the importance of singing from the heart and infusing one's music with genuine emotion and intention. In doing so, the singer can create a more meaningful and transcendent experience for both themselves and their audience.

This could be seen as a spiritual belief or a metaphorical way of describing the power and depth of music. Singing from the heart may allow a person to express themselves in a more authentic and vulnerable way, which can create a deeper emotional connection with listeners. It may also create a sense of unity or transcendence that goes beyond the physical realm.

Amma's statement suggests that when a singer sings from the heart, they are not just performing a musical act, but they are also connecting with a deeper aspect of themselves and the universe. This deeper aspect is what Amma refers to as divinity or beyondness.

By singing from the heart, a singer taps into emotions and feelings that are usually not expressed in everyday life. They are able to convey these emotions and feelings through their music, and this can create a powerful connection with their audience.

Furthermore, this connection with divinity or beyondness can be interpreted as a spiritual experience. It suggests that the act of singing can become a form of worship or a way to connect with a higher power.

Overall, Amma's statement highlights the importance of authenticity and emotional connection in singing. It also suggests that music can be a powerful tool for spiritual growth and connection.

Story

Once upon a time, there was a talented singer who had achieved great success in the music industry. However, despite all the fame and fortune, the singer felt a sense of emptiness inside. One day, while performing in front of a large audience, the singer had a profound experience. As he sang from his heart, he felt a deep connection to something beyond himself. He felt as though he was channeling a divine energy through his voice and that the music was flowing through him, rather than from him. This experience was so powerful that it changed the singer's life forever. He realized that true fulfillment came not from external success, but from a deep connection to the divine within. From that day on, he devoted his life to singing from the heart and sharing the beauty and power of music with others.

ॐ

Death

68. *"Transcending the cycle of death and rebirth is the real purpose of this life in human form. Dying to ego is real death. That death makes us immortal."* -Amma

According to the Advaita Vedanta, death is not the end but a transition from one state of being to another. It is a profound opportunity for spiritual growth and Self-realization. In vedanta, the true purpose of human life is to transcend the cycle of birth and death, and to realize our eternal nature.

sa yathā saindhavaghano'nantaro'bāhyaḥ kṛtsno
rasaghana eva, evaṃ vā are'yamātmānantaro'bāhyaḥ
kṛtsnaḥ prajñānaghana eva; etebhyo bhūtebhyaḥ
samutthāya tānyevānuvinayaṣyatiti, na pretya
saṃjñāstītyare bravīmīti hovāca yājñavalkyaḥ ||

– Brihadaranyika Upanishad 4.5.13

As a lump of salt is without interior or exterior, entire, and purely saline in taste, even so is the Self without interior or exterior, entire, and Pure Intelligence alone. (The self) comes out (as a separate entity) from these elements, and (this separateness) is destroyed with them. After attaining (this oneness) it has no more (particular) consciousness. This is what I say, my dear. So said Yājñavalkya.

The Pure Intelligence and Dissolution of Self in the Cosmic Oneness: The Yājñavalkya says, as illustrated in verse 4.5.13, the ultimate reality and nature of the Self. So, the essence of the Self, the dissolution of its individuality, and its union with the universal consciousness.

The Self: Without Interior or Exterior

He likens the Self to a lump of salt, without an interior or an exterior, but whole and purely saline. The analogy serves to drive home the point that the Self, in its truest form, is devoid of any distinction or division. It is whole and purely of one essence - Pure Intelligence. This understanding dissolves the perceived boundaries of inside and outside, highlighting the non-dual nature of the Self.

Emergence and Dissolution of Individual Consciousness

Yājñavalkya further explains that the individual self, or ego, is a result of the combination of the Pure Self with the elements. This combination gives rise to a separate identity, a particular consciousness. However, this separateness is temporary. With the dissolution of these elements, the individual self also ceases to exist. This dissolution signifies the end of personal identity and the associated limited consciousness.

Attainment of Oneness: Beyond Particular Consciousness

In the ultimate state of realization, the Self merges back into the state of pure, undifferentiated consciousness. It is akin to a lump of salt dissolving in the ocean, losing its individual identity to become one with the vastness. Yājñavalkya asserts that after attaining this oneness, the Self has no more particular consciousness. This refers to the transcendence of individual awareness and the awakening to a state of universal consciousness.

Conclusion: The Ultimate Teaching of Yājñavalkya

The essence of Yājñavalkya's teachings in this verse lies in understanding the transient nature of individual identity and the eternal, unchanging nature of the Self. It urges us to realize our true, undivided nature, which is Pure Intelligence. It is an invitation to dissolve the illusion of separateness, transcend the limitations of individual consciousness, and merge with the infinite ocean of universal consciousness.

Death

From the vedanta perspective, the true death is not the physical death of the body, but the death of the ego. The ego, with its identification with the body, mind, and individual identity, keeps us bound to the cycle of birth and death. It is the root cause of our suffering and separation from the eternal truth.

yathā nadyaḥ syandamānāḥ samudre'staṃ gacchanti
nāmarūpe vihāya |
tathā vidvānnāmarūpādvimuktaḥ parātparaṃ
puruṣamupaiti divyam ||

Mundaka Upanishad 3-2-8

Just as rivers flowing become lost in an ocean, giving up both their name and form, just so, the knower, freed from name and form, attains the bright Purusha which is beyond the avyakta (Unmanifest).

The Journey to the Divine: An Understanding of the Verse from Mundaka Upanishad 3-2-8

The verse from Mundaka Upanishad presents a profound metaphor for the spiritual journey of the individual self to the universal Self. The verse draws an analogy between rivers flowing into the ocean and the knower attaining the divine Purusha.

Rivers Merging into the Ocean: Losing Name and Form

In the first part of the verse, rivers are used as a symbol to illustrate the spiritual journey. Just as rivers, such as the Ganges, flow into the ocean and lose their individual identities, the same is true for the spiritual aspirant. Upon reaching the ocean, rivers relinquish their names and forms, symbolizing the dissolution of individuality and separateness. This metaphor beautifully encapsulates the process of unification and oneness.

The Knower's Journey: Transcending Name and Form:
Drawing a parallel to the rivers, the verse then speaks of the

'knower'. The knower, in this context, refers to the spiritual seeker who, through knowledge and understanding, transcends the limitations of name and form. These limitations, created by ignorance, represent our identification with the physical body and the ego, which binds us to the material world and blinds us to our true nature.

Attaining the Divine Purusha: The Ultimate Liberation

Upon freeing oneself from these shackles of name and form, the knower attains the divine Purusha. The Purusha, often translated as the universal Self or the cosmic man, is beyond the 'avyakta', the unmanifested or the indescribable. This attainment signifies the ultimate liberation, the union with the universal consciousness, mirroring the rivers' merging into the ocean.

Conclusion: The Essence of the Spiritual Journey

In essence, this verse from Mundaka Upanishad elucidates the spiritual journey from individuality to universality, from ignorance to knowledge, and from bondage to liberation. It underlines the need to transcend the limitations of name and form to realize and merge with the divine Purusha, much like rivers losing their identity in the vastness of the ocean.

Amma's words "Dying to ego is real death. That death makes us immortal" reflect a profound truth of Upanishads mentioned above, about the nature of existence. Ego, in this context, refers to our attachment to our own sense of identity, our desires, and our fears. It is the voice inside us that constantly seeks validation, recognition, and success.

Story

One day, a wise sage visited the king and challenged him to let go of his ego. The king scoffed at the suggestion, believing that his ego was what had made him successful and powerful.

Undeterred, the sage continued to visit the king and share stories and teachings about the importance of humility and compassion. Slowly but surely, the king began to see the value in these teachings and started to let go of his ego.

As he shed his attachment to his sense of self-importance, the king began to feel a sense of freedom and connection to something greater than himself. He realized that his previous sense of self had been limiting and had prevented him from experiencing true happiness and fulfillment.

The king continued on this path of self-discovery, eventually becoming known as a wise and just ruler who treated all of his subjects with kindness and compassion. He was beloved by his people and his legacy lived on long after his physical death. In this parable, the king's journey to let go of his ego represents the process of dying to the ego that Amma speaks of. Through this process, the king was able to shed his attachment to his individual identity and connect with something greater, ultimately achieving a sense of immortality through the positive impact he had on the world.

ॐ

69. *"Death is not complete annihilation. It is a pause. It is like pressing the pause button on a tape recorder." -Amma*

In the Advaita Vedanta view, death is not the end of our existence but rather a temporary cessation of the physical form. It is a transition from one state of being to another, much like pressing the pause button on a tape recorder.

Vedanta teaches us that our true essence is beyond the limitations of the physical body and the changing circumstances of life. We are eternal consciousness, the unchanging witness to the experiences of birth, life, and death. Death is merely a momentary pause in the grand tapestry of existence.

Just as a tape recorder continues to hold the recorded sound even when it is paused, our consciousness remains untouched and unaffected by the process of death. It transcends the temporary nature of the physical form and continues its journey in the realm of the eternal.

The understanding of death from the Advaita Vedanta perspective brings profound comfort and liberation. It reminds us that our true nature is beyond birth and death, beyond the transitory experiences of this world. We are not limited to the physical body; rather, we are infinite consciousness experiencing itself through the play of life.

Recognizing death as a pause rather than an end allows us to cultivate a deeper sense of peace, acceptance, and detachment. We can embrace the transient nature of life while simultaneously connecting with the eternal aspect of our being.

vāsānsi jīrṇāni yathā vihāya navāni gṛihṇāti naro 'parāṇi tathā śharīrāṇi vihāya jīrṇānya nyāni sanyāti navāni dehī

– Bhagavad Gita 2:22

As after rejecting worn out clothes a man takes up other new ones, likewise after rejecting worn out bodies the embodied one unites with other new ones.

The Metaphor of Change:
The nature of the soul and its relationship with the physical body. This verse presents a vision of the human body as a temporary garment for the eternal soul.

The Temporality of the Physical Body
The verse begins with a comparison: "As after rejecting worn-out clothes a man takes up other new ones." This analogy underlines the temporary nature of our physical existence. Just

as we discard old, worn-out clothes and replace them with new ones, so does the soul discard an old and worn-out body.
The Unchanging Nature of the Soul
The next part of the verse extends the metaphor to the spiritual realm: "Likewise after rejecting worn-out bodies the embodied one unites with other new ones." Here, the "embodied one" refers to the soul, which, unlike the body, is unchanging and eternal. While the physical body is subject to aging, decay, and death, the soul remains constant and immortal.
The Cycle of Birth and Death
This verse thus presents a perspective on the cycle of birth and death. The process of the soul leaving one body and entering a new one is likened to changing clothes. This metaphor provides a comforting image of death, not as an end, but as a transition to a new phase of existence.
Conclusion: A Shift in Perception
So, Amma invites us to shift our perception of life and death. By viewing the body as a temporary garment for the soul, we can understand death as a natural part of life's cycle, akin to changing clothes. This perspective can alleviate the fear of death, bringing peace and acceptance in its place.

jātasya hi dhruvo mrityur dhruvaṁ janma mritasya cha
tasmād aparihārye 'rthe na tvaṁ shochitum arhasi

– Bhagavad Gita 2:27

For death of anyone born is certain, and of the dead (re-) birth is certainty. Therefore you ought not to grieve over an inevitable fact.

Understanding the Certainty of Life and Death:
This verse presents a profound understanding of the inevitable cycle of life and death. The verse emphasizes the certainty of

death and rebirth, suggesting that grief over such an inescapable reality is unnecessary.

Life's Inevitable Cycle: Birth and Death

The verse begins by stating a universal truth: "For death of anyone born is certain." This phrase underlines that birth and death are two sides of the same coin. Every being that has taken birth in this physical world is subject to the law of mortality, making death a definite reality for all living beings.

The Certainty of Rebirth

The second part of the verse presents the concept of rebirth: "And of the dead (re-)birth is a certainty." The cycle of life, death, and rebirth, known as Samsara. The soul, which is considered eternal, takes on various physical forms through numerous cycles of birth and death. Thus, rebirth after death is seen as a certainty.

Transcending Grief over the Inevitable

Drawing on the inevitability of death and rebirth, the verse then advises against grief over such facts: "Therefore you ought not to grieve over an inevitable fact." This message encourages acceptance of the natural processes of life and death. It emphasizes that grief is unnecessary and unhelpful, as it cannot alter the fundamental truths of existence.

Conclusion: Embracing Life's Inevitability

So, Amma provides a profound understanding of the certainty of life's cycle. It invites us to accept and embrace the inevitability of birth, death, and rebirth as integral parts of existence. By doing so, it suggests we can transcend unnecessary grief, leading to a more serene and accepting approach to life's inevitable transitions.

Story

Once there was a wise man who lived in a small village. People would often come to him seeking his advice on various matters.

One day, a man came to him feeling very sad and said, "My dear wife has passed away. I feel so lost and alone. Is this the end of everything?"

The wise man replied, "Death is not the end, my son. It is just a pause in the journey of the soul. It is like pressing the pause button on a tape recorder. The recording is not gone, it is just on hold. Similarly, the soul continues on its journey, just as the recording will resume once the pause button is released."

The man was comforted by the wise man's words and went away feeling more at peace. He realized that his wife was not completely gone, but that her soul would continue on its journey, just as his own would one day.

The wise man's words brought comfort to many in the village who had lost loved ones. They began to see death not as an end, but as a transition to a new phase of existence. The wise man's teachings on death and the afterlife brought hope and comfort to many people in the village.

ॐ

Oneness

70. "Children, We must remember that man is not an island, totally isolated and disconnected from others. We are all part of a universal chain, or the universal consciousness. What happens to one happens to all. There are sparks of love inherent in everyone and God's grace is everywhere. Try and see the oneness in all of creation. " -Amma

In the Advaita Vedanta view, the concept of oneness is fundamental to understanding the nature of reality. It teaches us that despite the appearance of separateness, there is an underlying unity that connects all beings and things in the universe. This understanding of oneness has profound implications for how we perceive ourselves, others, and the world around us.

Vedanta tells us that at the deepest level, we are not separate individuals but expressions of the same universal consciousness. We are like waves in the vast ocean, seemingly distinct but ultimately part of the same infinite whole. This recognition of oneness invites us to shift our perspective and see beyond the boundaries of the ego, embracing a broader sense of identity that encompasses all of existence.

When we cultivate the awareness of oneness, we realize that the divisions we create based on race, nationality, religion, or any other external factors are merely illusory. We understand that behind the outer forms and differences, there is a shared essence that unifies all beings. This awareness fosters a sense of compassion, empathy, and interconnectedness, enabling us to treat others with love and respect.

In the Advaita Vedanta view, the realization of oneness is not merely an intellectual understanding but a direct experience of the unity of consciousness. Through practices such as meditation, self-inquiry, and contemplation, we can transcend the limitations of the ego and directly perceive the underlying unity that connects us all. In this state of expanded awareness, we recognize that every individual is a unique expression of the divine, and their well-being is intertwined with our own. The understanding of oneness brings a profound shift in our perception of the world. We begin to see the interconnectedness of all things and recognize that our actions and choices have ripple effects that extend far beyond our immediate circle. We develop a deep sense of responsibility towards the well-being of all beings and the environment, knowing that what we do to others, we ultimately do to ourselves.

maghavanmartyaṃ vā idaṃ śarīramāttaṃ mṛtyunā tada syāmṛtasyāśarīrasyātmano'dhiṣṭhānamātto vai saśarīraḥ priyāpriyābhyāṃ na vai saśarīrasya sataḥ priyāpriyayorapa hatirastyaśarīraṃ vāva santaṃ na priyāpriye spṛśataḥ ॥

Chāndogya Upaniṣad 8.12.1

Prajāpati said: "Mortal indeed, is this body, in the grip of death. But of the immortal Self, the bodiless, is this the abode. The embodied is surely In the grip of pleasure and pain, no release from these is possible for it. The unembodied these cannot touch, neither pleasure nor pain"

The purpose of Prajāpati's teaching in the Chāndogya, as of Yājñavalkya's analysis of the three avasthās, in the Bṛhadāranyaka, is to exhibit the true nature of the Self which is oneness, as free from the defects due to the association with the objects of the states of waking, dream and sleep.

The Mortal Body and the Unbodied Self: Understanding the Nature of Pleasure and Pain

The mortal body and the unbodied Self. It explores the relationship between the body and the Self, the nature of pleasure and pain, and how the understanding of one's true nature of oneness can lead to liberation from suffering. The mantra also highlights the significance of the distinction between the mortal body and the immortal Self in creating a sense of disgust for the body and illuminating the path to Self-realization.

I. The Mortal Body and the Immutable Self:

Expounding on the mortal nature of the body: The body is subject to death and decay, constantly held by the grasp of mortality.

The implications of perceiving the body as mortal: Understanding the mortal nature of the body evokes a profound sense of fear and discontentment.

The role of disgust in turning away from identifying the body as the self: By cultivating a sense of disgust for the body, one can detach from the notion of selfhood associated with it.

II. The Abode of the bodiless Self:

The body as the dwelling place of the self: The body, along with the senses, mind, and intellect, serves as the abode for the being experiencing the states of waking, dreaming, and deep sleep.

The distinction between the body and the self: The self is immortal and devoid of the qualities that afflict the body, senses, and mind.

Denoting the unbodied nature of the Self: The term "immortal" "oneness" signifies the bodiless essence of the self, emphasizing its indivisible and formless nature.

III. Becoming "Bodied" and the Experience of Pleasure and Pain:

The Self's identification with the body: Due to ignorance of their true nature, individuals mistakenly perceive themselves as the body, leading to the notion of "I am the Body."

The entanglement with pleasure and pain: As long as the Self considers itself embodied, it becomes susceptible to the continuous cycle of pleasure and pain caused by the merits and demerits accrued through actions.

The inability to escape the effects of pleasure and pain: While embodied, the Self perceives pleasure and pain as its own, and thus, they persistently influence its experience.

IV. Liberation from Pleasure and Pain through Self-Realization: Transcending the influence of pleasure and pain: Upon gaining knowledge of their true unbodied nature, individuals free themselves from the grip of pleasure and pain.

Pleasure and pain's inability to touch the realized Self: Merit and demerit, the root cause of pleasure and pain, cannot affect the unbodied Self, as it transcends the realm of actions and their consequences.

The absence of merit and demerit in the unbodied self: The inherent nature of the Self precludes the existence of merit and demerit, rendering the appearance of their effects distant.

Conclusion

The mantra explores the mortal nature of the body, the concept of the unbodied self, which is oneness and the relationship between pleasure and pain. By understanding the distinction between the body and the Self and realizing one's true nature, individuals can liberate themselves from the ceaseless cycle of pleasure and pain. This knowledge serves as a guiding light, leading individuals on the path to Self-realization and the transcendence of suffering.

Oneness also dissolves the barriers of separation and fosters a sense of love and compassion. When we recognize the inherent divinity in every being, we naturally treat others with kindness, understanding, and respect. We let go of judgments, prejudices, and divisive attitudes, and instead embrace the unity that binds us all.

In conclusion, the Advaita Vedanta view of oneness teaches us that we are not separate individuals but unity expressions of the same universal consciousness. By realizing our inherent unity with all beings, we cultivate compassion, empathy, and a deep sense of responsibility towards the well-being of others. Embracing the awareness of oneness allows us to live in harmony with the world, recognizing the divine spark that exists within each and every being.

ॐ

Unity

71. "May we all be able to light the inner lamp within ourselves and bring light to others as well. May everyone have the mental strength to achieve this. May the grace of the Paramatma bless my children." –Amma

Amma's Blessings: Illuminating the Inner Lamp and Spreading Light

Amma's blessings, which inspire individuals to ignite the lamp of Self-realization, cultivate mental strength, and receive the divine grace of the Paramatma.

Igniting the Inner Lamp:

Amma's blessings carry the profound message of lighting the inner lamp within ourselves. Just as a lamp dispels darkness and illuminates its surroundings, Amma urges us to awaken the divine light that resides within our hearts. Through her unconditional love, she instills in us the realization that we are not separate from the universal consciousness. Amma's blessings inspire us to embark on a spiritual journey, seeking Self-realization and discovering the innate divinity within.

Spreading Light to Others:

Amma's blessings extend beyond individual transformation; they also empower us to share our light with others. She reminds us that true spirituality lies in serving humanity and embracing the interconnectedness of all beings. By kindling the flame of compassion and selflessness, Amma's blessings encourage us to engage in acts of kindness, service, and support for those in need. Her profound love and blessings inspire us to become beacons of light, bringing hope, solace, and upliftment to others.

Cultivating Mental Strength:

Amma's blessings encompass the cultivation of mental strength. She recognizes the challenges and hardships faced by individuals in their spiritual and worldly pursuits. Through her divine grace, Amma imparts mental fortitude, resilience, and the power to overcome obstacles. Her blessings infuse us with inner strength, enabling us to navigate the complexities of life with clarity, determination, and unwavering faith.

Grace of the Paramatma:

Amma's blessings are intertwined with the divine grace of the Paramatma, the supreme reality that transcends all limitations. As a spiritual guide and embodiment of love, Amma invokes the grace of the Paramatma upon her children, encompassing both spiritual seekers and humanity at large. This divine grace brings solace, healing, and transformation, nurturing the growth of individuals and guiding them towards the path of Self-realization.

Conclusion

Amma's blessings are a source of profound inspiration, guiding individuals on their spiritual journeys and instilling in them the values of love, compassion, and selflessness. Her teachings and actions empower us to awaken the inner lamp of Self-realization, share our light with others, cultivate mental strength, and receive the grace of the Paramatma. May we all embrace Amma's blessings, illuminating our own lives and becoming beacons of light in the world, spreading love, peace, and joy to all beings.

ॐ

Amma & Advaita Vedanta

When we deeply reflect on Amma's words, her life and her love, expressed through her actions, glances, innumerable activities aimed at improving the lives of countless beings around the world, we cannot help but be drawn to Amma. Love and devotion towards Amma is a natural result for anyone who is blessed and fortunate enough to be in her presence.

At the same time, as we elaborate on Amma's words here, we cannot help but also draw parallels with the great verses from the Upanishads. To study Amma's words and to observe Amma's life, is to witness Advaita Vedanta in action. Amma lives as one who is established in Brahman. In Amma's 108 names, the first mantra is:

"Om purna-bramha-svarupinyai namah"

This verse salutes Amma as the complete manifestation of the Absolute Truth, which is often referred to as Brahman. It acknowledges her as a divine presence embodying the fullness and completeness of the ultimate reality.

In the second mantra:

"Om saccidananda murttaye namah"

This verse recognizes Amma as the embodiment of Sat (Existence), Chit (Knowledge), and Ananda (Bliss). It signifies her as a being of profound wisdom and divine bliss, representing the essence of existence itself.

Through these 2 mantras, Amma's state is being broadcasted. In Advaita Vedanta, the knower of Brahman is one with Brahman (Bramhavid Bramhaiva Bhavati).

For those unfamiliar with Advaita Vedanta, and come from a religious background where the word "God" is often used, it would be helpful to understand the concept of "Ishwara", and its relation to "Brahman".

Ishwara: Ishwara is often referred to as the non-dual aspect of the divine. It represents the aspect of the ultimate reality (Brahman) that is associated with creation, maintenance, and dissolution of the universe. Ishwara is characterized by qualities such as omniscience, omnipotence, and omnipresence. It is the divine presence that can be worshiped and approached through devotion and prayer. In the realm of duality, Ishwara is the manifestation of the divine that individuals relate to on a personal level, seeking guidance, protection, and divine grace. When most people refer to "God", they are referring to Ishwara.

Brahman: Brahman is the absolute, ultimate reality in non-dual Vedanta. It is formless, attributeless, and beyond all concepts and limitations. Brahman is described as the source, substratum, and essence of all existence. It transcends all dualities, including the duality of creator and creation. Realization of Brahman is the goal of spiritual seekers in non-dual Vedanta, leading to the direct experience of oneness and the dissolution of individual identity.

Non-dual Perspective: In non-dual Vedanta, the ultimate understanding is that Ishwara and Brahman are not fundamentally separate but are different expressions or aspects of the same underlying reality. Ishwara can be seen as the personalized, manifest aspect of Brahman, while Brahman is the unmanifest, transcendent source from which everything emanates. Ultimately, the journey of spiritual realization is to recognize the non-dual nature of reality, where there is no separation between the worshiper (Jiva), the worshiped (Ishwara), and the ultimate reality (Brahman). The goal is to move beyond dualistic perception and experience the oneness of Brahman, realizing that Ishwara is an expression of that oneness.

In directing our love and devotion to a Guru established in Brahman, with the awareness that by doing so, we are, in fact, connecting with the Truth that is within all of us, our love for Amma brings us to the recognition that we are also the same Sat-Chit-Ananda swarūpa (embodiment), just as Amma is.

ॐ

Conclusion

These pearls of wisdom guide us on a transformative journey, reminding us of the eternal truths that transcend time and space. Amma's teachings resonate with the essence of our interconnectedness and the profound impact of love and compassion in our lives. Her life itself is a testament to the boundless possibilities of a heart filled with love. Through her, we learn that true happiness lies in acts of selflessness and in fostering a deep sense of compassion for all beings.

Amma's teachings touch the depths of our hearts and awaken our innate potential to love unconditionally. We offer our heartfelt gratitude to Amma for her tireless dedication to humanity. Her life is a beacon of light that dispels the darkness of suffering and ignorance. Amma's wisdom knows no boundaries, and her love knows no limits.

Through these quotes, may her love and wisdom continue to inspire and guide us in our pursuit of a more compassionate and loving world. As we absorb the wisdom contained within these pages, may we, too, become instruments of love, peace, and transformation in the world.

Together, let us celebrate the extraordinary life and teachings of Amma and endeavor to carry her message of love and selflessness into every corner of our lives. With boundless love and gratitude.

Swami Amritachitswarupananda Puri

ॐ

Glossary

A

Abhāsa – fallacious appearance.

Abhāsa vāda – A causation theory in non-dualistic Vedanta, which maintains that the jiva or the individual soul is an illusory appearance of the Absolute, and has no real independent status

ācharya – a spiritual guide or teacher.

adhiśthana – substratum; that upon which something rests.

advaita – not (a) two (dvaita); non-dual philosophy.

aham – I; the ego

ahankāra – egoism; the concept of Individuality

ajñāna – (spiritual) ignorance.

akśhara – imperishable; unchangeable.

anādi – without any beginning

ānanda – "true" happiness; usually called "bliss" and is an aspect of our true nature

anirvachanīya – indescribable. Used to describe the nature of māya.

anitya – transient

aparoksha – immediate or direct (relating to gaining of knowledge, i.e. does not require application of reason).

asat – non-existent; unreal

ātma – the Self; the individual Self

āvaraṅa – the veiling power of māya. See māya, Vikśhepa.

avasthā – state; usually is used in the context of one of the three states of waking, dream or sleep

avidyā – ignorance i.e. that which prevents us from realizing the Self. See also māya.

avyakta – unmanifest

B

bādha - sublation. The adjective is bādhita, meaning negated, contradictory or false.

bhakti - devotion

bhāvana - contemplation.

bheda - separation; distinction; difference;

bhrama - confusion

bodha - knowing, understanding, awareness

Brahman - the universal Self, Absolute

buddhi - intellect

C

chaitanya - consciousness, awareness.

chidābhāsa - false appearance or reflection (Abhāsa) of Awareness (chit) - i.e. the ego.

chit - Awareness; consciousness. Also see satchidananda.

chitta - the aspect of the mind responsible for memory.

D

dama - restraint over the senses; one of the six qualities that form part of Shankara's chatushtaya sampatti.

darshana - audience or meeting (with a guru); viewpoint; one of the six classical Indian philosophical systems (purvamimamsa, uttaramimamsa, nyaya, vaisheshika, samkhya, yoga).

deha - body

dharma - Appropriate conduct, performed with the right attitude at the appropriate time. One of the four puruShArtha-s or aims of life, according to Sanatana Dharma.

dhyāna - meditation

duhkha - pain, sorrow, trouble.

dvaita - duality, philosophy of dualism; belief that God and the atman are separate entities. Madhva is the scholar most often associated with this philosophy.

G

guńa – According to classical sāmkhya philosophy, creation is made up of three "qualities," sattva, rajas and tamas. Everything - matter, thoughts, feelings - is 'made up of' these three in varying degrees and the relative proportions determine the nature of the thing in question.

guru – One's spiritual teacher

I

Isvara – God; creator of the material universe through the power of māya.

J

jagat – the world

jāgrat – the waking state of consciousness.

japa – the repetition of a mantra;

jijñāsā – the desire to know (oneself). One who desires to know oneself; a seeker is called a jijñāsu.

jīva – the identification of the Self with a body and mind;

jīvanmukti – liberation while still living in the body

jñāna – knowledge; wisdom

Jñāni – literally, one who is endowed with knowledge; a sage; often used to refer to one who has realized the Self.

K

kalpita – fabricated, artificial; invented; supposed.

karma – literally "action" but generally used to refer to the "law" whereby actions carried out now will have their lawful effects in the future

M

mahavākya – maha means "great"; vākya means "statement." These are the pointers to the non-dual Self used in Vedanta.

manana – Reflection on what has been heard (shravańa) from the guru. See also shravana, nididhyāsana.

manas – the aspect of mind acting as intermediary between the senses and the intellect (buddhi)

mantra – a syllable or a group of syllables with spiritual significance

māya – Illusion; it is the principle that brings about the illusory manifestation of the universe; it is beginningless; it is indescribable(anirvachanīya); it veils(āvarana) and projects(-Vikśhepa). See also āvarana and Vikśhepa.

mithyā – Unreal; illusory;

moha – delusion; infatuation

mokśha – liberation, enlightenment, Self-realization

mumukśhu – a spiritual aspirant with a burning desire for liberation

mumukśhutva – A strong desire to achieve enlightenment, to the exclusion of all other desires.

N

nāma-rūpa – name and form.

nāstika – atheist, unbeliever; usually refers to one who does not recognize the authority of the Vedas.

nididhyāsana – meditating on what has been heard at the time of teaching until there is total conviction. The third stage of the classical spiritual path. See also shravana and manana.

nidra – sleep.

nirodha – restraint.

nirvikalpa – without doubt

nisheda – negation, denial.

nishtha – firmness, steadiness.

nitya – eternal.

nivritti – giving up, abstaining, renouncing of desires that are contrary to the path to enlightenment.

P

paramārtha (noun); paramārthika (adj.) – the highest Truth or
reality; the Absolute
paramātman – The supreme Self, Brahman, the Absolute
paramparā – tradition, lineage
prajñā – wisdom, intelligence, gnosis.
prakriti – nature, primodial nature
prāna – the vital force in the body with which we identify in
the "vital sheath."
prānāyama – regulation of prana using the breath
prārabdha – Karma in action; remainder; accumulated past
actions
pratyagātman – the indwelling Self
prema – love, in its pure, unselfish form (as opposed to moha).
premaswarūpam - One whose essential Self-nature is love.
purusha – Individual soul, spirit
R
rāga – attachment.
rajas – the second of the three guńa. Associated with activity
and passion.
rishi – A seer or Sage.
rūpa – form, outward appearance
S
sadguru – the true teacher, a Self-realized being
sādhaka – a spiritual aspirant or, one who practices sādhana,
which is spiritual discipline
sādhana – the spiritual disciplines followed as part of a path
toward Self-realization
Sadhana chatuśtaya - the fourfold aid to the practice of Vedanta,
these four comprise the proximate aid to Self-realization. The
four are vivēka(discrimination), Vairāgya(detachment), the
sixfold treasures ending in one-pointedness and evenness of

mind, along with faith and lastly mumukshatvam(burning desire for freedom)

samādhana – contemplation, profound meditation; more usually translated as concentration; one of the "six qualities" that form part of Shankara's chatuśtaya sampatti. See chatushtaya sampatti, shamadi shatka sampatti.

samādhi – the state of total absorption and stillness achieved during deep meditation. Several "stages" are defined - see vikalpa, savikalpa samādhi, nirvikalpa samādhi and sahaja samādhi.

samsāra – the continual cycle of death and rebirth, transmigration, to which we are supposedly subject in the phenomenal world until we become enlightened and escape.

sanātana – literally "eternal" or "permanent"; in conjunction with dharma, this refers to our essential nature. The phrase "sanātana dharma" is also used to refer to the traditional (also carrying the sense of "original" and "unadulterated") Hindu practices or as a synonym for "Hinduism."

sankalpa – wish, intention, idea or notion formed in the mind

samskāra – The latent or residual impressions. Whenever an action is performed with an outcome in mind, a samskāra is imprinted in the jiva's mind. The accumulation of samskāras or tendencies dictate our nature leading people to behave in particular ways.

Sankhya - The school of philosophy founded by the sage Kapila, which professes dualistic realism with its two eternal entities Purusha(Individual Awareness) and Prakriti(Primordial matter)

sat – Existence, reality, Being, Truth . See also ananda, chit, satchitānanda.

Sat-asat - Real-unreal, Being-nonBeing

satchitānanda – the most commonly used word in Vedanta to describe our true nature, It translates as Being-Awareness-Bliss

satsanga – association with the good; keeping "holy company"

sattva – Pure, Steady, goodness, illuminating. It is the highest of the gunas, one of the three qualities. See guna.

shama – literally tranquility, absence of passion but more usually translated as mental discipline or self-control; one of the shamādi Shatka sampatti or "six qualities" that form part of the Sadhana chatuśtaya.

shamādi shatka sampatti – the six qualities that form part of the sadhana chatuShTaya sampatti. These are shama, dama, uparati, titikśha, samādhAna and shraddha.

Shankara – 8th Century Indian philosopher responsible for firmly establishing the principles of Advaita. Though he died at an early age, he commented on a number of major Upanishads, the Bhagavad Gita and the Brahmasutras, as well as being attributed as the author of a number of famous works, such as Atmabodha, Bhaja Govindam and vivēkachudamańi.

shāstra – Scripture, teaching, doctrine, which are the sacred books on Indian philosophy

shraddha – faith, trust or belief (in the absence of direct personal experience) - the student needs this initially in respect of what he is told by the guru or reads in the scriptures; one of the "six qualities" that form part of Shankara's chatuśtaya sampatti. See chatushtaya sampatti, shamādi shhatka sampatti.

shravańa – listening to the teachings of Vedanta from a qualified teacher. See also manana, nididhyāsana.

shruti – refers to the Vedas, incorporating the Upanishads. Literally means "what is heard" by the seers, the rishis.

sushupti – the deep-sleep state of consciousness.

svabhāva – one's natural disposition.

svadharma – one's own dharma.

svarūpa – the embodiment, or one's own nature (rūpa means 'form'); e.g., premaswarūpam (embodiment of love)

T

tamas – the "lowest" of the three gunas. Associated characteristics such as inertia and laziness.

Tattva jñāna - The knowledge of the Self, Self-realization

tyāga – renunciation

tapas – austerity

titiksha – forbearance or patience; one of the "six qualities" that form part of Shankara's chatuśtaya sampatti.

turīya – literally the "fourth" state of consciousness. It refers to the non-dual reality, the background against which the other states (waking, dream and deep sleep) arise. It is our true nature. The other three states are mithya.

U

upādhi – Limiting adjunct

upanishad – "to sit close by devotedly", the last portion of the Vedas

uparama or uparati – desisting from sensual enjoyment; one of the "six qualities" that form part of Shankara's chatuśtaya sampatti.

upāsana – worship, homage, used to refer to practices such as chanting, Japa and meditation on a deity, etc

V

Vairāgya – detachment; dispassion; nonattachment

vāsana – latent tendencies; conditioning;

Vedānta – literally "end" or "culmination" (anta) of the Vedas focused on the topic of liberation and the nature of the Absolute

vikalpa – doubt, uncertainty or indecision.

Vikśhepa – the "projecting" power of māya.

vishishtadvaita – qualified non-dualism; belief that God and the Atman are distinct but not separate. Ramanuja is the scholar most often associated with this philosophy. See advaita, dvaita.

vivēka – discrimination; the function of buddhi, having the ability to differentiate between the unreal and the real.

vyakta – manifested, apparent, visible, perceptible to the senses as opposed to avyakta - transcendental.

vyavahara (noun) vyavaharika (adj.) – the relative, practical, or phenomenal world of appearances; as opposed to pāramārthika (reality) and pratibhāsika (illusory).

Y

yoga – union; a process or a path leading to the realization of oneself as the seer, commonly used to refer to the approach propagated by Patanjali.

ॐ

www.ingramcontent.com/pod-product-compliance
Lightning Source LLC
Chambersburg PA
CBHW071206090426
42736CB00014B/2729